With great clarity and erudition, Derek Wall reveals the complexities of Elinor Ostrom's thinking as she formulated her brilliant insights about human cooperation and the commons. This book is a captivating intellectual biography that explains how Ostrom challenged the economic and political orthodoxies of her time, built a robust international network of scholars, and produced a body of literature that continues to nourish the contemporary commons movement.

David Bollier, independent commons scholar and activist, and author of *Think Like a Commoner*

One of our age's most elusive yet most necessary aspirations is an ecologically sustainable self-governing society. So how is it that so many of us managed to miss Elinor Ostrom for so long? She spent a lifetime exploring this aspiration, and drew on an extraordinary range of sources to do so. Derek Wall has written an inspirational book about this key figure of our times. We have much to learn from her – and from him.

Andrew Dobson, Professor of Politics, Keele University, and author of *Green Political Thought*

Elinor Ostrom's magisterial and influential work deserves engaging and full-length treatments such as this. Her innovative research opened new pathways and influenced both the left and the right. In this highly-engaging and well-written study, Derek Wall gives us a view from the left. It is a strong and valuable interpretation that will intensify the debate on her legacy.

Geoff Hodgson, editor of the *Journal of Institutional Economics*

The Sustainable Economics of Elinor Ostrom

Elinor Ostrom's Nobel Prize-winning work on common pool property rights has implications for some of the most pressing sustainability issues of the twenty-first century – from tackling climate change to maintaining cyberspace. In this book, Derek Wall critically examines Ostrom's work, while also exploring the following questions: is it possible to combine insights rooted in methodological individualism with a theory that stresses collectivist solutions? Is Ostrom's emphasis on largely local solutions to climate change relevant to a crisis propelled by global factors?

This volume situates her ideas in terms of the constitutional analysis of her partner Vincent Ostrom and wider institutional economics. It outlines her key concerns, including a radical research methodology, commitment to indigenous people and the concept of social-ecological systems. Ostrom is recognised for producing a body of work which demonstrates how people can construct rules that allow them to exploit the environment in an ecologically sustainable way, without the need for governmental regulation, and this book argues that in a world where ecological realities increasingly threaten material prosperity, such scholarship provides a way of thinking about how humanity can create truly sustainable development.

Given the inter-disciplinary nature of Ostrom's work, this book will be relevant to those working in the areas of environmental economics, political economy, political science and ecology.

Derek Wall is an Associate Tutor in the Department of Politics at Goldsmiths, University of London, UK.

Routledge studies in ecological economics

1 **Sustainability Networks**
Cognitive tools for expert collaboration in social-ecological systems
Janne Hukkinen

2 **Drivers of Environmental Change in Uplands**
Aletta Bonn, Tim Allot, Klaus Hubaceck and Jon Stewart

3 **Resilience, Reciprocity and Ecological Economics**
Northwest coast sustainability
Ronald L. Trosper

4 **Environment and Employment**
A reconciliation
Philip Lawn

5 **Philosophical Basics of Ecology and Economy**
Malte Faber and Reiner Manstetten

6 **Carbon Responsibility and Embodied Emissions**
Theory and measurement
João F. D. Rodrigues, Alexandra P. S. Marques and Tiago M. D. Domingos

7 **Environmental Social Accounting Matrices**
Theory and applications
Pablo Martínez de Anguita and John E. Wagner

8 **Greening the Economy**
Integrating economics and ecology to make effective change
Bob Williams

9 **Sustainable Development**
Capabilities, needs, and well-being
Edited by Felix Rauschmayer, Ines Omann and Johannes Frühmann

10 **The Planet in 2050**
The Lund discourse of the future
Edited by Jill Jäger and Sarah Cornell

11 **From Bioeconomics to Degrowth**
Georgescu-Roegen's 'New Economics' in eight essays
Edited by Mauro Bonaiuti

12 **Socioeconomic and Environmental Impacts on Agriculture in the New Europe**
Post-Communist transition and accession to the European Union
By S. Serban Scrieciu, Takayoshi Shinkuma and Shusuke Managi

13 **Waste and Recycling: Theory and Empirics**
Takayoshi Shinkuma and Shusuke Managi

14 **Global Ecology and Unequal Exchange**
Fetishism in a zero-sum world
Alf Hornborg

15 **The Metabolic Pattern of Societies**
Where economists fall short
Mario Giampietro, Kozo Mayumi and Alevgül H. Sorman

16 **Energy Security for the EU in the 21st Century**
Markets, geopolitics and corridors
Edited by José María Marín-Quemada, Javier García-Verdugo and Gonzalo Escribano

17 **Hybrid Economic-Environmental Accounts**
Edited by Valeria Costantini, Massimiliano Mazzanti and Anna Montini

18 **Ecology and Power**
Struggles over land and material resources in the past, present and future
Edited by Alf Hornborg, Brett Clark and Kenneth Hermele

19 **Economic Theory and Sustainable Development**
What can we preserve for future generations?
Vincent Martinet

20 **Paving the Road to Sustainable Transport**
Governance and innovation in low-carbon vehicles
Edited by Måns Nilsson, Karl Hillman, Annika Rickne and Thomas Magnusson

21 **Creating a Sustainable Economy**
An institutional and evolutionary approach to environmental policy
Edited by Gerardo Marletto

22 **The Economics of Climate Change and the Change of Climate in Economics**
Kevin Maréchal

23 **Environmental Finance and Development**
Sanja Tišma, Ana Maria Boromisa and Ana Pavičić Kaselj

24 **Beyond Reductionism**
A passion for interdisciplinarity
Edited by Katharine Farrell, Tommaso Luzzati and Sybille van den Hove

25 **The Business Case for Sustainable Finance**
Edited by Iveta Cherneva

26 **The Economic Value of Landscapes**
Edited by C. Martijn van der Heide and Wim Heijman

27 **Post-Kyoto Climate Governance**
Confronting the politics of scale, ideology and knowledge
Asim Zia

28 Climate Economics
The state of the art
Frank Ackerman and Elizabeth A. Stanton

29 Good Governance, Scale and Power
A case study of North Sea fisheries
Liza Griffin

30 Waste Management in Spatial Environments
Edited by Alessio D'Amato, Massimiliano Mazzanti and Anna Montini

31 The Green Fiscal Mechanism and Reform for Low Carbon Development
East Asia and Europe
Edited by Akihisa Mori, Paul Ekins, Soocheol Lee, Stefan Speck and Kazuhiro Ueta

32 Peak Oil, Climate Change, and the Limits to China's Economic Growth
Minqi Li

33 The Sustainable Economics of Elinor Ostrom
Commons, contestation and craft
Derek Wall

34 Green Industrial Policy in Emerging Countries
Edited by Anna Pegels

The Sustainable Economics of Elinor Ostrom

Commons, contestation and craft

Derek Wall

LONDON AND NEW YORK

First published 2014
by Routledge
2 Park Square, Milton Park, Abingdon, Oxon OX14 4RN

and by Routledge
605 Third Avenue, New York, NY 10017

First issued in paperback 2021

Routledge is an imprint of the Taylor & Francis Group, an informa business

Publisher's Note
The publisher has gone to great lengths to ensure the quality of this reprint but points out that some imperfections in the original copies may be apparent.

British Library Cataloguing in Publication Data
A catalogue record for this book is available from the British Library

Library of Congress Cataloging in Publication Data
Wall, Derek.
The economics of common pool property rights: the sustainable economics of Elinor Ostrom/Derek Wall.
pages cm. – (Routledge studies in ecological economics)
Includes bibliographical references and index.
1. Ostrom, Elinor–Political and social views. 2. Sustainable development. 3. Infrastructure (Economics) 4. Global commons.
I. Title.
HC79.E5W2685 2014
338.9'27–dc23 2013033371

ISBN 13: 978-1-03-209903-3 (pbk)
ISBN 13: 978-0-415-64174-6 (hbk)

Typeset in Times New Roman
by Wearset Ltd, Boldon, Tyne and Wear

To Emily Blyth, for all her love and all her help with this book.
And to all comrades, especially the comrades in Mindanao.

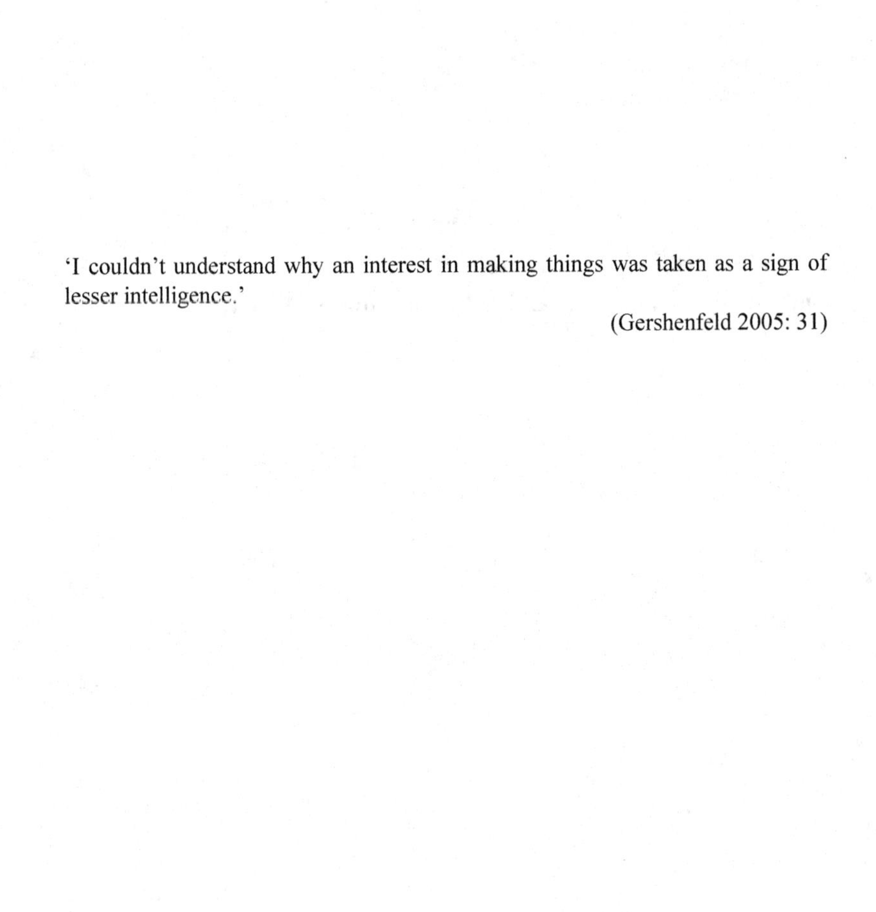

‘I couldn’t understand why an interest in making things was taken as a sign of lesser intelligence.’

(Gershenfeld 2005: 31)

Contents

Preface

It is impossible to write about Elinor Ostrom on her own; she was a cooperator and while her best known book *Governing the Commons* was a single author work, many of her publications and virtually all of her research was undertaken with others. She was part of a swarm or if you prefer she was a public entrepreneur who organised intellectual projects with others. Above all, she worked with her husband Vincent Ostrom.

Both Elinor and Vincent were, while by no means postmodernists or interpretivists, critical of positivism, which they viewed as naïve and unscientific. For example, Vincent Ostrom felt that researchers had normative positions and that different normative assumptions would lead to different research criteria. So it is appropriate to briefly explain my perspectives and how I came to write the book. I have taught economics at an introductory level for all my working life since graduating with a degree in environmental archaeology in 1986 from the University of London. My main political and academic interest has been in green politics. I am sceptical that our capitalist economy can sustain diverse and essential ecosystems and feel that we need to find new ways of promoting prosperity without wrecking our planet. Broadly speaking I am a Marxist, and my previous book before this title was *The Rise of the Green Left* (Wall 2010) which looked at ecosocialism.

I have never been convinced that a centrally planned economy would work efficiently, ecologically or democratically, so since reading Alan Roberts' book *The Self-Managing Environment* in the early 1980s I have been interested in the 'commons' and economics beyond the market and the state (Roberts 1979). I came across Elinor Ostrom's book *Governing the Commons* and included it on my course reading list for an undergraduate unit entitled 'New Radical Political Economy' that I teach in the politics department of Goldsmiths College. I was surprised to hear that Ostrom had won a 2009 Nobel Prize in Economic Sciences, or more strictly speaking a Swedish bank prize, for her work on the commons. There was little in the way of secondary accounts of her work that I could find and I thought it would be good to write a popular, accessible account of her work as well as an academic title. The popular account, so far at least, has not appeared but this is my attempt at an academic account.

I was also lucky to meet Professor Ostrom before her untimely death in 2012 when she visited London. I interviewed her for a piece I wrote for the Green

Party magazine *Green World*, at a major environmental conference. I didn't know she was dying with cancer but she seemed very frail. However, when I asked her questions, her voice and energy levels rose. She was a careful scholar but on meeting her I was impressed by her obvious passion. Two days later I went with a number of my students to her Hayek lecture at the Institute of Economic Affairs (IEA). Given that the IEA are a free market think tank, it amused me that when I talked to her after her lecture, we discussed Marx's interest in the commons. She was an open minded individual who respected different opinions and enjoyed what she termed 'contestation'.

I had assumed, until I learnt more about her work, that only Marxists were interested in the commons. After all, it was one of Marx's enduring concerns, and who else was even aware of the existence and characteristics of collective property? So I was rather surprised to find that Elinor Ostrom was not a Marxist. In fact she, apparently, came from a liberal free market perspective based on the ideas of Adam Smith, Friedrich Hayek and James Buchanan. Since reading her work exhaustively and thinking about her often unusual ideas, my conclusion is that she and Vincent are not easy to place in a pre-existing ideological category. They were not, of course, on the traditional (state-orientated or Marxist) left. Neither were they anarchists – at least not in the strict sense – because they believed in governance rules. However they of course felt that politics expanded beyond the state. It is probably more accurate to describe them as radical democrats or republicans in the sense of Italian city states, Spinoza and self-government. They could be described as liberals, but it is unusual to find liberals who make room for collective property rights and economics that includes, but extends beyond, monetary exchange. Neither Elinor nor Vincent were concerned about ideological labels but what they did care about was practical problem solving. My emphasis in this book is on 'craft', as they believed that academic work was a practical material endeavour. They built their own furniture and even their home. They were unusual in that they saw political economy as a process like cooking, furniture making or any other form of design practice. In this regard they of course referred to Tocqueville, but there is an intellectual relationship between their work and that of Herbert Simon; especially if we think of his book *The Sciences of the Artificial* (Simon 1996).

Elinor Ostrom was, along with Vincent, concerned with two essential questions. These were included in the syllabus for the course she taught at Indiana University. I am pleased that the University gave me permission to reproduce the introduction to the syllabus as an appendix in this book, so that readers can more easily judge her work by looking at what she taught. The two linked questions were as follows:

> How can *fallible* human beings achieve and sustain self-governing ways of life and self-governing entities as well as sustaining ecological systems at multiple scales?
>
> (See Appendix)

These questions that deal with ecologically sustainable self-governance will never be answered, at least not fully. To my mind these are the two big questions that economists, and those from other disciplines, ought to be researching, but generally don't. Elinor Ostrom moved not just beyond the market and the state but even beyond the commons, arguing that property rights and institutions are very diverse. She made, along with others, an impressive attempt to think about how economics could be more sustainable in two senses: sustainable in the ecological meaning but also sustainable as a serious academic discipline better able to address economic realities and to understand our economic behaviour. In a sense, she was never really an economist, despite winning the Nobel Prize for Economic Sciences. On meeting her in 2012, she gently corrected me when I addressed her as an economist, noting that she was a different species, that she was a 'political economist'. However I feel she made an important contribution to the creation of a sustainable economics.

There is an awareness that economics is in crisis but while a host of books come out with penetrating critiques and sophisticated analysis, the discipline becomes in practical terms, if anything, more conservative, with university departments closing courses on methodology and the history of the subject. Yet from behavioural economics to Deirdre McCloskey's essential work on rhetoric and metaphor (1998), intellectual developments that overlap with Elinor Ostrom's concerns, which challenge and could potentially enhance mainstream economics continue to grow. Such challenges come from a variety of directions. I think Elinor Ostrom would have smiled broadly to learn that two books were to be published on her work; one written by a Marxist and another by a researcher more sympathetic to Austrian economics (Aligică 2014). After all, she was a pluralist who loved debate, but what would have made her really happy was the knowledge that economists (and others) were using her work in a practical way. If those of us who are enthusiastic about her work, from whatever perspective, manage to persuade economists (and others) to use it in their teaching and for practical research, we will have helped provide Elinor Ostrom with a fitting tribute.

Derek Wall

Acknowledgements

I am not in a position to acknowledge generous research leave or grants from institutions. I have had none. However, I can say I enjoyed every second I spent on this book and would like to thank everybody who encouraged and helped me.

My fiancée Emily Blyth has read drafts, corrected my often dubious grammar, suggested books to read that would help with the topic and put up with me talking about Elinor Ostrom for roughly twenty five hours a day for a period of some years. She understood and shared the magic I felt about Elinor Ostrom's work and I love her all the more for doing so.

I like to write peer to peer, producing drafts, getting feedback and improving what I have done. I have had some very good peer-to-peer input from a number of friends. Ken Hunter read the first five chapters and gave me very useful help; I am in his debt.

Xanthe Bevis has been a great support as in previous projects. She also provided a critical eye and improved my work. Veronica Kotziamani likewise read chapter drafts and shared my enthusiasm for the topic. James Sheils was full of enthusiasm too especially for debates around Wittgenstein, republicanism, the philosophy of the social sciences and the sciences of the artificial. Daniel Whittal, Nandor Tanczos, Dr Debal Deb, James Moloney, Malcolm Bailey, Shahrar Ali, Anitra Nelson and Rowan Lubbock all read drafts and made useful comments.

Gareth Dale corrected some Polanyi misconceptions on my part.

I have shared perspectives with Eoin Flaherty. His research on the Irish rundales is a fine piece of work and he kindly commented on my chapters. Tony Gair read my knowledge commons chapter and has shared many thoughts on three-dimensional printing. It was a pleasure to share some thoughts with Len Vincent about engineering, design and Elinor Ostrom's work on the last day before handing this text to the publishers.

And of course Robert Langham, Andrew Humphries and Natalie Tomlinson at Taylor & Francis for their support with the book and to the anonymous reviewers who provided some important pointers for the development of this project.

A number of people associated with Elinor and Vincent Ostrom as colleagues or students of Elinor Ostrom were very helpful. I am inspired by the warmth, cooperative spirit and intellectual endeavour of those associated with her work. Charlotte Hess read a number of chapters and put me right in a number of places.

Keith Taylor who was a student of both Elinor and Vincent was a massive support, giving my words critical attention and encouraging me to keep working away at the book. I am hoping I can get out to Bloomington, Indiana to buy him a drink.

Patty Lezotte, also from the Ostrom workshop, was very helpful in tracking down a copy of the article 'The Ten Most Important Books' for me (Ostrom 2004); an essential piece of writing that it would have been difficult to have completed this book without.

I would also like to acknowledge my thanks to the IU Foundation for giving me permission to reproduce the syllabus of Elinor Ostrom's last course (see Appendix). James Walker and Philippa Marie Guthrie also deserve thanks for dealing with my request for permission so efficiently and swiftly. Michael McGinnis read my preface and gave me useful feedback. Ryan T.Conway was also supportive and dug out some useful information I needed.

Finally I have to thank Elinor Ostrom. While she was pretty universally known as 'Lin', I never felt that I could refer to her so informally. She was generous with her time and allowed me to interview her when she came to London in 2012. She was also willing to listen to me on a second occasion after the Hayek lecture, when I talked to her about Marx and the commons, E.P. Thompson and rioters. Tired as she obviously was, her eyes lit up when I told her about the Victorian women who had torn down the fences to preserve South London's Plumstead Common from enclosure. These two meetings were before I started serious work on this book but her generosity of spirit and intellectual commitment shone through. She was a truly inspiring and very practical thinker. To my mind there are two political ecologists or, to put it another way, two political economists who dedicated themselves to the puzzle of promoting democratic governance and ecological sustainability for the next seven generations. That she was one of this pair, in my opinion, her greatest achievement.

1 An accidental life?

> 'Vincent and I used to go on Thursday nights and all day Saturdays to (Unionville carpenter) Paul Goodman's,' she recalled. 'Yes, we made furniture there. Our dining room table, cabinets. Pretty much everything in our house except the padded chairs'.
>
> (Leonard 2009)

Introduction

It is said that on being woken by an early morning phone call on 10 October 2009 to inform her that she had won a Nobel Prize in economics, Elinor Ostrom turned to her spouse and colleague Vincent Ostrom and delivered the immortal words 'Wake up, honey. We have won a prize' (Sabetti 2011: 73). Her desire to see the prize as shared extended beyond Vincent, with whom she had worked for nearly a lifetime, to the members of their Workshop in Political Theory and Policy Analysis at Indiana University. It is also said that she took a draft of her Nobel lecture to a workshop session where her students and colleagues were encouraged to criticise it before she rewrote it. 'We' so often replaced 'I' in her work, which was collaborative and peer-to-peer, long before the term was first used. She was the first woman to win the prize, and while she did not even claim to be an economist, but instead a political economist, my argument developed in this book is that her work has the potential to transform economics.

We live in a world in crisis, and part of this crisis extends to economics. In 2011, uprisings toppled leader after leader in the Middle East and North Africa with governments falling like dominoes. Part of the reason for revolt was the sharply rising cost of basic food stuffs; rice, wheat, sugar and maize all accelerated in price during this period. While commodity prices are often volatile, there are real fears that an increase in extreme weather events was part of the reason for the increase in costs. For example, in 2010 fires raged in Russia, destroying wheat fields and pushing the price of bread upwards. In the same year, floods in Pakistan damaged cotton crops and the price of cloth rose. As I write in 2012, flooding is affecting much of Britain. Some scientists believe that climate change has led to these and other disruptive weather events.

No one can tell with certainty, whether climate change is already having an impact. However, there is little doubt that if greenhouse gas levels continue to rise, the climate will become more unstable, extreme events will increase, crops will be disrupted, commodity prices will rise further and millions of people are likely to become refugees. Climate change is just one facet of an environmental crisis; biodiversity is declining and basic ecological cycles are under pressure. Many commentators also argue that high oil prices are here to stay. During the 1990s, oil was priced around $10 a barrel, in 2013 it sat at $100. Higher oil prices push up the general level of inflation and stifle economic growth.

Economists appear to have problems rising to such a challenge; simply allowing supply and demand to act as an invisible hand may be inadequate. Economists have been widely derided for their failure to predict, let alone correct, real world crises. Such crises have extended to the global economy. In 2008, imbalances in the international economy, a credit balloon and financial instability led to a global financial collapse and severe recession. In 2012, the Eurozone is in deep crisis and four years after the financial crash the US economy remains fragile. Growth in China, which has been helping the global economy, seems to be slowing. While events move fast, the global economy appears to have shifted in a dangerous and unstable direction. Economists have failed to provide policy advice that has helped to heal a wounded world economy. Events will no doubt move on; sustained growth may return, commodity prices may fall and technological innovation may make environmental problems less intractable. Yet critics argue that mainstream economics demands revision.

In turn, the research techniques and even the basic assumptions used by economists have also been criticised with increased force. The argument that a basic rethink of the discipline is necessary can be heard more loudly and from diverse quarters. So, if conventional economics demands a critical eye and perhaps even a fundamental shift in orientation, where will an alternative come from? If we need a new economics, where will we find it? This title argues that one source is via a seemingly obscure professor of politics from a Mid-Western university. A woman forgotten by most economists, and even academics on the left that are critical of the current discipline and its role in determining policy. The person under discussion is, of course, Professor Elinor Ostrom.

In 2009, when Professor Ostrom became the first woman to win the Nobel Prize in Economic Sciences, which she shared with Oliver E. Williamson, most economists probably sighed with surprise and said something along the lines of 'Elinor who?'. Ostrom was not well known among economists at the time. Strictly speaking, she was not even an economist, but worked in a politics department and preferred to be known as a political economist. Steven Levitt, who wrote *Freakonomics*, a bestselling popular economics title, noted on his *New York Times* blog:

> If you had done a poll of academic economists yesterday and asked who Elinor Ostrom was, or what she worked on, I doubt that more than one in

> five economists could have given you an answer. I personally would have failed the test. I had to look her up on Wikipedia, and even after reading the entry, I have no recollection of ever seeing or hearing her name mentioned by an economist.
>
> (Levitt (12 October 2009))

Despite this apparent obscurity, the awarding team judged her work to be vitally important. Indeed, it will be suggested that the late Professor Ostrom, who died in 2012, has produced a body of work that contributes to some of the most important questions of the twenty-first century, from tackling climate change to conserving cyberspace. With her unusual but rigorous emphasis on qualitative as well as purely quantitative research, her work also has important implications for debates about economic methodology.

It is possible to overstate Elinor Ostrom's apparent obscurity; she was a former President of the American Political Science Association and a Professor at both Indiana and Arizona State Universities. She won numerous awards. For example, in 1999 she became the first woman to win the Johan Skytte Prize in Political Science. Other prizes include the National Academy of Sciences John J. Carty Award in 2004, as well as the James Madison Award and William H. Riker Prize in Political Science. She was one of only a few women to become members of both the National Academy of Sciences and the American Academy of Arts and Sciences. In 2010, *Utne Reader* magazine included her as one of the '25 Visionaries Who Are Changing Your World.' In 2012, *Time* magazine listed her as one of the hundred most influential individuals on the planet. However, it is true to say that as a pioneer of inter-disciplinary research, she was probably better known among academic ecologists and political scientists than economists.

She won the Nobel Prize in Economic Sciences for her work on common pool resources and property. Traditionally, economists have argued that there are two forms of property, private and state. Economies are mixed, i.e. some activities such as policing are largely controlled by the state, while others are provided by the market. Ostrom argued that a third form of property, neither privately owned nor state controlled, but based on common ownership, is also significant. In turn, economic activity is not merely split between the alternatives of market and state but can be regulated by collective social activity. Even where property is privately owned, user rights may exist for a variety of individuals and communities rather than only for a single owner. In fact, she conceptualised a wide diversity of property rights, ownership systems and forms of governance.

Her work, and that of Oliver Williamson, with whom she shared the Nobel Prize in Economic Sciences, is rooted in institutional economics. While institutional economics is made up of a number of different schools of thought, all tend to suggest that economics is shaped by forms of governance (Rutherford 1996). The political economy of institutions extends to community management as well as formal state activity. The Nobel authorities on awarding their joint prize noted:

> Economic transactions take place not only in markets, but also within firms, associations, households, and agencies. Whereas economic theory has comprehensively illuminated the virtues and limitations of markets, it has traditionally paid less attention to other institutional arrangements. The research of Elinor Ostrom and Oliver Williamson demonstrates that economic analysis can shed light on most forms of social organization.
>
> (Nobel Prize 2009a)

While Williamson (1985) examined how corporations can resolve conflict and manage transaction costs, Ostrom's institutional research focussed on common pool resources and property. Indeed Ostrom can be seen as the economist or political economist best placed to conceptualise the explosion in web-based activity and social media, which are largely built on commons-based platforms. The accelerating growth of the World Wide Web, peer-to-peer production and Wikipedia have been investigated by economists, but forcing them into the pre-existing categories of market and state is far from satisfactory.

Ostrom's practical research examined how communities succeeded or sometimes failed to maintain marine fisheries, forests, grazing land and other forms of common pool resource. Ostrom challenged the notion of the tragedy of the commons, showing that while commons can fail, we should not assume that they will always do so. Neither is commons, Ostrom (1990) insisted, an absence of property rights but often is based on carefully constructed rules for management of a resource.

Ostrom argued that people can, in some circumstances, construct rules that allow them to manage the environment without destroying it. In a world where ecological realities increasingly threaten material prosperity, her work provides a way of thinking about how humanity can create truly sustainable development, maintaining key ecosystems while meeting human needs.

Ostrom's approach is often difficult to categorise with traditional notions of economics or political philosophy. At first glance, she seems to draw upon concepts and schools of thought that appear, without further study, contradictory. Yet, I would argue, further examination suggests clarity and coherence in her thinking.

Elinor Ostrom might, for example, be understood as an Austrian-influenced thinker. 'Austrian' refers to the work of market-based European economists such as Friedrich von Hayek and Joseph Schumpeter. Indeed, in March 2012, shortly before her death, Ostrom delivered the Institute of Economic Affairs Annual IEA Hayek Memorial Lecture to a large audience in London. The Institute of Economic Affairs (IEA) is a free market think tank, which advocates privatisation, tax cuts and curbs on trade union power. While the IEA does not deny the reality of climate change, it is concerned that interventionist policies that seek to reduce rising levels of carbon dioxide and other greenhouse gases may damage industrial competitiveness.

Elinor, however, had little interest in industrial competitiveness. She increasingly came to see promoting sustainability as her vocation, speaking at international environmental conferences and writing articles about social-ecological systems for scientific journals. Her experience as a woman has also shaped her thinking. As we shall see, she faced difficult challenges as a woman academic in a sexist climate during the first decades of her career. Her awareness of the need to fight gender-based prejudice and other forms of discrimination seemed to set her apart from market-based liberal economists. While she did not research gender she was happy to be associated with feminist economics (May and Summerfield 2012). Yet issues that might be seen as left orientated, such as environmental concern and female empowerment, were approached from new perspectives. For example, while she was an advocate of policies for tackling climate change, she remained critical of the very notion of policy if it is imposed from above. Equally, she distanced herself from statist forms of socialism, but perhaps paradoxically endorsed collectivist solutions to economic and environmental problems in some situations. She believed that governments should fund public services, but leave their production to firms or community organisations. Ostrom, who once described herself 'as a stubborn son of a gun', is a thinker who is difficult to pigeonhole within existing categories in economics and political philosophy. Ostrom's work, and that of her husband and co-worker Vincent, is unusual and requires careful examination. To introduce her work, at a superficial level, we can contrast Hayekian market-based interpretations with normative concerns that seem firmly on the left. While this is a good way perhaps of introducing a debate about the orientation of her work, it has to be discarded relatively quickly. Her work does not fit into the usual categories; she and Vincent Ostrom were highly independent scholars who drew upon astonishingly varied theorists and schools of thought.

It is also clear that the thinker with whom they identified most was the nineteenth century French political commentator Alexis de Tocqueville. His two-volume study *Democracy in America* helped inspire the Ostroms' fascination with self-governance, reflected in all of their work.

To get an idea of Elinor Ostrom's work from her own perspective, it is worth reading her syllabus for the last course she taught at Indiana University (see Appendix). She begins with a question linking concerns with sustainability to Tocqueville's fascination with grassroots democratic self-government, asking how can '*fallible* human beings achieve and sustain self-governing ways of life and self-governing entities as well as sustaining ecological systems at multiple scales?'.

However, many of her most innovative insights are derived not only from particular thinkers or schools of thought, important as these were, but were shaped by her life experience, which is outlined briefly below.

An accidental life?

Elinor Ostrom died on 12 June 2012, having been diagnosed with pancreatic cancer in late 2011. In the months before her death at the age of 78, she wrote several new papers and travelled extensively, speaking at a number of important international conferences. Her academic career spanned five decades but was far from easy at first. Indeed, after winning the Nobel Prize in Economic Sciences, she noted 'To an outside observer, my career may look rather successful at the current time. Has it always been this way? To be honest, the answer is no. My entry into an undergraduate major in political science was almost accidental' (2010a: 2).

She was born in Los Angeles on 7 August 1933 to Adrian and Leah Awan. Adrian was a set designer for the Hollywood Bowl and the Civic Light Opera. Leah was a musician and for a time managed the San Francisco Symphony Orchestra. Born in South Dakota, Leah was said to have been a musical prodigy with perfect pitch. As a child, Elinor accompanied her father on Saturday mornings to watch music rehearsals and set construction. Such early exposure to musical performance inspired her to become a ballerina, but she suffered disappointment in this regard because of her flat feet.

She also faced prejudice in her early years. Her mother was Protestant, her father Jewish. She was brought up as a Protestant, yet she remembers children shouting 'Jew' at her in the Sunday school playground:

> 'I got circled in the schoolroom, out on the playground.'
>
> 'You Jew! You Jew!' she recalled, her voice rising, imitating the taunts.
>
> 'Having that experience as a kid and being a woman, and having that challenge as it has been at different times to be a woman, I've got pretty good sympathy for people who are not necessarily at the center of civic appreciation.
>
> (Leonard 2009)

Elinor developed a love of what she termed 'contestation', by which she meant debate and argument, from an early age. She believed that her passionate attachment to debate was first inspired by family discussion of religion. While neither of her parents were especially religious, she spent time with her aunt who was committed to kosher practices.

'That was a wonderful experience for me, [. . .] It was a serious kosher home, and the Friday night discussions were very serious' (Leonard 2009). Her father lost his job, life was difficult during the economic crisis of the 1930s, and the war years that followed in the 1940s. She felt that the tough times taught her that it was important to work hard and be independent because the 'world isn't going to come with you with all sorts of gifts' (The Big Think (14 November 2009)).

Her almost Gandhian commitment to a low impact lifestyle was also inspired by such an early experience of austerity. While later she was to take economics courses and excel in them, she never seems to have had a desire to accumulate wealth. She apparently lived modestly, and later recycled her Nobel Prize winnings into funding for research:

> We need to get people away from the notion that you have to have a fancy car and a huge house. Some of the homes that have been built in the last 10

> years just appal me. Why do humans need huge homes? I was born poor and I didn't know you bought clothes at anything but the Goodwill until I went to college. Some of our mentality about what it means to have a good life is, I think, not going to help us in the next 50 years. We have to think through how to choose a meaningful life where we're helping one another in ways that really help the Earth.
>
> (Korten (26 February 2010))

Gardening was one of a number of childhood passions shaped by the Depression and life during the Second World War, 'Our house had a large backyard that we filled with a vegetable garden and fruit trees. I learned how to grow vegetables and how to can apricots and peaches during the heat of summer' (Nobel Prize 2009b).

To the amusement of Elinor and her friends she enrolled at Beverly Hills High School, which provided one of the accidents that propelled Elinor towards an academic career. An unusually large percentage of Beverly Hills students went on to higher education. If Elinor had gone to another high school, her academic career might have ended long before it began. Beverly Hills is associated with Hollywood and high living, and is famous for its star-studded alumni including the actors Richard Dreyfuss and Carrie Fisher, and film director Roger Corman. The school has also appeared in numerous films including *Clueless* and *It's a Wonderful Life*. It was a school whose typical students included the rich and glamorous, rather than children of divorced parents struggling to get by:

> Technically, we lived in Los Angeles, but the high school was literally across the street [...] I'm very grateful for that opportunity, because 90 per cent of the kids who went to Beverly Hills High School went on to college. I don't think I would have gone to college if not for being in that environment.
>
> (Leonard 2009)

She noted, '[W]hile it was a challenge being a poor kid in a rich kid's school, it did give me a different perspective on the future.' (Nobel Prize 2009b)

The school also saw her interest in politics blossom; perhaps ironically, because of her stuttering problem. 'Colleagues have asked what led me to become a political scientist. One answer is that I became a political scientist because I stuttered in high school.' To help her stuttering, she was encouraged to join a poetry club and then the debating society for two years, where she competed with groups from other high schools. She often had to debate one side of an argument and then argue against what she had just said. She felt this was a good preparation for academic life:

> You learn that there are always at least two sides to every issue, because in the diverse rounds of one tournament you are likely to be assigned both sides of the debate topic, and you must be prepared to make an effective argument for whichever side you are assigned.
>
> (Ostrom 2010a: 2)

Sexist assumptions were rife at school and Elinor was prevented from taking an advanced mathematics course because of her gender. 'I had to take calculus as an assistant professor,' she remarked in one interview at Indiana University (Nobel Prize 2009b).

She joined the University of California, Los Angeles (UCLA) to study politics in 1951. She gained an early interest in economics and seems to have excelled in the course units she took. Graduating in 1954, she married Charles Scott, a fellow UCLA graduate. They moved to Boston, where he enrolled at law school. She looked for work and helped support him through his studies. However her degree apparently made little impression on prospective employers; they wanted women primarily as secretarial staff:

> Looking for a job in the 1950s as a female and as a new college graduate was an 'instructive' experience. The first question in every interview was whether I had typing and shorthand skills. After working for a year as Export Clerk in a Cambridge electronics firm, I finally landed a position as Assistant Personnel Manager in a distinguished Boston firm that had never hired a woman before.
>
> (Ostrom 2010a: 3)

She decided that she wished to return to education to study for a PhD, but her husband was apparently less than enthusiastic. Eventually she and Charles Scott divorced. The divorce was amicable, and Ostrom saw it as an example of the kind of politics of negotiation that inspired her work on the commons. 'That's problem solving, too, [...]. Sometimes, with couples, it's OK to say it's not working and it's not going to work and you move on' (Leonard 2009).

She returned to Los Angeles to study at UCLA. In 1957, she also gained a recruitment position in the Personnel Office of UCLA. She was pleased to work in the office and her attitude to recruitment is indicative of a lifelong commitment to diversity and inclusion. 'This was particularly gratifying because I had been able to diversify the firm's staff, previously all white and Protestant or Catholic, to include several new employees who were black or Jewish' (Ostrom 2010a: 3).

Returning to education proved to be something of a battle for Elinor. UCLA prevented her from taking a PhD in economics because of her lack of mathematics. Deciding instead to focus on political science, she was also discouraged:

> The graduate advisor in political science strongly discouraged me from thinking about a doctorate, given that I already had a very good 'professional' position. He indicated that the 'best' I could do with a Ph.D. was to teach at some city college with a very heavy teaching load. My earlier experience with finding a professional position in Cambridge led me to ignore this warning and apply for an assistantship so I could pursue a Ph.D. on a full-time basis. Fortunately, I was granted an assistantship.
>
> (Ostrom 2010a: 3)

The climate of the times was so hostile to women that enrolling women graduate students led to a departmental row:

> It was a big controversy at UCLA in the political science department. They had not had a woman in their program for many years and there were four of us out of forty admitted in the year I was admitted to a doctoral program and there were many of the faculty who were extremely upset.
>
> (The Big Think (14 November 2009))

She took seminars with Vincent Ostrom whom she later married. Vincent's research interest was in governance and administration and he asked students to research the governance of water basins:

> My assignment was the West Basin, which underlay a portion of the city of Los Angeles and 11 other cities. During the first half of the twentieth century, water producers ignored the facts that the level of groundwater underlying Los Angeles was going down and seawater was intruding along the coast. Toward the end of World War II, several municipal water departments asked the U.S. Geological Survey to conduct a major study of the area and agreed to fund one third of the study. The report detailed a grim picture of substantial overdraft and threat of further saltwater intrusion that could eventually ruin the basin for human use.
>
> (Ostrom 2010a: 4–5)

Elinor gained her MA in 1961 and her PhD in 1965. Both Ostroms became fascinated with how individuals could cooperate to conserve environments like the West Basin, without destroying them.

> [My] dissertation was a great big thick thing on how ground water producers in Southern California, earlier in an urban area, in LA, were able to solve a very very tough problem. They were pumping water down and the salt water was going in and they developed a whole series of strategies to solve it and solve it very successfully.
>
> (Gupta (22 March 2011))

It is important to see her work as a partnership with that of her husband Vincent Ostrom, who she married in 1963:

> Both scholars are complementary and mutually reinforcing. The one serves as the base and source of inspiration for the other: Vincent is more philosophical and ideational, coming from political theory and administrative sciences, strongly rooted in the constitutional tradition in which the study of American public administration had its origin. Elinor is more analytic, empirical, and operational, with a strong drive to confront assumptions with social reality and to test hypotheses in an experimental laboratory setting or

> operational field survey against painstakingly defined conceptual indicators and self-collected data, even using satellite observations in later years.
>
> (Toonen 2010: 193)

She remarked to one interviewer after her Nobel win, 'There is no way you can write about my work without paying attention to the work of Vincent' (Toonen 2010: 193).

There was a division of labour between them. Although this was not exclusive, Elinor specialised in empirical research, particularly into commons, while Vincent's work emphasised constitutional systems in books such as *The Intellectual Crisis in American Public Administration* and *The Meaning of American Federalism*. However much was shared, as Elinor noted they had a common institutional emphasis: 'We simply study institutions, that is what we do' (Toonen 2010: 193). She also observed, 'it should not be over-looked that it was Vincent, not me, who discovered and first used the concept of common pool resources in his teaching and writing on common property resource management at the end of the 1950s' (Toonen 2010: 194).

Vincent's ancestors were Swedish, the name Ostrom is derived from *ö* which means 'island' and *ström* which is 'river' thus the island in the river. Born in Washington State, he received a BA in political science in 1942 and an MA in 1945. He worked as a high school teacher in California before becoming a lecturer at the University of Wyoming in 1945, where he was assigned a research project looking at cattle ranching:

> I followed an empirical, bottom-up approach. Cattle turned out to be an important locus of interest. Systems of brands on cattle could be perceived in terms of property rights. The arrangement was that, in the winter, the cattle were on private land, but in the summer they were in the open, i.e., a common area. The roundup was a collective enterprise. Brands served as a way to appropriate young calves, for example. Part of the land was private, but in the summer feeding was on the open range. This made me aware of the need to think about ways to conceptualize common property in the domain between private and public ownership as part of the system of governing. I saw stockowners associating privately to commonly establish and enforce property rights.
>
> (Toonen 2010: 195)

His interest in environmental sustainability was sharpened by a personal experience. The contrast between attitudes to water use in Los Angeles and Wyoming intrigued him:

> After leaving the Los Angeles area, I became a resident of a small city in Wyoming where the problem of an adequate water supply was a daily concern to the community. The normal water consumption of the householder was subject to detailed regulation by municipal ordinance. The

> irrigation of lawns and gardens was limited to certain days of the week for even- and odd-numbered street addresses. Then, watering was permitted only for specific hours in the day. Nozzles and sprinklers were required to prevent the waste of water. All of these regulations were enforced subject to penalties for a misdemeanor if violated.
>
> (V. Ostrom 1950: v)

His PhD in political science from UCLA in 1950 was entitled *Government and Water: A Study of the Influence of Water upon Governmental Institutions and Practices in the Development of Los Angeles*. Vincent's thesis focussed, in his words, on the influence of water on the 'human ecology' of Los Angeles, showing how the water basin was a commons that had to be governed by a variety of overlapping institutions so that it would not be degraded by overuse or the intrusion of salt water (V. Ostrom 1950: v). From their earliest years as academics, the Ostroms examined how political institutions, often of a local and informal nature, might be developed to allow sustainable use of resources. While Elinor won the Nobel Prize and wrote *Governing the Commons*, neither Ostrom could have produced their innovative work without the other. While Vincent started to work on problems of sustainability and commons before meeting Elinor, she developed ever more detailed and sophisticated techniques for studying these concepts during her long academic career.

When, during the 1950s, Vincent was invited to contribute to the creation of a constitution for the State of Alaska, he advocated a participatory approach (Wohlforth 2010: 225). Elements of the constitution stressing collective rather than state ownership of resources, and the establishment of a fund that distributed a dividend from the oil industry to Alaskan citizens, have been seen as inspired by his work. He was fascinated by the Federalist tradition in US politics that saw citizens develop a democratic constitution after the War of Independence.

He was also intrigued by the work of Herbert Simon, who later won a Nobel Prize in Economic Sciences on administration. While the topic of administration might be seen as prosaic, compared to, say, an intellectual interest in continental philosophy, Vincent viewed academic work as a practical task and was fascinated by questions of grassroots governance, acting as editor of the journal *Public Administration Review* between 1963 and 1966.

Among many other areas of study, Vincent retained an interest in indigenous political institutions. For example, with an anthropologist he studied the termination agreement between the Federal Government and the Klamath of Southern Oregon in 1954. A fictional account of the termination is instructively entitled *Buy the Chief a Cadillac* (Steber 2006). Vincent was appalled by the treatment of indigenous people by the US authorities.

His continued collaboration with Elinor Ostrom is a theme of any study of her work. Beginning when he was her teacher and she his graduate student, while they were married to other partners, it became a lifelong personal and intellectual partnership. After marrying, they moved to Bloomington, Indiana in 1964.

First Vincent and then Elinor were given posts in the politics department of Indiana University. While Vincent was engaged as Professor of Political Science, Elinor's position was rather more humble. In her words, she began at the 'bottom of the totem pole' teaching American government at 7:30 a.m. on Tuesdays, Thursdays and Saturdays. At first she had a heavy workload as a teacher and combined lectures with research, often working cooperatively with her students. For example, African-American students encouraged her to undertake research into policing in Indianapolis and Chicago (The Big Think (14 November 2009)). It was felt at the time that public administration worked best when simplified and centralised. Small and often overlapping police authorities were thought to be inefficient, and the views of users, especially minorities, were not a priority. Vincent and Elinor had different ideas, inspired in part by Herbert Simon's contention that much administrative theory was based on 'proverbs' rather than scientific assumptions (Simon 1997: 29). Elinor started on collaborative, grassroots fieldwork:

> Roger Parks had a fantastic idea for a research design to study policing in Indianapolis. He pointed out that there were three independent, small police departments serving neighborhoods immediately adjacent to socioeconomically very similar neighbourhoods being served by the much larger Indianapolis City Police Department. That gave us a natural experiment.
>
> (Ostrom 2010a: 8)

This research suggested that economies of scale in administration were limited and 'polycentric' systems of policing often worked well. Her research was interdisciplinary from the start, and based on diverse methodological strategies. The Ostroms agreed that political science was a craft, and that human beings are political artisans who create systems of governance in the same way they produce art or great works of cuisine. Indeed Elinor and Vincent, in wanting to make political science a practical, experimental endeavour, were inspired by the perhaps unlikely pursuit of furniture making. Setting up home, they visited Paul Goodman, a local carpenter who they asked to make their furniture. Instead, he offered to teach them how to make what they wanted. Their collaborative experience making furniture items reinforced the Ostroms' interest in collective problem-solving:

> One of the reasons we called this place a workshop instead of a center was because of working with Paul and understanding what artisanship was.
>
> You might be working on something like a cabinet and thinking about the design of it, and thinking this idea versus that idea, and then Paul could pick up a board and say, oh, you shouldn't use this one because it will split. He could see things in wood that we couldn't. So the whole idea of artisans and apprentices and the structure of a good workshop really made an impression on us.
>
> (Leonard 2009)

The Ostroms also built their own home. Elinor drafted the plans, having learnt from her set designer father.

In 1973, they created the Workshop in Political Theory and Policy Analysis at Indiana University, which after their deaths in 2013 was renamed the Ostrom Workshop in Political Theory and Policy Analysis. The Ostroms used words with care, and the original workshop title was designed to emphasise that political theory was to be accompanied by practical analysis of policies, rather than remaining abstract and unconnected. Design was also a major concern for Herbert Simon, whose influence on their intellectual development is significant. Another intellectual stimulus to the Ostroms was their involvement with the Center for Interdisciplinary Research (ZiF) at Bielefeld University, in what was then West Germany. During the early 1980s several visits were undertaken and Elinor Ostrom learnt game theory, which is the formal study of strategic decision-making, from Reinhard Selten (Ostrom 2010a: 12). They were also exposed to European schools of sociological thought. Vincent had a long-standing interest in the work of the German theorist Walter Eucken who, while an economist, read the philosopher Husserl with care.

During the 1980s after 15 years of work on policing and local government, Elinor returned to the study of commons. Elinor's renewed focus on the question of commons led, after the urging of her friend the institutional economist Douglass North, to the publication of *Governing the Commons* in 1990 and Nobel recognition for her work in 2009. In her last years, while extending her analysis of commons, she became increasingly intrigued with the concept of social-ecological systems, seeking to link social and natural sciences to understand the ecological systems within which human beings are embedded. She once noted, has 'anybody mentioned that I'm a bit of a workaholic?' (Leonard 2009). She wrote or co-wrote thirty books and was a principal director of thirty-five externally funded research projects, according to one obituary (Ecological Society of America 2013). The Ostroms inspired considerable affection from their colleagues and students. From her brightly coloured clothes and headscarf, which made her look like a native American matriarch or a particularly relaxed member of the Amish, to her and Vincent's fascination with furniture making and indigenous art, an eccentric demeanour provided continued interest. The often unusual life experiences of Elinor Ostrom shaped her innovative approach to economics, politics and the other disciplines to which she contributed.

Garrett Hardin, Karl Marx and the tragedy of the commons

The biographical sketch of Elinor Ostrom shows that there is a huge overlap between her ideas and those of her husband Vincent Ostrom. This is unsurprising, given that they worked as a team for decades. However, Elinor is better known than her husband, despite his initial interest, for her specific focus on the concept of commons. Her work on the commons can be seen as a critique of Garrett Hardin's 'Tragedy of the Commons' paper published in the journal

Science in 1968. Hardin, a biologist, argued that an absence of property rights was a cause of many environmental problems. He felt that commons, where property was not owned by a private individual, would lead to abuse of resources. Unowned resources are unprotected and so open to over-exploitation. Hardin gave the example of a field used for cattle grazing to illustrate his argument. If too many cattle are placed on the common, it will be overgrazed and destroyed. The common is tragic, not because it is a sad situation but an inevitable one. Like the original ancient Greek use of the term 'tragedy', the situation unfolds inexorably; none of the characters within the play can change the plot. Each individual knows that overgrazing is a problem but believes that any action they take is too small to be effective. If they put fewer cattle on the common, others will continue to put on more. Disaster is the result:

> [...] the rational herdsman (*sic*) concludes that the only sensible course for him to pursue is to add another animal to his herd. And another.... But this is the conclusion reached by each and every rational herdsman (*sic*) sharing a commons. Therein is the tragedy. Each man (*sic*) is locked into a system that compels him to increase his herd without limit – in a world that is limited. Freedom in a commons brings ruin to all.
>
> (Hardin 1968: 1244)

The alternative to 'ruin' according to Hardin, is either to privatise the commons or for the state to nationalise it. His paper gained huge attention and was very widely read:

> It is extraordinary indeed when the same paper is cited by electrical engineers (writing in *Systems Methods*, *Spectroscopy*, etc.), medical and biological workers (publications such as the *Journal of Forestry, Bioscience*, the *Australian Medical Journal*) and even social scientists (for example in the *Journal of Applied Psychology, Current Anthropology* and the *Journal of Conflict Resolution*).
>
> (Roberts 1979: 147)

The phrase 'tragedy of the commons' appeared to be obvious common sense, providing an unambiguous morality tale of ecological catastrophe. Hardin was not without his critics, for example, writing in the 1970s the Australian physicist and social commentator Alan Roberts, noted:

> The Commons Tragedy, in Hardin's sense, is a myth without historical foundation. But in the widespread and largely uncritical acceptance of its false assumptions, the elements emerge of a tragedy far from mythical, and curiously classical: a search for salvation along paths which all unwittingly lead to destruction. We might call it *the tragedy* of 'The Tragedy of the Commons.'
>
> (Roberts 1979: 161)

Roberts argued that commons were seized from local people and enclosed, and that before such enclosure, commons worked well because local people organised collectively to prevent overuse:

> [...] the commoners did not simply throw up their hands in despair and watch the remorseless tragedy of their livelihood being destroyed. Their answer was a direct and simple one: where resources were limited and threatened, each commoner was given a 'stint' – that is, he (*sic*) was rationed as to the number and the type of beasts he (*sic*) could graze.
>
> (Roberts 1979: 150)

For Roberts, the commons often worked because human beings have the potential to solve problems creatively without external direction. The notion of commons, as a positive institution under threat, has also been noted by Antonio Negri and Michael Hardt:

> There has been a continuous movement throughout the modern period to privatize public property. In Europe the great common lands created with the break-up of the Roman Empire and the rise of Christianity were eventually transferred to private hands in the course of capitalist primitive accumulation. Throughout the world what remains of the vast public spaces are now only the stuff of legends: Robin Hood's forest, the Great Plains of the Amerindians, the steppes of the nomadic tribes, and so forth.
>
> (Hardt and Negri 2001: 300)

Alan Roberts, Michael Hardt and Antonio Negri are self-described Marxists, although rather heterodox and libertarian. Many other Marxists have discussed the commons. While Hayek and other liberal thinkers were not noted for their investigation of the topic, an examination of Karl Marx's work shows that the commons was one of his key areas of interest. One of his earliest pieces of political journalism dealt with the erosion of customary rights from commons in the Rhineland. Marx wrote about the debates on the law on thefts of wood in the provincial assembly in the radical newspaper *Rheinische Zeitung* in 1842, noting that peasants' customary right to pick up fallen wood for their fires was being criminalised. While the forests were privately owned by the local gentry, they were commons, because traditionally the local community had the right to use them. That was until enclosure, when harsh penalties for those who dared to continue taking fallen branches were introduced. His co-author Friedrich Engels suggested that this episode inspired Marx to become interested in economics and to develop a radical critique of society:

> I heard Marx say again and again that it was precisely through concerning himself with the wood-theft law and with the situation of the Moselle peasants that he was shunted from pure politics over to economic conditions, and thus came to socialism.
>
> (Callinicos 2011: 6)

Marx and Engels frequently alluded to 'communal property' which they distinguished from state property (Marx 1976: 885). Marx, for example, identified the commons in the eighteenth century Scottish Highlands:

> To the clan, to the family, belonged the district where it had established itself, exactly as in Russia, the land occupied by a community of peasants belongs, not to the individual peasants, but to the community. Thus the district was the common property of the family. There could be no more question, under this system, of private property, in the modern sense of the word, than there could be of comparing the social existence of the members of the clan to that of individuals living in the midst of our modern society.
>
> (Marx (1853))

He argued that the commons were enclosed and that such enclosure, long before Hardin's paper, was justified by economic doctrine. In an angry passage from *Capital* he notes how the Duchess of Sutherland expelled Scottish clanspeople from their communal land:

> Between 1814 to 1820 these 15,000 inhabitants, about 3,000 families, were systematically hunted and rooted out. All their villages were destroyed and burnt, all their fields turned into pasturage. British soldiers enforced this mass of evictions, and came to blows with the inhabitants. One old woman was burnt to death in the flames of the hut, which she refused to leave. It was in this manner that this fine lady appropriated 794,000 acres of land which had belonged to the clan from time immorial. [...] She divided the whole of the stolen clanland into twenty-nine huge sheep farms, each inhabited by a single family, for the most part imported English farm-servants. By 1835 the 15,000 Gaels had already been replaced by 131,000 sheep.
>
> (Marx 1976: 891–892)

Perelman (1983) has argued that the enclosure of the commons was an essential but unspoken element of the classical market-based economics of Adam Smith. Private property is, of course, one of the key defining features of market-based economics. While Marx argued that communism required the withering away of the state, commons can be seen as the source of his alternative to both the state and the market. Commons appears to be a socialist economic concept that provides a fundamental point of opposition between private and collective ownership. Marx, before his tragically premature death in 1883, became ever more focussed on the commons, writing voluminous notes on the anthropology of indigenous peoples, with a particular focus on communal property rights, instead of finishing *Capital* (Krader 1972). Critical discussion of the commons in Marx's thought is beyond the scope of this book. Yet having established that the commons were a source of immense, even all-consuming fascination for Marx, we might ask, can Elinor Ostrom be described as a Marxist?

From Adam Smith to Amartya Sen

While commons looks like communism and was a key concept for Marx, it is highly misleading, as I have noted, to define Ostrom as a socialist or communist thinker. She is often conceptualised as a follower of free market economists from Adam Smith to Hayek. Indeed Boettke has noted, '[W]hat Vincent and Elinor Ostrom and their students are trying to do is to look at how it is that you can have Smithian solutions to Hobbesian dilemmas' Boettke (24 November 2009).

Although Hobbes suggested that society potentially meant the war of all against all, Adam Smith's belief in barter and trade informs Elinor's notion of the cooperative commons, where conflict is settled by negotiation. Both Elinor and her husband Vincent came from a pedigree that values many market-based thinker like Smith. Indeed Ben Fine has argued that Elinor Ostrom was an exponent of economics imperialism because she tried to apply economic analysis to the wider study of human behaviour (Fine 2010). Fine has criticised this tendency, perhaps best represented by Gary Becker, in some detail (2000). If even the commons, that most collectivist of institutions, can be understood via rational choice theory and the array of prominent liberal thinkers, cited on the last page of *Governing the Commons* 'such as Hobbes, Smith, Madison, Hamilton, Tocqueville', the academic left seems injured beyond recovery (Ostrom 1990: 216). In a scathing review of *Governing the Commons*, Fine argues that her 'approach is an ingenious variation on the core themes of mainstream economic theory [...] from the vantage point of social and political theory, that is precisely the problem' (Fine 2010: 585). Such a view will be debated throughout this book. Critics like Fine can point to evidence of Elinor Ostrom's connection with market-based economics, rational choice approaches and the concept, damning for him, of social capital.

Both Ostroms were founder members of the Public Choice Society. Elinor served as president of the society between 1982 and 1984, and Vincent between 1967 and 1969. Public choice theory extends classic free market economics to the study of politics. It suggests that, while market failure has been used to justify government intervention, such intervention often, and perhaps more often than not, fails. In turn, far from being neutral servants of the people, politicians and civil servants include rent-seeking individuals who introduce policies that benefit them personally. Accordingly, if economics is based on the actions of rational individuals, who seek to maximise personal benefit, so too are other areas of life including politics. However, while economic competition is beneficial, politicians can monopolise power, leading to inefficiency and gross exploitation. I will argue in later chapters that James Buchanan, the economist most associated with public choice, was a very strong influence on the work of both Ostroms.

A major academic study of the Ostroms' Bloomington workshop by Aligică and Boettke stresses their roots in classical liberal thought, via Adam Smith onwards, seeing them as developing a new school of public choice theory in the form of institutional analysis and development (IAD) (Aligică and Boettke 2009).

When Elinor won the Nobel Prize, Hayekians and other market-orientated economists celebrated her victory. Yet her normative concerns, including a commitment to dealing with climate change, seem to distance her from many of those who embrace the market. When asked what she felt were the most important issues facing global society she replied:

> The melting of the glaciers, rising sea levels, extreme storms, and the many other impacts of global warming are grave and need to be considered among the major environmental problems of our era. We should not, however, ignore environmental problems facing local communities and regions throughout the world.
>
> (Ostrom 2009b: 246)

While Ostrom rejected Malthusian ideas of the population bomb and stressed the creativity of human attempts to tackle environmental problems, she felt that environmental problems such as climate change had to be addressed. In turn, her stress on sufficiency, arguing as we have seen, that humans should live better on less, seems to have little do with the traditional view of economics as a science of accumulation. Equally, her strong personal commitment to advancing women and minorities seems to place her on the left rather than the free market right.

Her apparent support for public choice and allied rational choice is also confusing. While associated with such perspectives, she has also been supportive of their well-known critic Amartya Sen. In his paper *Rational Fools*, Sen challenged the idea that selfish maximising behaviour explained economic activity. In the following parable he ridicules its basic assumptions:

> 'Where is the railway station?' he asks me. 'There', I say pointing at the post office, 'and would you please post this letter for me on the way?' 'Yes' he says determined to open the envelope and check if it contains something valuable.
>
> (Sen 1977: 32)

Ostrom when asked, 'What is it about Amartya Sen's work that you find interesting?' replied:

> His concern with equity, and that instead of just efficiency, we should be thinking of how to enhance equitable arrangements. He also has a pretty good sense of local levels and the higher – they can be quite fair or they can be quite over-powering and corrupt. Why should we think that people who are now in the government are all good and people at the local level are all bad?
>
> SG: Where do you disagree with Amartya Sen?
>
> Right at this moment, I can't think of any place I disagree.
>
> (Gupta (22 March 2011))

Closer examination shows that both Sen and Ostrom were unapologetic about their apparently conflicted approach to rational choice theory. Both rejected many of its assumptions but also found part of it useful to explore human motivations analytically.

Elinor Ostrom was also, like Sen, an advocate of greater social equality, bluntly telling one German newspaper that being 'born rich is always bad'.

> Inequality is dangerous. When the rich are floating at too extreme altitudes, they are completely unable to understand the needs of the poor. When there are more and more rich, and thereby people who think that they are something better, that is not good for a democracy.
>
> (*European Tribune* (14 October 2009))

Indeed many on the left celebrated, just as loudly as the Hayekians, when she won her Nobel Prize, typically the *Huffington Post* observed:

> Ostrom's body of work is inherently radical, demonstrably anti-corporate, and implicitly socialistic. Her basic premise is that the purported 'tragedy of the commons' – in which privatization of resources is viewed as the only realistic antidote to their complete exploitation – is actually an inversion of logic and reality, and that in fact the most sustainable forms of resource management are collective, cooperative, egalitarian, and decentralised in nature. [...].
>
> In choosing to honour her, the Nobel selection committee has provided an intriguing buttress against the self-referential 'only money matters' work of people like Milton Friedman, and has extended its influence into a new generation of economics premised on sustainability and community-based management.
>
> (Amster (2009))

Yet Elinor Ostrom rejected a socialist label, observing:

> Do you take issue with those who call your theories 'implicitly socialistic?'
>
> Elinor Ostrom: Yes. I don't think they are supporting socialism as a top-down theory. A lot of socialist governments are very much top down and I think my theory does challenge that any top-down government, whether on the right or the left, is unlikely to be able to solve many of the problems of resource sustainability in the world.
>
> (The Big Think (14 November 2009))

Apparently 'leftist' concerns over issues such as equality, ecology and feminism, were never presented by her as existing within an anti-capitalist or anti-market framework. She noted that she 'was a stubborn son of a gun' and expressed relief at winning the Nobel Prize because she felt that her work had been seen as marginal, if not worthless, by many of her academic peers especially during the early years of her career (The Big Think (14 November 2009)). She remembered being criticised for reading a book about peasants: 'Once while waiting at a meeting of the Political Science Association I was asked why I was reading a book on peasants. Political science was about presidents, parties, and Congress' (Toonen 2010: 197).

Both Ostroms noted the importance of polycentric approaches to governance. By this, they meant that there is no one prescription that can be applied universally; different methods can sometimes produce results which are equally appropriate and valuable. Different approaches can be combined, and while this looks messy both practically and intellectually, relative strengths can potentially be meshed together and weaknesses overcome. It is no surprise from a polycentric perspective that her work contains insights from very different and apparently diametrically opposed schools of thought. Neither Vincent nor Elinor approached theory in a binary fashion.

Another element of Ostrom's polycentric thought is her debt to indigenous people. Indigenous, in this respect, is a little difficult to define but should be seen as a sociological concept rather than an ethnic one. At one political prize-giving speech she thanked the indigenous people of North America for their seven-generation rule, 'indigenous people in this country had a way of thinking seven generations into the future. We need to do more thinking about seven generations into the future' (Ostrom (2008)). References to the indigenous are often found in her work, typically, a paper on climate change suggested that support for the management of the world's forests by indigenous people is vital (Ostrom 2009a: 29).

Ostrom's scepticism of universal rules extended to indigenous peoples. While indigenous thought, she felt, was too often ignored, indigenous people are not automatically correct in all circumstances:

> I urge people to respect the indigenous people. In terms of health knowledge, there is a lot of indigenous knowledge about herbs and other things that work for illness and how to manage illness in an effective way. But we also find that sometimes indigenous knowledge is wrong and as we do tough science, we say 'no, that's wrong'.
>
> What I object to is the presumption that the government officials have got all the knowledge and locals have none. On the other hand, I don't want to say the government officials don't have any because there are times when you can have access to good scientific information at a large scale.
>
> (Gupta (22 March 2011))

It is also worth noting that while she is best known for her work on common pool resources and collective property, she did not advocate one particular form of property ownership. She viewed her work as dealing with a puzzle rather than advancing a particular ideological solution. Discussing knowledge commons with her colleague, Charlotte Hess, they noted:

> […] use of the word commons is not infrequent. It can be constructive and often provides the impetus to collective action around the commons. But a commons is not value laden—its outcome can be good or bad, sustainable or not—which is why we need understanding and clarity, skilled decision-making abilities, and cooperative management strategies in order to ensure durable, robust systems.
>
> (Hess and Ostrom 2011: 14)

The sustainable economics of Elinor Ostrom

Ostrom's work, and indeed that of her husband and the wider network of scholars they worked with, has varied and important implications. This title argues that the creation of a sustainable economics, both in the theoretical sense of an economics fit for purpose in the twenty-first century and beyond, and specifically in terms of environmental sustainability, can be enhanced by examination and extension of Elinor Ostrom's thought.

While her work is most associated with the concept of commons, it should also be associated with 'contestation'. She believed that strong argument was a technique necessary to the production of knowledge. Her work is 'contestable' and must be open to criticism and debate. How, for example, is it possible to combine insights rooted in methodological individualism with a theory that stresses the possibility of communal forms of organization? Is it possible that, while noting the existence of the commons, like many other economists she under-theorises questions of power, conflict and culture? Is an emphasis on grassroots local solutions to climate change adequate to deal with a fast emerging crisis propelled by global factors? These questions are discussed throughout this text as her ideas are introduced and situated in more detail. Chapter 2 outlines some of the individuals and groups who influenced Elinor Ostrom, including Friedrich Hayek, Michael Polanyi, John R. Commons, Alexis de Tocqueville, Herbert Simon, Jane Jacobs and the Haudenosaunee. Chapter 3 examines Ostrom's often novel methodology which combined such diverse research techniques as laboratory experiments, case studies, historical examination, quantitative analysis and satellite surveys. Chapter 4 outlines the tragedy of the commons thesis in greater detail and shows how Ostrom's work indicates that, in particular circumstances, it can be overcome. Five focuses on her response to climate change and her work examining social-ecological systems. Chapter 6 looks at the contribution Ostrom's work makes to understanding cyber space, software and information commons. Chapter 7 examines whether common pool property systems can be extended to industrial production and expands the notion of social sharing to physical goods as well as environmental resources and information systems. Chapter 8 looks at the politics and power issues inherent in conserving and extending the commons. The final chapter discusses the extent to which Ostrom provides the basis for a form of more sustainable economics.

2 Signs and wonders

> *Question*: *If you could have dinner with anybody, who would it be?*
> Elinor Ostrom: Well, I would like to have a dinner with John R. Commons, who was a very distinguished labor economist at the University of Wisconsin and whose work I've read multiple times and I still assign to my students. He was struggling with trying to understand how to enable labor to organize more effectively and wrote some of the initial legislation for labor law in Wisconsin and elsewhere. And he had a very interesting philosophy about rights having a counterpart to duties. And so if somebody has a right, somebody has to have a duty! And I would love to discuss with him some of those philosophical foundations.
>
> The Big Think (14 November 2009)

Both Reinhard Selten and his wife suffered from diabetes, a condition that gave rise to a number of ill effects. Frau Selten's legs were amputated beneath the knees and her eyesight declined but she continued to care for their three cats and to cook, although such tasks took longer. Reinhard observed, 'what is most important, she maintains a cheerful attitude towards life. We have learnt to adjust to our situation' (Selten 1994). Despite illness, Reinhard continued to take an interest in wildflowers. Botany was just one of a number of varied pursuits including political activism. In 2009, he contested the European Parliamentary elections in Germany as the lead candidate for 'Europe – Democracy – Esperanto', which promotes a universal language and human rights. Reinhard was born in Breslau, then in Germany, in 1930. During the Second World War the city became part of Poland. Half-Jewish, his parents, who had no faith, had hoped that when he was an adult he could decide his own religious opinion. However in Hitler's Germany, rising anti-Semitism meant they felt it was prudent for him to be baptised a Protestant. Reinhard survived the war but became a refugee and never returned to Breslau. He was first attracted to game theory after reading an article in *Fortune* magazine as a teenager. In 1994, he won a Nobel Prize in Economic Sciences, shared with John Nash and John C. Harsanyi, for his work on game theory. He was also a friend of Elinor Ostrom and taught her game theory.

This chapter outlines how 11 schools of thought and thinkers contributed to Elinor Ostrom's intellectual development. Each supplied at least one significant concept that shaped her practical research. Jane Jacobs, for example, helped her to think about complexity, design and the potential dangers of centralised planning systems. It is important to outline each in order to better understand the origins of Elinor Ostroms' ideas.

The list could be extended. For example, none of those examined in this chapter directly studied common pool resources. Elinor Ostrom's work on the commons drew on researchers like Robert Netting, who examined Swiss commons, and Margaret McKean who surveyed examples of commons from Japan. These researchers are referenced more fully in Chapter 4 which looks specifically at her work on commons and her book *Governing the Commons* (Ostrom 1990). I was tempted to include discussion of Frank Knight and Joseph Schumpeter, two interesting economists who she had clearly read. Ostrom referenced both in her PhD for their work on the concept of public entrepreneurship (Ostrom 1965). She argued that outside of purely market relations, individuals or groups might act as entrepreneurs, organising activity and taking risks, in her study of water management in California. Nonetheless this concept of the public entrepreneur, important as it was to her work, did not seem to involve her in detailed or extensive discussion of either Schumpeter or Knight, so I resisted their inclusion in this chapter. I also considered discussing Amartya Sen's influence on her thinking, as she admired his work (Gupta (22 March 2011)). The intellectual relationship between Sen and Ostrom was no doubt close. It is also clear that there are very strong parallels and equivalent paradoxes in their work. They are both figures who are often seen, rightly or wrongly, as on the 'left' but who built upon market-based economics. For example, both Ostrom and Sen drew upon rational choice theory but also critiqued it. Yet, I think it is more illuminating to understand how both Elinor and Amartya took insights from thinkers like Reinhard Selten and Robert Axelrod who took rational choice theory in new more cooperative and humanistic directions, than to discuss Sen as a direct influence on her work.

It would have been possible to discuss more of her influences from institutional economics. This would be a book-long project on its own rather than part of a chapter and the traffic has been two-way, with institutionalists like Douglass North informing her work and learning from her. The two dominant institutionalists who cannot be ignored if we are to understand her work are of course John R. Commons and James Buchanan who are discussed here. Ostrom's understanding of institutional economics in general was essential to her work.

Elinor Ostrom was an inter-disciplinary thinker and not averse to engaging with those with very varied and sometimes contradictory views. Her principle concern, however, was to find intellectual tools that could be used practically to study how institutions worked or failed to work in sustaining collective resource use. Starting with perhaps the most significant intellectual influence on her and Vincent Ostrom, Alexis de Tocqueville, this chapter moves on to the importance for her thought of the institutional economist John R. Commons. An eccentric but reformist thinker, he believed in intervening in the market to help workers and others who might suffer injustice. His thought, at least on the surface, contrasts strongly with that of the free marketer Friedrich Hayek. Political philosophers Harold Lasswell and Abraham Kaplan enriched her thought, along with the market-based institutional economist James Buchanan. Michael Polanyi's approach to knowledge and the Haudenosaunees' notion of a seven-generation rule were also important to her. She read the biologist Ernst Mayr whose approach to the philosophy of science influenced her thinking. A number of theorists who took rational choice theory in new directions, showing that economics might be about more than selfish self-interest, including Reinhard Selten, Robert Axelrod and Herbert Simon are also vital if we are to understand Elinor Ostrom's work. The iconoclastic opponent of modernist city planning Jane Jacobs also inspired her. The greatest influence on her intellectual development was without doubt her husband Vincent and they learnt from each other. The individual who inspired and fascinated them most was a French nineteenth century writer Alexis de Tocqueville (1805–59).

Alexis de Tocqueville

> When de Tocqueville discussed the 'art and science of association' he was referring to the crafts learned by those who had solved ways of engaging in collective action to achieve a joint benefit. Some aspects of the science of association are both counterintuitive and counterintentional, and thus must be taught to each generation as part of the culture of a democratic citizenry [...]. A democratic citizenry who do no more than vote in national elections cannot sustain a democracy over the long term.
>
> (Ostrom 2006a: 9–10)

If one figure could be used to describe their thinking, in the way that we may label individuals as Keynesians, Marxists or Hayekians, the nineteenth century French writer and politician Alexis de Tocqueville, could be used to describe the Ostroms as Tocquevillians. One of Vincent Ostrom's most important books *The Meaning of Democracy and Vulnerability of Democracy* is subtitled 'A Response to Tocqueville's Challenge' (V. Ostrom 1997); the Ostroms helped establish a Tocqueville endowment at Indiana University and often discussed his work; and a portrait of Tocqueville hangs in the main seminar room in their workshop, which they founded on the Bloomington campus. Perhaps the nearest Elinor came to embrace an 'ism' was that of 'Tocquevillism'.

Born in Normandy in France, Alexis de Tocqueville was a member of an aristocratic family traumatised by the French Revolution of 1789 (Epstein 2006: 10). He can be understood, along with John Locke, Adam Smith and John Stuart Mill, as one of the classical liberal political philosophers. He wrote a number of books and had a varied political career during the often-tumultuous era of nineteenth century French politics. At various times a government minister and a member of the French Parliament, he made journeys to Algeria, Britain and Ireland, recording his observations about political and social life. In 1831, he was sent by the French government to the USA to write a report on their prison system. While he did produce the report, he is better known for the two-volume book *Democracy in America*, which records his experience during his nine months in North America. He was fascinated by many aspects of US politics that he saw as a largely successful experiment in the creation of a democratic system. Tocqueville also wrote an account of the French Revolution of 1789 *L'Ancien Régime et la Révolution*, published in 1856. A democrat, he felt that the revolution had replaced one centralised political system with another. Tocqueville died of tuberculosis in 1859 and was buried in the family plot in Normandy. He was an abolitionist who opposed slavery, a Roman Catholic who was sympathetic to the Irish population before the great famine; he advocated free trade and challenged the working class French socialist movement.

Tocqueville's extensive analysis in *Democracy in America* provided a number of insights necessary for Elinor Ostrom's study of common pool property and Vincent's writings on politics. He believed that for governance to be truly democratic it had to involve citizens constructing their own rules of political association. Politics and government should not just involve a formal state but institutions at varied levels of society. Like Adam Smith, Tocqueville viewed people as self-interested. In this sense, he was an individualist, but also like Smith, he argued that people could come together for meaningful association. Smith's theory of market exchange was underpinned by the suggestion that virtues such as trust were vital to the economic order, which Smith described as 'moral sentiments' (Smith 2010). Tocqueville argued, in turn, that cooperative behaviour based on similar moral sentiments was vital for a functioning democracy. These were all insights that the Ostroms found useful and instructive.

Elinor Ostrom's asssumption that commons work best when they are controlled by the commoners who use them, fits well with Tocqueville's belief in grassroots democracy. He argued that democracy involved practice and renewal and was underpinned by shared cultural norms. Above all, he believed that democracy should be participatory. He was particularly enthusiastic about the township meeting held in New England. Similar to classic Athenian democracy, citizens would meet and directly make decisions. He noted:

> Town meetings are to liberty what primary schools are to science; they bring it within the people's reach, they teach men (*sic*) how to use and how to enjoy it.
>
> (Tocqueville 1980: 87)

Tocqueville rejected the idea that politics was simply about power over others. While politics could involve manipulation, he was interested in politics as negotiation, with individuals learning how to live best with each other even if they had contradictory interests. Neither did he believe in any structural explanation or what postmodernists since Lyotard (1984) refer to as 'grand narratives'. While Marx and Engels famously argued in *The Communist Manifesto* that all written history was the history of class struggle, Tocqueville rejected what he saw as causal explanatory systems of social change. Jon Elster (2009) has referred to him as the first social scientist. While this claim is debatable and Tocqueville's work was based on his travel rather than a focussed programme of research, he was keen to examine how societies worked in practice through observation.

The notion of politics as a craft, advocated by the Ostroms, was strengthened by their reading of Tocqueville. Vincent Ostrom notes that Tocqueville sought a 'new science of politics. [...] for a new world' (V. Ostrom 1997: 29). Tocqueville's participatory liberalism is essential to the Ostroms' thinking, together with their interest in *The Federalist Papers* and other sources that show the American revolutionaries' attempts to create a working participatory democracy. Like the Ostroms, Tocqueville combined a liberal belief in individual action with an emphasis on cooperation and collective action. Above all, his work helped inspire the Ostroms' view that politics was wider than the study of the state. Vincent noted the importance of Tocqueville's concept of self-governance:

> [...] in which each individual is first one's own governor and then capable of working out appropriate patterns of rule-ordered association with others through mutual agreements based on common knowledge and shared understanding as the foundations for conjoint activities in communities of relationships [...]. From this perspective, I consider Tocqueville to be correct in this presupposition that democratic societies are self-governing societies, not State-governed Societies.
>
> (V.Ostrom 1997: 59)

The Ostroms also argued that their attempt to show how individuals worked within an institutional setting, can be described as 'Tocquevillian analytics' (McGinnis 2005: 170).

Tocqueville combined political philosophy with practical study; his examination of American democracy was based on personal observation rather than abstract philosophy His notion of language as a key influence on political life is another feature of his work embraced by both Elinor and Vincent Ostrom. Any examination of Elinor's work that ignores Tocqueville's influence is likely to be misleading.

Lasswell and Kaplan

> The book by Harold D. Lasswell and Abraham Kaplan on *Power and Society* is certainly one of the most important books in my early career. What was so important was that Lasswell and Kaplan saw multiple values that could be used in efforts to achieve multiple outcomes. They included power as one of the values that people might use as a resource as well as an outcome. They might search for using power to get power or knowledge to get power or to get any of the other eight values that they included in their analysis. This broadened my perspective on individual choice and behaviour in a way that was very instrumental.
>
> (Ostrom (22 March 2012))

Harold Lasswell (1902–78) was a political scientist and Abraham Kaplan (1918–93) a philosopher. In *Power and Society*, they attempted to construct an analytical basis for political science. In their introduction to the book they noted, 'the present work is an attempt to formulate the basic concepts of political science. It contains no elaborations of political doctrine, of what the state and society *ought* to be' (Lasswell and Kaplan 1950: xi). *Power and Society* is a textbook of political definitions, an attempt to define concepts precisely, so they can be used to draw solid conclusions.

The concern with a pragmatic focus on research has been important throughout Elinor Ostrom's career. She was not principally interested in developing a broad social, political or economic philosophy as Marx or Hayek tried to accomplish, but instead she tried to understand how institutions worked or failed in practice. While neither sustainability nor common pool resources are mentioned in *Power and Society*, political science is introduced as a pragmatic and focussed field of investigation. The notion that the outcomes that individuals sought might be based on multiple values, which Elinor gained from reading Lasswell and Kaplan, contrasted with the assumption of mainstream economics that material benefit was the sole outcome that self-interested individuals sought. Her understanding of Lasswell and Kaplan's work contributed to her search for more complex ways of understanding human motivation, pursued by thinkers such as Robert Axelrod and Herbert Simon, who she also read.

Like the Ostroms, Lasswell and Kaplan were inter-disciplinary scholars, who argued that politics could not be understood without reference to economics, sociology and psychology, they argued 'since the subject matter of political science is constituted by power as a process, its scope cannot be sharply differentiated from that of other social sciences' (Lasswell and Kaplan 1950: xvii).

Vincent Ostrom noted that Lasswell believed that politics did not mean the study of the state alone:

> Lasswell and his generation, who were my teachers, presumed political science to be a science of State, or a science of Government. Lasswell attempted to break out of that mold. Lasswell's genius was his deep appreciation that the characteristics of a democratic society did not conform to a theory of command and control by relying on some single center of Supreme Authority.
>
> (V. Ostrom 1997: 58–59)

However, Lasswell was associated with behavioural approaches to politics and studied Nazi propaganda during World War Two. He and Kaplan were aware that politics might be reduced to the study of power based on manipulation of individuals. Lasswell and Kaplan were not interested in political ideas or values but in studying systems. Despite Vincent's assessment, an observation of the clinical and apparently authoritarian manipulation of systems by sets of experts seems to mark their work. Indeed, it has been suggested that their approach was technocratic:

> Lasswell believes that through the rigorous application of scientific methods, democracy is made to operate smoothly and efficiently. [...] there does not seem to be much of anything that is democratic about either the context in which the policy process is supposedly embedded or the policy process itself.
>
> (McGovern and Yacobucci 1999: 7–8)

The dry analytic content and often seemingly cynical approach of *Power and Society* and their other publications contrasts with the outlook of both Ostroms, who were inspired by participation rather than systems of political control. Nonetheless, the need to define concepts used in research exactly to make comparisons possible is a feature of *Power and Society* utilised by both Ostroms. Elinor's enthusiasm for *Power and Society* contributed, perhaps, to her belief that key terms had to be defined with care, to enable researchers from different disciplines to reach a shared understanding and promote effective work in the social sciences. As will be discussed in Chapter 3, the Ostroms, along with colleagues including in particular, Ronald Oakerson and Larry Kiser created an Institutional Analysis and Development (IAD) framework for examining institutions, which can be seen as an attempt to extend the task of *Power and Society*; of enhancing the practical research potential of political science. Both the Ostroms and Lasswell and Kaplan sought to make political analysis more precise so that it could function to help solve practical problems. Of course, the Ostroms rejected the notion that politics was a top-down academic pursuit; instead, they believed that it could be used to provide tools for citizens to cope better with the governance problems they faced. Practical policy considerations were also a concern of John R. Commons, who after Vincent Ostrom and Tocqueville was perhaps the most important influence on Elinor's work.

John R. Commons

John R. Commons (1862–1945) was an institutional economist, social reformer and labour historian. Born in Ohio, he grew up in Indiana and after a somewhat convoluted career, taught economics at the University of Wisconsin (Harter 1962: 9). He was also a highly successful policymaker helping to write a number of laws protecting workers and citizens, covering health and safety legislation, labour protection, pension and trade union rights. Much of the progressive social and labour legislation in twentieth-century USA can be traced back to Commons or his students and colleagues. He was the architect of welfare and has been seen as waging an assault on laissez-faire (Harter 1962). His zeal for social reform was linked to his role as an institutional economist. He argued that institutional forces shaped economic transactions, including buying, selling and wage setting, particularly the legal framework of a society (Commons 1893). He did not agree with the idea that the market would automatically benefit all; coercion helped shape the transactions undertaken in ways that might reward those with power and disadvantage others. He suggested, for example, that monopolies were an example of how those with influence could push up prices. He rejected the idea that monopolies existed only as a consequence of government intervention, which could be removed by further freeing market forces to create competition (Harter 1965). In his view, the institutional framework of an economy shaped who benefitted and who bore greater costs. While he flirted with a range of heterodox and radical schools of thought including that of the land reformer Henry George, he believed that the market economy was beneficial in a number of ways. Yet he felt that the market left to its own devices would tend to generate inequality and injustice so legislation was important to reduce forms of market failure. For example, legislation could be used to improve the bargaining power of trade unionists against powerful firms who might otherwise use their strength to push down wages. As he outlined in *The Legal Foundations of Capitalism*, law provides part of an institutional framework that shaped economic decision-making (Commons 1968). Geoffrey Hodgson, a contemporary institutional economist, has argued that according to Commons, 'the law was constitutive. In particular, as Commons fully recognised, common law itself requires frequent legal interpretation, choice, and judgment. It never works in an entirely spontaneous fashion, entirely outside powerful legal institutions' (Hodgson 2003: 566).

John R. Commons' reformist institutionalism was, in almost all respects, rejected by the free market institutionalists like Buchanan and Tullock after his death in 1945. These 'new institutionalists' to whom both Elinor and Vincent Ostrom were affiliated via their membership of the Public Choice Society, argued that government action might lead to various other forms of injustice and that government failure was perhaps a greater problem than market failure. It could be said that Commons belonged to the era of the New Deal and the Keynesian welfare state, despite never being a Keynesian and dying in 1945 before the introduction of 'The Great Society'. Buchanan and Tullock, as we shall see, can be linked to the Reaganite counter-revolution in US politics that sought to sweep away restraints on the market.

As her statement, which opens this chapter, indicates, Elinor Ostrom valued Commons' role as a reformist labour economist. As we have seen, she was keen to advance workers' rights, at least, in terms of the participation of women and ethnic minorities. Both Commons and Ostrom noted the importance of negotiation and compromise to achieve political solutions. His understanding of property rights was essential to Elinor Ostrom's research. He argued that legal frameworks helped shape market outcomes and that property was a legal construct. In her Nobel Prize lecture, Elinor Ostrom noted how she had drawn upon Commons' notion of property rights as a bundle of rights, rather than a single right to own a resource (Ostrom 2010b: 652). Commons argued that it is misleading to merge an object with its ownership and to assume that ownership means we can do whatever we like with it. In contrast, he distinguished property from property rights and argued, in turn, that property rights were often a bundle of rights. He provided in the bundle of rights notion an important way of understanding common pool property. Drawing upon his work, Elinor Ostrom made a crucial distinction between property rights and particular items, physical or non-physical, to which they were applied. For example, she believed that common pool property systems were different from the land, sea or cyberspace that they might govern. Thus a field might be owned by a private individual, a community or the state; it would remain a field but the nature of the property rights governing it would change with such different forms of ownership. The notion of a bundle of rights can be used to show that different communities or individuals hold different rights. Typically in the UK, individuals, institutions or the state can privately own common land. Commoners, usually limited to those who live locally, can use commons to graze animals or gather plants. In turn, in many cases, anyone can use the common for walking or other recreational activity but only a precisely defined group of commoners have the right to graze animals on the common. Land which is held as common property, is physical land governed by a property rights regime. Objects are different from their defined forms of ownership, for example, a book can be owned by an individual, owned by the state in a library or shared with friends. As will be discussed in later chapters, Elinor Ostrom was carefully to distinguish between common pool resources and common property systems; ownership is not the same at the object owned. Ownership, in turn, may be multiple and mixed.

John R. Commons also noted the existence of legal pluralism, with different systems of overlapping authority, a notion that was important to both Elinor and Vincent Ostroms' work. Instead of rejecting customary law as outdated, he stressed how it was based on accumulated wisdom, a notion that, despite his very different approach to welfare and social justice, links Commons' thought to that of Hayek. Customary law and legal pluralism are important concepts to understanding indigenous approaches to economic governance and property rights. His institutionalism, concern with justice and sophisticated understanding of property rights were all important to Elinor Ostrom's intellectual development. While she was identified as a practitioner of the new institutional economics of the post-war period, together with figures such as Buchanan and North, she drew upon the old institutionalism of John R. Commons. Oliver Williamson, whom Ostrom shared the Nobel Prize with, praised the contribution of John R. Commons' work repeatedly and 'singled out Commons as an "old" institutionalist whose work is especially close to the "new" institutional economics' (Hodgson 2003: 547).

Friedrich Hayek

> For the purposes of our paper, Hayek's classic analysis of the essential two types of knowledge in order to bring, a clear understanding remains crucially relevant in the construction of scientific knowledge and information policy. He wrote in 1945 that while we are used to respecting scientific knowledge gathered by experts, it is only in combination with 'local knowledge' that the knowledge takes on a real value. All of the valid research on common-pool resources involves this combination of scientific knowledge

> with time and place analysis, or as Hayek puts it, the 'special knowledge of circumstances.'
>
> (Hess and Ostrom 2001: 20)

Friedrich Hayek (1899–1992) was an Austrian-born economist and political philosopher. Critical of collectivism, he viewed communism as brutal and regressive, linked in his mind to the supposedly allied totalitarianism of Hitler's Germany. He was perhaps the most successful intellectual opponent of the left during the twentieth century. In response to the Keynesian consensus that dominated policymaking during the 1950s, 1960s and 1970s, he mounted an ultimately successful assault on government economic intervention. He was dismissive of efforts to create greater social equality, arguing that the very notion of social justice was literally meaningless:

> I believe that 'social justice' will ultimately be recognized as a will-o'-wisp which has lured men [*sic*] to abandon many of the values which in the past have inspired the development of civilisation – an attempt to satisfy a craving inherited from the traditions of the small group but which is meaningless in the Great Society of free men [*sic*].
>
> (Hayek 2012: 67)

Regardless of whether one views him as the emblematic hero or villain of free market economics, Hayek's work is complex and subtle. He argued that markets tended to work and state intervention tended to disempower citizens and prevent economic development. Like John R. Commons, he suggested that legal institutions put in place by government were necessary. Both he and Commons also acknowledged the importance of customary or informal law, based upon tradition, which grew from the grassroots. He also argued, despite his antipathy to redistribution and social justice, that the state should provide a minimal safety net to prevent citizens falling into absolute poverty.

It has been suggested that Hayek's theory of knowledge 'is his most distinctive contribution to both economics and to social science' (Gamble 1996: 111). Economists generally argue that markets work better the more closely they conform to an ideal type, that of perfect competition. Perfect competition assumes an infinite number of buyers and sellers, an unrealistic assumption perhaps, but economists generally think that competition leads to greater efficiency and choice. Perfect competition also assumes perfect knowledge. While this is also an unrealistic assumption, economists have generally assumed that the closer to perfect knowledge a market is, the more efficient it will be. If we have perfect knowledge of all the prices in a market for a particular good, we will tend to buy the cheapest, which will force firms to cut their prices, promoting efficiency and empowering the consumer. In contrast, Hayek argued instead that because knowledge in society is poorly distributed, this makes markets necessary because markets are better at dealing with the information failure that would make central planning of economic activity unworkable. It is not that markets rest upon perfect knowledge but, for Hayek, the fact that knowledge in society is imperfect that meant that markets were a vital necessity. Identified with contemporary free market orthodoxy, Hayek's critique of mainstream economic theory, nonetheless, made him a methodological radical.

Hayek was a strong opponent of what he termed 'rationalism' or 'scientism'. This does not mean that he valued irrational or purely emotional approaches to problem-solving but that he felt that a plan rationally developed for society would always be oppressive and flawed because of the knowledge problem. 'Utopian' plans for a better society were always dangerous because a single thinker or group of thinkers lacked the information needed to create such a plan. Hayek opposed socialism because he saw it as based on just such a utopian plan instigated by a strong state. Knowledge, he argued, was divided into two types. The first was scientific knowledge gathered by experts, while the second type was local and often highly informal. An understanding of both was necessary if policies were to be implemented effectively. Central planners could not gather enough knowledge of local condition in his view and their plans were likely to end in disaster.

Elinor Ostrom stressed how a top-down approach can lead to such disaster. Garrett Hardin's notion of the 'tragedy of the commons' is based on the assumption that local people are powerless to prevent disaster and therefore control from an external body is needed. Yet according to Ostrom, government action or indeed privatisation, can lead to the loss of local knowledge and local systems of governance that have evolved over time. While Hayek was a strong advocate of private property rather than commons, his theory of knowledge suggests that local action may be more effective than central action. This is because local people are better informed in many circumstances than experts in the centre are. A Hayekian approach to knowledge was essential to his anti-socialist views and advocacy of the market; it also influenced Ostrom's sympathy for local solutions to resource management.

Both Ostroms drew upon Hayek's theory of knowledge but seemed to echo the conservative philosopher Michael Oakeshott's criticism that 'a plan to resist all planning may be better than its opposite, but it belongs to the same style of politics' (Gamble 1996: 119). There is a danger of using Hayek's theory of knowledge dogmatically to reject all government intervention and as Elinor Ostrom often noted, local people might sometimes get things wrong and fail to manage resources sustainably. However, she agreed with Hayek that government officials were often less knowledgeable than local people.

Hayek argued that markets were an example of spontaneous order, what he termed *catallaxy*. The Ostroms suggested that such human self-creation of functioning institutions takes place both in markets and beyond in varied forms of polycentric governance. Their colleague Michael McGinnis suggested that to describe the Ostroms as believing in spontaneous order is misleading:

> In my view, there is not much that is spontaneous about a polycentric system of governance. [...] A polycentric system can be said to be spontaneous only

> if one restricts that term to mean that no one person or collective entity purposively designed a system meant to operate in this manner. However, this lack of planning is only apparent if you are looking at the system from the outside. From the inside, each of these jurisdictional units contains creative individuals who have acted to design and implement these multiple units of governance in order to pursue their own goals and resolve their disputes more effectively. Skills at planning and leadership are essential requirements in the establishment and maintenance of each of these organizations.
>
> (McGinnis 2005: 168)

Ultimately, all human action might be thought to require planning; nonetheless both Hayek and the Ostroms suggested that a single central plan is likely to lead to failure.

The British political scientist Andrew Gamble argues that Hayek held an almost ecological view of markets, seeing both ecosystems and markets as evolving spontaneously without a conscious external plan. Yet Gamble suggests that Hayek failed to address whether 'the market order is compatible with the natural ecosystem [...]. The contemporary global economy based on neoliberal rules is a success of Hayekian principles. But whether Hayekian principles can preserve the ecosystem poses a new and sterner test' (Gamble 1996: 138).

Michael Polanyi

One might assume that Karl Polanyi inspired Elinor Ostrom. Using anthropological sources, he challenged the idea that markets have been dominant throughout human history, finding evidence for wide spread non-market economic activity (Polanyi 1957). However, Elinor's work drew instead upon his younger brother Michael's.

Karl was born in Vienna and both brothers grew up in Budapest. Karl was best known for his book *The Great Transformation* and was very much an anti-capitalist intellectual (Dale 2010). In contrast, Michael (1891–1976) was a chemist and his experience of visiting the Soviet Union transformed him into a strong defender of the market economy. His work, which influenced Hayek, focussed on the philosophy of science with forays into economics, politics and ethics. He argued that knowledge is both conceptual and tacit. Scientists might discover concepts of universal application, but to translate such concepts into a useable form requires that they be combined with more informal and localised understanding. What we know but cannot explain is 'tacit'. Riding a bicycle, baking a cake or running a marathon can be described by concepts that can be written down in recipe books, manuals or 'how to do' guides. Yet such conceptual descriptions do not adequately explain the processes involved. Conceptual knowledge, which is written down or perhaps presented as a set of mathematical codes is, Polanyi argued, incomplete. He felt that even scientists rely to some extent on tacit knowledge. A positivist form of knowledge that rejects personal non-verbal learning is incomplete. Rich personal experience is vital for tasks to be carried out. In short, as he stated '[W]e can know more than we can tell' (Polanyi 2009: 4).

He rejected codification of all forms of knowledge because tacit knowledge is too subtle to be easily transmitted. He believed that scientists worked best when they were like entrepreneurs and trying to develop their knowledge through exchange. In a messy, complex world, multiple individuals and institutions worked best. In his 1951 book *The Logic of Liberty*, he first used the term 'polycentricity' which means 'many centres'. In his view, decentralised market activity led to efficient production and should be accompanied by plural political institutions.

During the 1970s, Elinor's study of policing suggested that multiple, small and overlapping police authorities delivered better services than centralised bodies (Ostrom *et al.* 1978). She was a keen advocate of polycentricism in several senses. Rather than focussing on one type of institution she argued that commons, markets and state intervention all had a role. Polycentricism, perhaps, also led to her methodological pluralism with the notion that different approaches to research can complement each other. Polycentricism is vital to her work and reinforces the Hayekian distrust of central planners. However, as Barbara Allen, who edited two volumes of Vincent Ostrom's work noted, when Vincent first used the word polycentricism in 1961, he was unaware of Michael Polanyi's previous use of the concept (Allen and V. Ostrom 2011: 351).

Elinor Ostrom also sought to show that her work and that of Vincent differed in at least one important respect from that of Michael Polanyi. She and her colleague Michael McGinnis argued that for Polanyi, 'polycentrism connotes an automatic dynamic process that does not recognize the pivotal role of public entrepreneurs in making connections between units of a governance system or the critical importance of explicit coordination among distinct actors within that system' (McGinnis and E. Ostrom 2011: 18).

In contrast to Polanyi, the Ostroms felt that while central planning was potentially damaging, it was not enough to rely on spontaneous action to solve problems, conscious human action to craft appropriate institutions was vital. Yet despite such differences, the Ostroms and Polanyi shared a polycentric approach and an appreciation of the informal status of some vital forms of knowledge. Michael Polanyi helped deepen the Ostroms' philosophy of knowledge and appreciation of the role of pluralistic approaches to governance.

James Buchanan

> Honoring James Buchanan is an honor and a privilege. I review the influence of his work on my own research and that of colleagues associated with the Workshop in Political Theory and Policy Analysis. *The Calculus of Consent* helps to explain the capabilities and limits of citizen self-organization and led to a number of studies in metropolitan areas across the United States. In more recent years, efforts to understand how and when

users of a common-pool resource would self-organize to manage resources have also been strongly affected by Buchanan's work.

(Ostrom 2011: 370)

James Buchanan (1919–2013) was, like Elinor, a Nobel Prize winning economist who practised political economy as a new institutionalist (Rutherford 1996). In contrast to the 'old' institutionalists such as John R. Commons and Thornstein Veblen, Buchanan argued that politics could be better understood using economic analysis and was critical of increased state control of the economy. John R. Commons sought to show how political, in particular legal structures shaped the economy, whereas Buchanan, while accepting this insight, placed a much greater emphasis on how market behaviour instead affected political activity. The notions of methodological individualism and self-interest assumed by economists were extended to the behaviour of political actors. In the preface to *The Calculus of Consent* his best-known book written with Gordon Tullock, it is noted:

> This is a book about the *political* organization of a society of free men (*sic*). Its methodology, its conceptual apparatus, and its analytics are derived, essentially, from the discipline that has as its subject the *economic* organization of such a society.
>
> (Buchanan and Tullock 1965: v)

While Buchanan and Tullock did not claim that politicians were more self-interested than the rest of the population, they argued that their motives were similar to private individuals in general. Thus, people might enter politics for self-interested reasons and civil servants might seek to improve their personal lot. Politicians might try to find ways of helping key groups of voters to improve their own chances of being re-elected. Economic motives, as much as ideological or social commitment, explained why individuals might become politicians or civil servants.

Buchanan helped develop these insights into the public choice framework and this was followed by a wider move to use economic analysis to explain other areas of human behaviour. Rational choice theory evolved partly out of his and Tullock's work, to understand how self-interest shaped human behaviour in a variety of contexts. Gary Becker has been associated with this approach and, in turn, has been criticised as an economics imperialist by the political economist Ben Fine (Fine 2000). While it might be argued that Buchanan and Tullock felt that politics was, in a sense a branch of economics, this is slightly misleading. While 'old' and 'new' institutionalists took opposite sides of an ideological debate, both sets of institutionalists felt economic activity demanded a role for some kind of non-market governance. All economies were, in their eyes, political economies. However, Buchanan feared, like Hayek, that increasing government intervention would act as the road to serfdom. Politicians would intervene more and more to gain the support of voters, and as the scope of government expanded, human freedom would be stifled in a top-down managed society.

Both of the Ostroms were close to Buchanan and both became President of the Public Choice Society. They were enthusiastic about his advocacy of decentralisation as a way of making political systems more competitive. His study of constitutions linked ideas from Tocqueville to formal analysis and game theory. Such constitutional economics informed the Ostroms' development of an institutional analysis and development framework. His key concepts of constitutional design shaped Elinor Ostrom's analysis of the features most likely to give rise to a sustainable commons. He argued constitutions worked at different levels, a set of rules might exist that determined how new working rules could be constructed. He felt that despite political conflict which almost inevitably arose between different groups in a society, political solutions would be adhered to if there was a broad consensus on constitutional design.

Buchanan and Tullock, along with other public choice theorists, criticised the assumption that states provided an automatic solution to market failure, while the Ostroms agreed they were opposed to a purely laissez-faire alternative. Elinor Ostrom felt that Vincent had been wrongly associated with a simplistic notion of public choice and was critical of the way public choice theory developed. An article co-written by Michael McGinnis and Elinor Ostrom noted:

> First, public choice theory brings to the study of politics a relentless focus on the importance of efficiency in public policy. [...] but [Vincent] Ostrom never presumed that this would be the only goal under consideration. In a polycentric order, individuals or communities might decide, for whatever reason, to sacrifice efficiency for the pursuit of other goals, such as accountability, fairness, or physical sustainability.
>
> (McGinnis and Ostrom 2011: 19–20)

The Ostroms rejected the model of rational behaviour invoked by public choice theorists, based on pure material self-interest, arguing instead that human motivation is more subtle and complex. While Buchanan was generally seen as a right wing libertarian-tinged thinker who was hostile to taxation, like John R. Commons he argued that individuals needed to come together to deal with collective problems. If collective action reduced costs for individuals enough, it would be likely they could cooperate. Buchanan believed that voluntary associations to provide for services such as policing or fire protection were possible without a formal state. In turn, a state might be necessary but a constitution constructed by citizens was vital to provide a set of rules so that different individuals could cooperate. Like other thinkers or sets of thinkers discussed in this chapter, James Buchanan provided Elinor Ostrom with intellectual tools she could use in practical research. Buchanan's work shines out in her *Governing the Commons* study, where she sees the creation of a working system to sustain a common resource as a form of constitution making (Ostrom 1990: 2001). From Maine lobster fishers to Cree hunters, Elinor analysed systems of political consensus and sustainable environment governance, with insights from his work.

Charlotte Hess who worked with both Vincent and Elinor, observed:

> Both Lin and Vincent have noted the important influence of Buchanan and Tullock's 1962 volume *Calculus of Consent* because of its focus on public choice as well as individuals' capacity for self-governance and collective action. Vincent's thesis traces the institutional structure of L.A.'s water system to the shared property of the original pueblo system of El Pueblo de Nuestra Señora la Reina de Los Angeles, the original name of the city of Los Angeles, California.
>
> (Hess 2010: 3)

Ernst Mayr

In an article entitled 'The Ten Most Important Books' Elinor Ostrom (2004) included *The Growth of Biological Thought: Diversity, Evolution and Inheritance* (Mayr 1982). This might appear to be an unusual choice for a political economist. One interpretation of Ostrom's work is to see her, along with Vincent, as drawing upon classical liberal thinkers including Adam Smith and Tocqueville. This is true but she was not interested in being part of a 'tradition'; she and Vincent focussed on problem-solving and looked for intellectual tools to do so. Such tools came from diverse sources. She was also a political ecologist, concerned with how human beings could act sustainably, so it is important to recognize that she read widely within the natural sciences as well as the social. Ernst Mayr's book the *The Growth of Biological Thought* was important to her for a number of reasons.

Ernst Mayr (1904–2005) has been described as 'one of the principal architects of 20th century evolutionary biology' (Gadagkar 2005: 87). He became interested in biology, when as a young man, he spotted a pair of rare ducks known as red-crested pochards that had not been seen in German for 77 years. His scientific achievements were extensive but Elinor Ostrom was most interested in his approach to the philosophy of science. She and Vincent believed that human society could not be studied in isolation from the rest of nature, we are another species amongst many and have a biological nature as well as a social one. She did not advocate socio-biology and she rejected the idea of static human nature, especially one based on supposed 'natural' features. She and Vincent argued that ecological considerations had to be taken into account. She was also interested in the evolution of economic systems. She did not of course advocate social Darwinism nor see natural and social evolution as identical but she believed that culture changed over time and was subject to some form of selection. The topic of evolutionary economics is complex and beyond the scope of this title but Elinor Ostrom was fascinated by Mayr's account, which showed how the concept of evolution in biology developed.

Mayr wrote *The Growth of Biological Thought* because he thought it was important for his students to understand how historical biological thought had advanced so that they could better understand contemporary theory. His emphasis was on practical problems. He looked at how biologists had tried to solve particular scientific puzzles in the discipline, noting:

> In the problematic approach the chief emphasis is placed upon the history of attempts to solve problems – for instance, the nature of fertilization or the direction-giving factor in evolution. The historian not only of the successful but also of the unsuccessful attempts to solve these problems is presented. In the treatment of the major controversies in the field, the endeavour is made to analyse the ideologies (or dogmas) as well as the particular evidence by which adversaries supported their opposing theories. In problematic history the emphasis is on the working scientist and his [*sic*] conceptual world.
>
> (Mayr 1982: 7)

Elinor Ostrom was a strong advocate of intellectual practice as a way of dealing with puzzles and problems. She felt that Mayr's book was important because rather than focussing upon the biographical details of scientists or setting different ideological schools against each other, instead it showed how biologists had aggregated knowledge (Ostrom 2004). Mayr stressed that 'contestation' in the form of strong debate meant that even theories that proved flawed helped contribute to greater understanding in the field. Ostrom noted that her second benefit from reading Mayr was an understanding of emergence. In contrast to economists who stress methodological individualism, Mayr showed that a system could not be understood by looking only at its constituent elements. She quotes him as noting that systems 'almost always have the peculiarity that the characteristics of the whole cannot (even in theory) be deduced from the most complete knowledge of the components, taken separately or in other partial combinations' (Mayr 1982: 63 in Ostrom 2004). Thus emergence occurs: a human being is not simply an aggregate of its cells and cells are not simply aggregates of their molecules. Elinor Ostrom's work includes an apparently paradoxical combination of an acceptance of emergence especially in complex adaptive systems together with a commitment to methodological individualism. Certainly she felt, as we shall see in later chapters, challenged by Mayr's understanding of emergence. Although she does not discuss this aspect, it is also possible that she was influenced by Mayr's anti-essentialism and anti-historicism. He did not believe that evolution was moving in a particular direction guided by an essential spirit or external influence. He also notes that a widespread commitment to Aristotle's essentialism that 'found everywhere well-defined species, fixed and unchanging' slowed the acceptance of evolution (Mayr 1982: 306). Because Aristotle could not imagine origins, did not believe that species changed and stressed their distinct essences, his ideas made it difficult for a concept of evolution to emerge. Elinor Ostrom's thought stresses pluralism, relational factors and rejects unchanging essences, in regard to political economy. However, above all, Ostrom valued the idea, supported by Mayr, that social sciences could attempt to develop knowledge in a cumulative way, building on previous researchers' work. She hoped to understand human governance problems better by doing so. Her reading of Mayr strengthened her intellectual approach and *The Growth of Biological Thought* helped her reconsider her understanding of the questions of individualism and emergence.

Selten and Axelrod

> I was fortunate that Reinhard Selten invited me to join his game theory seminar on the Bielefeld campus. During long walks in the woods behind the campus, Reinhard and I discussed an evolving framework for institutional analysis and the centrality of game theory to its development.
>
> (Ostrom 2010a: 11–12)

Elinor Ostrom took the rational choice assumptions of new institutional economics in a cooperative direction. While she never claimed human beings were intrinsically cooperative, during her career, she distanced herself from notions that we are innately selfish. While such an approach might seem to be a rejection of the market-based economic consensus, it should not be forgotten that, while Adam Smith argued that humans were motivated by self-interest, he also observed that trust was necessary to make exchange possible. Elinor Ostrom's lifelong project challenged the implications of rational choice theory which suggested that competitive behaviour is apparently ubiquitous.

She often cited Axelrod's work and became interested in game theory through working with the Nobel winner Reinhard Selten. Of Axelrod, she noted:

> Few scholars have been able to integrate participation in antiwar protests, computer chess tournaments, working on a campaign staff for a presidential contender, biological evolution, agent-based modeling, and building rigorous methods of policy analysis. Robert Axelrod has a strong interest in all of the above. More important, he has made major contributions to all of them including: (1) the development of a general theory of the emergence of sustainability of cooperation relevant for many repeated settings.
>
> (Ostrom 2006b: 171)

Robert Axelrod, born in 1943, has been Professor of Political Science and Public Policy at the University of Michigan since 1974. His first degree was in mathematics and he has consistently applied mathematical approaches to the development of political science. His best-known book *The Evolution of Cooperation* argues that even a society of egoists may be able to develop cooperative forms of behaviour. Evolutionary processes, in his view, promote collective sharing behaviour because this benefits individuals more than purely competitive and aggressive practices. President of the American Political Science Association between 2005 and 2006, he was often praised by Elinor Ostrom and they shared an inter-disciplinary approach to research.

Selten, who won a Nobel Prize with John C. Harsanyi and John F. Nash Jr in 1994, as we have seen, is a fascinating character. Born in Poland in 1930, half Jewish, he was lucky to survive the Holocaust. The brutality of the Second World War meant that he became strongly attracted to humanitarian causes. He worked on game theory with particular emphasis on the well-known prisoners' dilemma. In the prisoners' dilemma, two prisoners are held in separate cells. The police have no real evidence that either of the prisoners, who have previously committed a robbery, are guilty. If both prisoners refuse to confess, they will be set free. Silence will give rise to freedom. However, if one prisoner confesses and the other does not, the prisoner who confesses will receive a lighter sentence and is under pressure to confess. If the first prisoner remains silent but the other confesses, he or she will receive a heavier sentence. Rational choice assumptions suggest that self-interest means that because neither prisoner can trust the other, they will both confess. Rationality and selfish behaviour gives rise to a worse outcome for an individual player than altruistic trusting behaviour. Nash equilibrium, as conceptualised by John F. Nash, predicts this outcome.

Selten won his part of the Nobel Prize, along with Nash and Harsanyi, for his 'trembling hand' equilibrium, the idea that during a game, participants would factor in unintentional mistakes on the part of the other players. Axelrod showed that, in repeated games, cooperative behaviour could evolve despite egotistical self-interest. In essence, Ostrom who worked with both Axelrod and Selten, was fascinated to see how game theory could give rise to cooperative behaviour during such uncooperative game scenarios. Such insights were extended to Ostrom's study of commons to show how the free rider problem identified by Garrett Hardin might be overcome.

Hartmut Kliemt, who met Elinor during her and Vincent's visits to Bielefeld University, in what was then West Germany, noted:

> [...] it became almost immediately clear that Elinor Ostrom was more inclined towards the modeling aspects of economics and game theory than Vincent and thereby even closer to my interests. [...]. We both admired Reinhard Selten's philosophical approach to game theory and Vincent Ostrom's approach [...]. Both of us had worked on building a bridge between these two seemingly disparate strands of social theory for about a decade. Trying to bring together the two approaches we had, somewhat paradoxically, become both more optimistic and more pessimistic about the contribution of formal modeling to social theory. We had become increasingly convinced of the value of non-cooperative game theory or rational choice modeling (RCM) as a tool of representing complex interactions. At the same time we became increasingly skeptical about the prospects of rational choice theory (RCT) as a means of explanation.
>
> (Kliemt 2011: 38)

Game theory powerfully influenced Elinor Ostrom's practical research and was a major theme of her work. There are many references to game theory and the specific contribution of Selten within *Governing the Commons* (Ostrom 1990). Often associated with selfish rationality, inspired by Selten and Axelrod, she used experimental work in behavioural game theory to explore how to promote cooperation. Paradoxically her interest in rational choice theory led to conclusions, supported by research findings from formal models and experiments, which undermined the simple model of rationality suggested by mainstream economists. In seeking to understand human motivation in a more subtle way, she also made extensive use of the insights of another Nobel Prize winning political economist, who was of course, Herbert Simon.

Herbert Simon

> [...] the narrow rational choice model of the individual used in neoclassical economics and by some formal theorists of human behaviour is characterized by assumptions that the individual possesses complete information, the individual values a single, externally measurable value (such as profits or the probability of being re-elected), and the individual selects the strategy which maximises this value. A model of the individual drawing on the work of Herbert Simon would instead posit an individual with limited information and bounded capacities for processing information, with multiple goals, and a calculation process involving limited search for satisfactory outcomes.
>
> (Ostrom 1982: 24)

Herbert Simon (1916–2001) won a Nobel Prize in economics for his concept of bounded rationality. Like Elinor, he was a political scientist as well as an economist. A wide-ranging thinker, he was concerned with administration, design, artificial intelligence and a host of other fields. Like Ostrom, the binary choice between state and market seems to have little to do with his understanding of economics. Reading his extensive writings, it sometimes appears that he practised his own unique discipline that was not really economics or politics or psychology but a study of human resource use and governance of social and technological activities.

Simon's notion of bounded rationality, as he noted in his Nobel speech, can be traced back to John R. Commons and other institutionalist economists such as Veblen. Simon's uncle Harold Merkel had:

> studied economics at the University of Wisconsin under John R. Commons. Uncle Harold had died after a brief career with the National Industrial Conference Board, but his memory was always present in our household as an admired model, as were some of his books on economics and psychology. In that way I discovered the social sciences.
>
> (Simon/Nobel Prize Org (2013a))

Simon read social sciences and mathematics at the University of Chicago in the 1930s:

> My most important mentor at Chicago was the econometrician and mathematical economist, Henry Schultz, but I studied too with Rudolf Carnap in logic, Nicholas Rashevsky in mathematical biophysics, and Harold Lasswell and Charles Merriam in political science.
>
> (Simon/Nobel Prize Org (2013a))

Lasswell, as we have seen, was another powerful influence on both Elinor and Vincent Ostrom. This quest for rigor encouraged Simon to challenge the methodological assumption of rational self-interest suggested by mainstream economics. While imagining that individuals might try to act rationally to maximise personal benefit, like other economists influenced by institutional context, Simon was aware that their ability to do so rested on imperfect knowledge. He argued that bounded rationality is a result of such imperfect knowledge. According to Simon, instead of maximizing, 'satisficing' behaviour may be more common for both firms and individuals because it is impossible to process the information necessary to maximise either utility or profit. Instead, particular but limited goals are set and we attempt to achieve them. Rationality is better served by more modest aims than an aim of trying to achieve the maximum possible in all economic situations. *The Economist* described his approach:

> Contrary to the tenets of classical economics, Simon maintained that individuals do not seek to maximise their benefit from a particular course of action (since they cannot assimilate and digest all the information that would be needed to do such a thing). Not only can they not get access to all the information required, but even if they could, their minds would be unable to process it properly. [...]
>
> Humans, for example, when in shopping mode, aspire to something that they find acceptable, although that may not necessarily be optimal. They look through things in sequence and when they come across an item that meets their aspiration level they go for it. This real-world behaviour is what Simon called satisfiying.
>
> (*The Economist* (20 March 2009))

Simon was a strong advocate of making social sciences more rigorous by introducing mathematics to study human behaviour and blurring the boundary between natural and social sciences. Such an approach might be associated with rather crude positivism that over-simplifies human behaviour. However, Simon argued that while more could be learnt about human behaviour, much would always remain unknown. He believed in using empirical research to study economics rather than becoming over-dependent on abstract, often unproven, theoretical assumptions and complex formal models:

> The social sciences have been accustomed to look for models in the most spectacular successes of the natural sciences. There is no harm in that, provided that it is not done in a spirit of slavish imitation. In economics, it has

> been common enough to admire Newtonian mechanics (or, as we have seen, the Law of Falling Bodies), and to search for the economic equivalent of the laws of motion. But this is not the only model for a science, and it seems, indeed, not to be the right one for our purposes. Human behavior, even rational human behavior, is not to be accounted for by a handful of invariants. It is certainly not to be accounted for by assuming perfect adaptation to the environment.
>
> (Simon/Nobel Prize Org (2013b))

Elinor Ostrom assumed bounded rationality in her work and Simon's approach to methodology that utilised mathematics but rejected 'physics envy' was important to her practical work. Simon's work, which is the product of an institutionally sophisticated economist, was clearly of great importance to her. The assumption of bounded rationality also implies that institutions are necessary as a way of gathering and transmitting knowledge. Institutions are economically vital because they make decision making easier in a world where collecting information is costly, by collecting and transmitting knowledge. Elinor Ostrom cited Herbert Simon's book *The Sciences of the Artificial* as one of ten books that she felt was most important to her work (Ostrom 2004). In it, he attempts to develop a discussion of how to research the artificial world created by human action. The products of human action, from language to cyberspace to gardens and recipes, are all around us and need to be understood. Contingent products of human ingenuity can, Simon argued, be studied scientifically and understood better (Simon 1996). Vincent Ostrom sought to understand artificial human artifacts such as constitutions more effectively. Like Vincent, she was inspired by the US constitution, an artifact constructed by human action. She also took a key principle from another constitution as an inspiration for her work on commons and social-ecological systems. This, of course, was the seven-generation rule, derived from the Haudenosaunee confederation's constitution.

The Haudenosaunee Confederation

Elinor Ostrom was an advocate of indigenous rights and was inspired by the seven-generation rule (Ostrom 2008). The seven-generation rule, which suggests that in major decisions we should think of the impact on future generations, is apparently also found amongst indigenous people in India but is best known from the Haudenosaunee, a confederation of six nations, who live in the twenty-first century, mainly in what is now New York State and Ontario. The Haudenosaunee, are perhaps better known as the Iroquois. However, Haudenosaunee, which means 'They are building a longhouse' is their preferred self-description (Racusin and McArleton 2012: 3).

Few of the thinkers who inspired Ostrom that are discussed in this chapter were concerned explicitly with environmental sustainability. Neither were they concerned with indigenous rights. Some of them can be seen as at best Eurocentric; others at worst racist. John R. Commons, while a social reformer and insightful thinker, depressingly embraced crude racial stereotypes in his work on labour markets (Leonard 2005: 215). Tocqueville believed that indigenous Americans were doomed, noting 'our well-digested plans are met by the spontaneous instincts of savage life' (Tocqueville 1980: 327). In contrast, and like Amartya Sen, both Ostroms have been happy to go beyond the canon of European and white American theorists. Elinor Ostrom's fieldwork and use of case studies covered every continent and she strongly rejected the idea that communal peoples were 'backward'. Vincent Ostrom's work, while focussing on US politics drew from thinkers across the planet. As we noted, he studied the Klamath with interest. One of his students related (Loveman 2008) that he recommended *The Cheyenne Way* (Llewellyn and Adamson Hoebel 1941). While fascinated by indigenous Americans, he also referred, sympathetically to Islamic, Chinese and African thinkers (V. Ostrom 1997). Neither of the Ostroms were Eurocentric thinkers.

When I interviewed Elinor Ostrom in March 2012, she told me that it was important to respect North American indigenous people and discussed the seven-generation rule. The Ostroms noted that indigenous people have developed institutions of governance, crafting political rules and using customary rights to manage their economies, societies and interactions with the rest of nature.

Political theorists have long been drawn specifically to the Haudenosaunee. Their sophisticated political system has been seen by some as a model for the US constitution (Johansen 1982). The Haudenosaunee were studied in depth by the nineteenth century anthropologist Lewis Morgan. Karl Marx read Morgan avidly and noted Haudenosaunee communal forms of property ownership (Shaw 1984). Marx's notebooks on anthropology provided the basis of Engel's *The Origins of the State, the Family and Private Property*.

The Haudenosaunee were originally the five nations. The Mohawk, Oneida, Onondaga, Cayuga and Seneca created a federation to end conflict and were joined by the Tuscarora in 1722. Allied with the British, they were defeated by the American revolutionaries and their influence rapidly diminished. The confederation of the six nations dissolved after US independence but Haudenosaunee peoples are politically active in the twenty-first century in environmental and land rights campaign. They also retain the right to hold their own passports. The Haudenosaunee developed a sophisticated political constitution which fascinated Morgan, Marx and other thinkers. Their system was democratic and led by women. Decisions were made directly by consensus rather than through majority voting. 'Leaders' acted as speakers for the community rather than commanding them and checks on power were built into their system.

Sustainability, economic equality and respect for previous and future generations were part of their constitution. Fenton (1998) attempted to summarize their political principles. He noted their primary commitment to sustainability, 'The Earth, our mother, is living and expanding continually, imparting its life-giving force to all growing things on which our lives depend.' Rule by women is also clearly identified by Fenton, '[I]t is us women that count. A chain of kinship connects all members of society, running through mothers to the smallest child and reaching even those as yet unborn.' Sharing is of great importance, he noted 'the law of the kettle'. Hospitality 'is a right and a duty to share. Throwing ashes is the negation of the hospitality, sharing, friendship, peace, harmony, and accord.' (Fenton 1998: 49). He further observed 'Equanimity. Restraint is important. One must not exert too much power and "spoil it". The equable person succeeds.'

While Elinor Ostrom focussed on the seven-generation rule, we shall see the principles of the Haudenosaunee parallel many of her more general concerns. The Haudenosaunee built a political constitution as an attempt to provide an institutional answer to the questions posed later by the Ostroms. The Haudenosaunees attempted to deal with self-interest and potentially damaging conflict not by assuming that humans were 'naturally' cooperative and nurturing but by building appropriate political institutions in an attempt to create better governance. Like James Buchanan they advocated 'politics without romance', noting that fallible human beings had to work hard to remain at peace. They were perhaps better Tocquevillians than Tocqueville. Like him, they studied how to build better political association. While Elinor Ostrom undertook no detailed investigation into their system, their work closely parallels hers and it is instructive that in embracing the seven-generation rule, she sought to show their importance as political thinkers with lessons for policymaking today.

Jane Jacobs

> Before the speech, Ostrom met with students from various colleges around the Twin Cities, discussing her commons research in subjects beyond natural resources. She cited Jane Jacobs – the passionate advocate of neighborhoods who believed that local people usually know more about what's best for their communities than expert planners – as an influence on her work.
>
> (Walljasper (2 November 2011))

Elinor Ostrom's intellectual influences might seem to be made up exclusively of dead white men. This is not quite the case but as she acknowledged it was often hard for women to become academics when she started her career. She has been compared to and she cited Jane Jacobs who was best known for writing *The Death and Life of Great American Cities* (Jacobs 1961).

Jane Jacobs was not an academic but a popular writer. Her book on urban planning became a widely cited best-seller that fundamentally changed how cities were designed. She was highly critical of what she described as modernist, paternalistic and utopian attempts to redevelop cities. Such plans were based on good intentions and aimed to remove 'slums' and to replace them with new housing. Unfortunately, according to Jacobs, because experts who failed to consult city dwellers created these plans they went horribly wrong. She was very upset by the destruction of communities to make way for roads and saw the expansion of freeways as damaging. She argued that automobiles were a symptom of a wider problem of paternalistic and undemocratic planning.

Planning from above, however well intentioned, was likely to go wrong in her view. Elinor Ostrom's work on co-production and study of policing can be seen as similar to Jacobs, in that diversity was valued and production worked best when it involved participation from relevant consumers.

Elinor Ostrom was also interested, although aware of criticism, in the concept of social capital. She noted that Jacobs was one of the originators of this concept that stressed the informal creation value through personal networks. Jacobs examined 'reciprocity and networks' that helped neighbourhoods and entire cities to function (Ostrom and Ahn 2003: xxvi).

The messy, diverse, socially mixed cities that Jane Jacobs celebrated, like the governance systems that interested the Ostroms, were designed. They were the product of intelligent human planning but not planning purely from one centre or planning by experts alone. You might think there was nothing offensive in a lawn but Jane Jacobs, who loved vivid examples, recounts the hostility of Harlem residents to a patch of green grass.

> In New York's East Harlem there is a housing project with a conspicuous rectangular lawn which became an object of hatred to the project tenants. A social worker frequently at the project was astonished by how often the subject of the lawn came up, usually gratuitously as far as she could see, and how much the tenants despised it and urged that it be done away with. When she asked why, the usual answer was, 'What good is it?' or 'Who wants it?' Finally one day a tenant more articulate than the others made this pronouncement: 'Nobody cared what we wanted when they built this place. They threw our houses down and pushed us here and pushed our friends somewhere else. We don't even have a place around here to get a cup of coffee or a newspaper even, or borrow fifty cents. Nobody cared what we need. But the big men come and look at that grass and say, "Isn't it wonderful! Now the poor have everything!" '
>
> (Jacobs 1984: 25)

There are many parallels between Jacobs' work and that of Elinor Ostrom. The notion of adaptive complex systems that came to be more important in Ostrom's work in her last decade looking at social-ecological systems is implicit in Jacobs' writing. Indeed she noted, that her book suggested changes in 'in housing, traffic, design, planning, and administrative practices, and discusses, finally, the *kind* of problem which cities poses – a problem in complexity' (Jacobs 1984: 24).

Cities are complex social and natural systems; informal governance and institutions and practices that look untidy or redundant are often essential. Elinor Ostrom's work promotes sustainable environmental governance but is cautious of plans that do not take into account social and ecological knowledge at the grassroots. A green plan imposed by experts might lead to unpredicted negative consequences and might be the subject, like the East Harlem lawn, of popular wrath. Jacobs noted of Ebenezer Howard's plans to create garden cities, with belts of agriculture 'where the city poor might live close to nature' that good intentions can lead to negative consequences:

> His aim was the creation of self-sufficient small towns, very nice towns if you were docile and no plans of your own. As in all Utopias, the right to have plans of any significance belonged only to the planners in charge.
>
> (Jacobs 1984: 27)

Jacobs' work is not without its critics who might say that the good intentions of planners to tackle poverty and environmental degradation should not be lost and that large-scale projects were necessary. Her work has justified tower block demolition but blocks have often been replaced by expensive homes displacing local people in schemes of gentrification. Jacobs would no doubt have agreed with much criticism of such practical interpretations of her work. She did not reject planning or the concerns of thinkers like Howard and Mumford but she believed that the world was a little messy and rather diverse and democratic choice was essential. Experts need to be partners, not parents. It seems likely that from her early work on local government onwards, Elinor Ostrom gained inspiration from Jane Jacobs. Elinor Ostrom, always cautious, acknowledged the need for nested systems, noted the contribution of government agencies in providing useful knowledge, for example, geological surveys. Whereas some would argue for a purely decentralist approach, Elinor Ostrom noted that there were 'No panaceas!' (Korten (26 February 2010)). Nonetheless Jane Jacobs seems a kindred spirit.

Ostrom beyond Ostrom

The varied intellectual influences on Elinor Ostrom's thought can appear both obscure and eclectic. John R. Commons or Lasswell and Kaplan appear almost forgotten in the twenty-first century and were far from prominent in much of the twentieth century. John R. Commons drew opposite conclusions to Hayek or Buchanan regarding the need for government intervention. Yet study reveals coherence. Ostrom was not a dogmatic or consciously ideological thinker, she rarely drew upon the entire approach of any particular thinker but instead she tended to use individual thinkers or broad approaches to generate concepts that helped in her quest for institutional knowledge. Her work was about trying to understand governance in a practical way, to see how human beings could come together to try to solve real-life problems; whether in the area of policing or sustainable use of environmental resources. From John R. Commons' notion of property rights as a bundle of rights to approaches to game theory from Axelrod and Selten or Simon's assumption of 'bounded rationality', Elinor Ostrom collected concepts that were used in her lifelong project.

It is interesting that parallels to Ostrom's work can be found from other thinkers, who have followed different routes, but were fascinated by similar problems.

For example, the social ecologist and anarchist Murray Bookchin was also inspired by the New England township meetings identified by Tocqueville and other similar forms of grassroots self-governance:

> You know this is an ideal that is ages old. It belonged to the early Swiss confederacy, not the present one. It was an ideal that existed in New England. Farmers in New Hampshire and Vermont and the upper valley tried to establish a republic of towns and cities during the American Revolution, and in the aftermath of the American Revolution against the federal centralized state. These are notions that Americans can understand and that have meaning in contrast with the old socialist notions of nationalizing the economy. Remember too that there is an economic program of municipalization, not just collectivization. The township should have control over the land; it should have control over the industries.
>
> (Bookchin 1986: 8)

Many of the thinkers discussed here were critical of mainstream economics as a social science. James Buchanan noted:

> As it is practiced in the 1980s, economics is a 'science' without ultimate purpose or meaning. It has allowed itself to become captive of the technical tools that it employs without keeping track of just what it is that the tools are being used for. In a very real sense, the economists of the 1980s are illiterate in basic principles of their own discipline [...]. Their motivation is not normative, they seem to be ideological eunuchs. Their interest lies in the purely intellectual properties of the models with which they work, and they seem to get kicks from the discovery of proofs of propositions relevant only for their own fantasy lands [...] I do deplore the waste that such investment of human capital reflects.
>
> (Buchanan 1986: 14–15)

While such polemical tones do not reflect Elinor Ostrom's way of writing or speaking, she was aware of such criticism of economics. Austrian-influenced economists like Hayek and indeed Buchanan, of course combined an enthusiasm for the market with a deep critique of mainstream economic methods. A strong concern with methodology is clear from Elinor Ostrom's work. She sought a rigorous approach to solve practical problems yet felt that conventional economic tools and assumptions had to be adapted to be relevant to her work. Like property rights, methods, for her, were multiple. She was critical of positivism and believed in an inter-disciplinary approach (Ostrom 1982). The next chapter examines her innovative approach to methodology.

3 On method

> Despite references to 'revolutions' and paradigm shifts, new social science theories and methods have not fully displaced their predecessors. Rather, each new theory and method has added another strand. Constructivists, institutionalists, and postmodernists coexist with behavioralists and structuralists. Despite the history of theoretical and methodological competition and critique, scholars also engage in creative synthesis. The current appreciation for methodological pluralism may be interpreted as a product of the survival and adaptation of approaches that were once perceived to be under existential threat. Promotion of methodological pluralism favors a theoretical eclecticism that should decrease concerns about existential threats to particular approaches, and should thus decrease the intensity of methodological debates.
>
> (Poteete *et al.* 2010: 11)

Debates about methodology, a term that deals with how research is undertaken, can be fierce. Positivists, structuralists and postmodernists may resemble angry tribes, who generally prefer to ignore the existence of each other and, where they do interact, do so via vicious polemics. The existence of 'existential threats' may sound like an exaggerated claim. However, debates about research into human institutions and practices can have surprisingly grave implications. Occasionally these are illustrated in popular culture. The 1964 film *Dr. Strangelove or: How I Learned to Stop Worrying and Love the Bomb* horrified and delighted audiences reeling from the 1962 Cuban missile crisis. The film was black comedy dealing with not only the Cold War and international relations but also social science method in the form of game theory.

An insane US General orders a nuclear attack on the Soviet Union. While the US and USSR authorities cooperate in an attempt to prevent mutually assured nuclear destruction, the film ends with the triggering of the doomsday weapon. The Soviets, according to the plot, decided that game theory indicated that it was rational for them to construct a weapon that would annihilate all higher forms of life on the planet. The existence of such a weapon, at a fraction of the cost of more traditional nuclear arms, would prevent the US from launching an attack:

> There were those of us who fought against it, but in the end we could not keep up with the expense involved in the arms race, the space race, and the

> peace race. At the same time our people grumbled for more nylons and washing machines. Our doomsday scheme cost us just a small fraction of what we had been spending on defense in a single year. The deciding factor was when we learned that your country was working along similar lines, and we were afraid of a doomsday gap.
>
> (McAfee 2002: 115)

The film satirised the work of the United States' RAND Corporation. The corporation was a private sector body, which quite literally 'researched' and 'designed' scientific approaches to war. One of its main purposes was to develop game theory to investigate how to develop strategies for possible nuclear war (Amadae 2003). The film character Dr Strangelove was said to be an amalgam of RAND's director Herbert Kahn and the mathematician John von Neumann. The Hungarian-born von Neumann is generally credited with the invention of game theory in the book he co-authored with Oskar Morgenstern *The Theory of Games and Economic Behavior* (Von Neumann and Morgenstern 1944). He also, apparently, invented the cold war doctrine of mutually assured destruction (MAD). In the film, Dr. Strangelove is an insane wheelchair-bound advisor to the US President. Both roles are played by the British comedian Peter Sellers. Von Neumann is said to have taken part in high-level US strategy meetings in his wheelchair as he battled with the cancer that killed him in 1955.

Research methodology during the era of the Cold War was associated with conflicting world views and indeed produced existential threat. Structuralist approaches drawn from Marxism might be seen, right or wrongly, as products of a totalitarian system. Methodological individualism, as an alternative, was strongly linked to the idea of personal freedom and political autonomy but via institutions like RAND might also, paradoxically or not, be associated with militarism and imperialist domination.

While the Cold War has passed into history, methodology can still be associated with what Elinor and her co-authors have termed 'existential threats'. Interpretivist approaches, especially those associated with postmodernism and post-structuralism, raise fears amongst those with opposing methodological assumptions. They are often associated, correctly or not, with an 'anything goes' moral relativism and by arguing that social reality cannot be objectively mapped, appear to preclude research that generates practical conclusions. Alternative methodological approaches that assume that human behaviour in economics, political science and similar disciplines can be studied 'scientifically' are, in contrast, sometimes seen as threatening to reduce living human beings to mere things. Methodological debates can, thus, be sharp.

While Elinor Ostrom is best known for her work on common pool resources and property, she also made interesting contributions in the area of research methodology. She was fascinated by methodological debates and was well aware of the often emotive and polarised nature of such discussions.

Elinor Ostrom's work moved forward and changed; she was an innovator. She was also a collaborator. It is often useful to think of her as a node in a network rather than an old style academic author working largely on her own. One of her most important methodological contributions was published in 2010, written with her collegues Amy R. Poteete and Marco A. Janssen, under the title *Working Together: Collective Action, the Commons, and Multiple Methods in Practice*. This collaboration built on Elinor's work with her husband Vincent, and research with their other colleagues, but took it in new directions. It is useful to see how the book, the most complete piece of writing outlining Elinor's practical and theoretical research assumptions, was shaped by her encounters with many of the thinkers and schools of thought discussed in the last chapter.

This chapter outlines Elinor Ostrom's inter-disciplinary perspective, which links social and natural sciences. Ostrom's broad methodological approach is discussed and the Institutional Analysis and Development (IAD) framework is introduced. Some of the many practical research methods used by Ostrom including case studies, quantitative analysis, experiments, agent based models and satellite surveys, are described. These practical methods provide data that can be used within the broader IAD framework. Finally, Ostrom's approach to methodological individualism is discussed in the context of her broader work.

Beyond positivism

Discussion of social science methodology is extensive, complex and, as I have already noted, often tribal. Methodology refers to the philosophical assumptions that determine how and why practical research is undertaken. Methodological considerations are linked to the philosophy of knowledge and the related field of the philosophy of science. A difficult question, which no doubt will never be answered to consensual satisfaction is the relationship between the natural sciences and the human or social sciences. What is meant by the word 'science' and whether human behaviour can be studied scientifically is the subject of some debate.

Economists have often been accused of 'physics envy' and of seeking to reduce people to atoms, to predict their behaviour in a mechanistic way. Economists, in turn, have on occasions dismissed subjects such as sociology and anthropology as somewhat vague. Mainstream economics links micro foundations derived from assumptions of human rationality to broadly Keynesian macro perspectives to understand how markets work. Keynes argued that the assumptions of microeconomics were inadequate in explaining how an economy worked at a macro, i.e. national level. Yet discussion of his macro analysis moves beyond the focus of this book. The micro foundations of mainstream economics are relatively simple. Humans, according to economists, are assumed to wish to maximise their individual utility or well-being. While subjective benefit is impossible to measure, it is assumed that 'indifference' or the relative worth of different choices can be identified. Economics is monetised and monetary exchange can be measured. Knowledge is expected to be 'perfect' or close enough to perfection to be adequate to allow economic agents such as consumers of business people to make effective choices. Human economic behaviour, according to mainstream economists, adheres to law-like patterns that allow for broad prediction. While human behaviour cannot be utterly predicted it can be studied in a broadly scientific manner.

Much of the mainstream methodological approach has been criticised. Economists have had an indifferent record of predicting economic events. As we have seen, while recognised as strong advocates of the market, Austrian economists such as Hayek or Schumpeter, have been seen as methodological radicals and critical of the economic mainstream. Hayek, for example, dismissed assumptions of perfect knowledge as unrealistic. Schumpeter argued that economic situations are dynamic and change over time; therefore the assumption that markets moved towards equilibrium might be over-simplistic. Marxist critiques of mainstream economics have stressed such an emphasis on dynamic change, noting that markets change over time and that, beyond the simplest assumptions, economic rules change radically from one society to another. For example, in the twenty-first century corporations are significant economic actors; in the fifteenth century, at least in Europe, guilds were major players. Marxists, of course, also note the existence of class inequalities, which they argue help shape economic and indeed most social activity. Institutional economists, while very diverse, generally note that transaction costs, imperfect information and power differentials, mean that economics cannot be understood without examining varied governance institutions. Diverse methodological challenges to economics suggest that the mainstream approach demands reform if it is to provide useful conclusions.

Elinor Ostrom thought deeply about methodology and practical research methods. While her work has profound implications for both the methodological assumptions of economics and the practical research undertaken by economists, she did not set out to challenge or change economics but instead to investigate practical problems, such as sustainable resource use, that crossed the divide between economics and politics, as well as other disciplines. While she was influenced by a number of thinkers, as we have seen, she can be described most simply as an institutionalist. It is therefore important to understand what she meant by an 'institution' and to outline the broad assumptions behind the institutional analysis and development (IAD) framework she developed with Vincent Ostrom and other colleagues.

Institutional analysis and development

Elinor Ostrom defined institutions as 'the prescriptions that humans use to organize all forms of repetitive and structured interactions including those within families, neighborhoods, markets, firms, sports leagues, churches, private associations, and governments at all scales' (Ostrom 2005: 3). The British institutional economist Geoffrey Hodgson, noted that:

> Institutions are the kinds of structures that matter most in the social realm: they make up the stuff of social life. The increasing acknowledgement of the role of institutions in social life involves the recognition that much of

> human interaction and activity is structured in terms of overt or implicit rules. Without doing much violence to the relevant literature, we may define institutions as systems of established and prevalent social rules that structure social interactions. Language, money, law, systems of weights and measures, table manners, and firms (and other organizations) are thus all institutions.
>
> (Hodgson 2006: 2)

Institutional economists have differed in their conception of institutions. For example, both Douglass North and Elinor Ostrom distinguished, in contrast to Hodgson, between organisations and institutions (Cole 2013). Organizations were players in their view and institutions were sets of rules. A theoretical concern with institutions links to particular assumptions on Ostrom's part in regard to causality, ontology and epistemology. Causality examines the causes of a particular event; ontology discusses being, while epistemology is the study of knowledge. Epistemology asks how we know what we know; ontology examines what is meant by existence; causality asks why something happened. The IAD approach to causality, ontology and epistemology is pluralistic or, to use the term preferred by the Ostroms, polycentric. The Ostroms were suspicious of the idea that a single factor might act alone to produce a discrete event. The causation of a particular event tends to be seen as multiple; a series of nested processes generally generates an occurrence. Institutions, physical factors, language, culture and strategic human action all come into play.

Their ontological approach assumes that human existence cannot be reduced to one factor or set of factors. Our social reality is plural; human beings live in a physical world, which can be studied by the natural sciences, cultural factors also shape us and we are beings that within constraints can change our lives. Any human being or society is complex, at the same time, both social and 'natural'.

The epistemological approach of IAD is also, unsurprisingly, pluralistic. The model building of economists and a broadly scientific method that investigates 'law-like' human behaviour is criticised if it is used in a narrow and simplistic way. The pursuit of useful knowledge of human behaviour can use tools such as statistics, experiments and formal modelling. Yet the Ostroms felt that cultural factors including language cannot be investigated with such techniques alone.

Like Hayek, both Ostroms were critical of the 'scientism', the idea that experts could investigate human behaviour, derive certain conclusions and use such conclusions to make unambiguous policy pronouncements. The Ostroms did not reject scientific approaches but argued that knowledge was always likely to be incomplete, so caution is necessary. The IAD approach demands consideration of how to define success or failure. 'Scientism' assumes neutrality; however the choice of criteria is almost inevitably normative, different groups and individuals may have different priorities and thus different criteria for success. If the objective sought is cost efficiency, this might challenge alternative criteria such as long-term ecological sustainability, social equality or democratic governance.

Different assessments of success or failure will be derived, depending on the criteria chosen. One overwhelming normative consideration that can be found in the work of the Ostroms is an emphasis on self-government. The aim of research using an IAD framework is to help individuals to understand institutional puzzles. More information from practical research helps in problem-solving and institutional design. In the Institutional Analysis and Development syllabus she taught at the Workshop in 2011, Elinor Ostrom noted:

> The thesis that we advance in this seminar is that individuals, who seriously engage one another in efforts to build mutually productive social relationships – and to understand why these are important – are capable of devising ingenious ways of relating constructively with one another.
>
> (See Appendix)

Model building might be useful in aiding such a process but, according to the Ostroms, considerable caution is needed. Models should be used as tools but the danger is that a messy reality is made to conform to restrictive assumptions, especially in economics. Thus Vincent Ostrom observed that the economist Walter Eucken:

> [...] writing in the late 1930s, called attention to what I regard as the basic epistemological problem in the cultural and social sciences. Eucken asserted that economic theorists rely on a single, simple, general model that is presumed to have universal application in the conduct of economic analysis. By so doing, he argued that economists increasingly distanced themselves from economic 'reality.' Abstractions lose meaning, theory is confined to doctrine and lacks contact with 'reality.' [...] A fully specified model bounded by limiting assumptions is presumed to have universal applications. Model thinking may serve the purposes of rigorous mathematical reasoning but neglects empirical 'realities' and problematics in human affairs.
>
> (V. Ostrom 1997: 97)

While 'model thinking' was problematic, a purely empirical approach, where facts are heaped up, was also flawed. Vincent Ostrom felt that 'facts' on their own have little meaning and made great use of John Searle's notion of the distinction between 'brute facts' and 'institutional facts'. John Searle, best known for his book *Speech Acts* (1969), developed a philosophy of language, drawing upon a tradition of pragmatism and the work of Austin and Wittgenstein.

Searle felt that 'facts' have to be understood in context or they have little or no meaning. This understanding is also reflected in John R. Commons' notion of 'a going concern', which describes an organization, such as a firm, with working rules (Commons 1968: 145). Aligică and Boettke in their useful summary of the IAD approach, note that Searle's perspective is both essential to the Ostroms' work and has devastating implications for positivist or indeed any purely empirical approaches to methodology. Empirical study can be highly misleading unless combined with an understanding of often invisible or semi-visible sets of rules. Typically, observation of a football pitch tells us little about the game being played, 'an understanding of the living reality in human societies cannot take place other than by an understanding of how rules are constituted of social facts as 'institutional facts' (Aligică and Boettke 2009: 79). Without an understanding of the rules of the game, that might not be discovered, by direct observation, the game would be incomprehensible:

> Let us imagine a group of highly trained observers describing an American football game in statements only of brute facts. What could they say by way of description? Well, within certain areas a good deal could be said, and using statistical techniques certain 'laws' could even be formulated. For example, we can imagine that after a time our observer would discover the law of periodical clustering; at statistically regular intervals, organisms in like colored shirts cluster together in a roughly circular fashion (the huddle). Furthermore, at equally regular intervals, circular clustering is followed by linear clustering (the teams line up for the play) and linear clustering is followed by the phenomenon of linear interpenetration.
>
> (Searle 1969: 52)

Rules need to be understood and relationships identified rather than simply assumed. In turn, from an IAD perspective, research into the human condition was impossible without reference to language. Vincent Ostrom argued:

> The words we use and the ideas with which we work are the most fundamental part of human reality. How we communicate with one another, think, act, and do whatever we seek to achieve is shaped by the ambiguities of language. What we presume to be true is expressed and mediated through the conventions of language and the experiences that human beings share in talking with, relating to, and working with one another. The exigencies of language and culture apply to what people profess as knowledge, what they do, and how they relate to one another in whatever they manage to achieve.
>
> (V. Ostrom 1997: 8)

Elinor Ostrom referenced Winch's book *The Idea of a Social Science and its Relation to Philosophy* that drew upon the insights of Wittgenstein, to suggest that social sciences were flawed unless they placed attention on language and culture (Ostrom 1982: 12). Creating a shared terminology is important for research to take place. Dialogue is also vital to the IAD approach. The principal normative goal of promoting self-government demands debate with the individuals within the institutional setting under study. Dialogue allows a researcher to check their findings because participants may identify errors made. Dialogue also demands a shared understanding of words and reinforces the importance of language within Elinor Ostrom's work.

Vincent Ostrom saw an IAD approach as an attempt to move beyond mainstream economic methodology in a number of respects:

> Absurd doctrines can meet standards of logical rigor and mathematical proof but yield disastrous consequences when used to inform actions. Human actions need to draw on general principles that can be applied to particular time and place exigencies that vary with ecological and cultural circumstances.
>
> (V. Ostrom 1997: 97)

Vincent's reference to 'ecological' circumstances is important. Human behaviour occurs both within an institutional setting but also within a wider physical reality. This too must be acknowledged if we are to understand human institutions and action. Of course, physical factors can range in significance for human action within institutional settings:

> *The relative importance* of the *rule configuration* and the physical world in structuring an action situation varies dramatically across different types of action situations. The rule configuration almost totally constitutes some games, like chess, where physical attributes are relatively unimportant. There is little about the size of a chessboard or the shape of the pieces that contributes to the structure of a chess game. On the other hand, imagine, for a moment, *switching the balls used in American and European football. The strategies available to the players in these two games, and many other sports, are strongly affected by the physical attributes of the balls used, the size of the field, and the type of equipment.*
>
> (Ostrom *et al.* 1994: 44)

To summarize, an IAD approach acknowledges ecological and other physical factors where relevant, and assumes that economic and wider social behaviour is embedded in institutions, whether formal or informal. In turn, the IAD framework acknowledges that human experience is mediated by language and that institutions are based on culturally determined rules. Human beings from the perspective of the Ostroms have creative agency, they are neither prisoners of structures that determine absolutely what they do nor the atomistic units assumed by mainstream economics. Putting these insights into practise meant moving from broad methodological assumptions to a specific framework, and from the framework to practical research. For the Ostroms, the IAD framework had practical implications for focussed attempts at problem solving. To understand Elinor Ostrom's methodological assumptions it is important to understand how she and co-workers understood the construction and operation of rules and norms. Most important in this regard is the grammar of institutions she put together with the political scientist Sue Crawford (Crawford and Ostrom 2005).

A grammar of institutions

Elinor Ostrom's central concern was institutions. Institutional economics in its very diverse manifestations is based upon the assumption that economic activity requires governance. Governance, in turn, is impossible without sets of rules, so one way of understanding an institution is by mapping its rules' From her doctoral research into water basin management to her work in the twenty-first century on social-ecological systems, Elinor Ostrom learnt more about institutions by trying to understand their rules. Rules and ruling making are at the heart of the IAD framework.

Elinor Ostrom noted:

> [...] rules as used in this book are defined to be shared understandings by participants about *enforced* prescriptions concerning what actions (or outcomes) are *required, prohibited,* or *permitted* (Ganz 1971; V. Ostrom 1980; Commons 1968). All rules are the result of implicit or explicit efforts to achieve order and predictability among humans by creating classes of persons (positions) who are then required, permitted, or forbidden to take classes of actions in relation to required, permitted, or forbidden outcomes or face the likelihood of being monitored and sanctioned.
>
> (Ostrom 2005:18)

As she noted in *Understanding Institutional Diversity*, the term 'rule' can be used in at least four different ways as a regulation, instruction, precept or principle. Regulations are set by an authority and variously allow, expect, permit or outlaw a form of action. The rules of a game of football can be seen as rules, which are regulations. Instructions refer to strategies to solve a particular problem such as solving with a mathematical equation. Precepts, according to Ostrom, are examples not of instructions to solve a problem or regulation to determine an action, but moral principles seen as beneficial. Finally, rules as principles, cover law-like behaviour and can be tested empirically. For example, the fact that water freezes at 0°C, is a principle.

Ostrom referred to rules in the first sense of the word as regulations. They are, she suggested, similar to genetic material. They shape an institutional setting, which she describes as an action situation (Ostrom 2005: 17). Rules are shared understandings of prescriptions backed by an authority, which require, permit or prohibit particular actions. If rules are followed, they tend to rule in some actions and rule out others. Traffic laws that prevent speeding are one example. Such rules do not have to be written down but, of course, often are. She also discussed 'strategies' and 'norms'. She used the term 'strategy' to cover the second meaning of the term rule, i.e. a procedure for solving a particular problem. She used the term 'norm' to describe the third use of the word 'rule' as a precept noting that norms 'are part of the generally accepted moral fabric of a community' understood as 'cultural prescriptions'. (Ostrom 2005: 17). Rules are backed by sanctions such as fines, while norms are enforced by negative social sentiment. In practice, it may be difficult to separate rules from norms.

Elinor Ostrom believed that it is important to understand the origin of rules to understand a process of governance. She noted that diverse sets of rules exist in society; they are not, even in a totalitarian state, monolithic. Associations, businesses, even families all make rules. Rules in use can be contrasted with rules in form. Rules in form, may be written down, but may be unknown to participants so have no real effect. Rules in use are shared and relevant to the functioning of given institutions. Working rules can be ignored, interpreted in a variety of ways but if followed consistently can become social habits. She noted that this can make attempts to map working rules challenging:

> The capacity of humans to use complex cognitive systems to order their own behaviour at a relatively subconscious level makes it difficult at times for empirical researchers to ascertain what the working rules for an ongoing action arena may actually be in practice. It is the task of an institutional analyst, however, to dig under surface behaviour to obtain a good understanding of what rules participants in a situation are following.
>
> (Ostrom 2005: 19)

Such working rules can be an example of Michael Polanyi's tacit knowledge in this sense but even when they are consciously held, the fact that they are expressed in language can cause confusion. Rules are enforced but enforcement can be broken and ignored. If rules are not widely accepted and shared, it may be too costly for authorities to enforce them, so they break down.

Elinor Ostrom worked with another political scientist Sue Crawford to construct 'a grammar of institutions' which aimed to provide a syntax 'for analyzing and expressing institutional statements.' (Crawford and Ostrom 2005: 139). The word 'grammar' refers to a set of structural rules that order a language and the word 'syntax' refers to the 'the study of the principles and processes by which sentences are constructed in particular languages' (Chomsky 2002: 11). An institutional grammar refers to the rules that help constitute an institution, a particular rule can be expressed in a form that can be analysed using an appropriate syntax.

Crawford and Ostrom assumed that rules, even when they are initially tacit, potentially may be expressed linguistically. A typical institutional statement might be expressed 'No villager may graze more cattle on the village common during the summer than they can support during the winter.' This example, which is quite often found in rules governing common land, promotes usufruct, i.e shared sustainable use of a resource. Crawford and Ostrom provided a number of examples including:

1. All male, U.S. citizens over eighteen years of age must register with the Selective Service by filling out a form at the U.S. Post Office or else face arrest for evading registration.

2. All senators may move to amend a bill after a bill has been introduced, or else the senator attempting to forbid another senator from taking this action by calling him or her out of order will be called out of order or ignored.

(Crawford and Ostrom 2005: 139)

Such statements can include five components (1) Attribute, (2) Deontic, (3) Aim, (4) Conditions and (5) Potential sanctions for evaders. The attribute refers to the individual, individuals or groups that the statement applies to; for example, villagers, senators and male US citizens over the age of 18. 'Deontic' refers to the nature of the rule to distinguish prescriptive and non-prescriptive clauses in a statement. For example, 'may' or 'must'. More precisely, it indicates permitted, obliged and forbidden acts. 'Aim' denotes 'the specific description of a working part in an action situation to which an institutional statement refers.' (Crawford and Ostrom 2005: 148). For example, a process such as putting the cattle on the common or filling in a form at the post office. 'Conditions' include when and where an institutional statement is relevant. If conditions are not specified they will be universally relevant to the villagers, senators or US males over the age of 18, etc.

This attempt to classify rules of institutional behaviour proved controversial to some observers. Elinor Ostrom noted that when she delivered a lecture on institutional grammar in 1982 at Biefeld, Germany, she was criticised for building a complex intellectual framework to explain something that was, apparently, obvious and needed no analysis (Ostrom 2005: 174). Sue Crawford and Elinor Ostrom turned statements into logical strings using algebra, a technique that was threatening and confusing to some observers. However, they argued that a detailed institutional grammar was needed to communicate ideas clearly and to move beyond slogans. Such a grammar was an essential part of the IAD framework.

Institutional analysis and development in practice

In practice, an IAD framework has been described as 'a metatheoretical conceptual map' (Poteete, Janssen and Ostrom 2010: 40). Frameworks, theories and models are often utilised as interchangeable methodological terms. However, Elinor Ostrom sought to define the concept of a framework with particular care. For her a framework provided a structure to test particular theories or to attempt to deal with particular problems. Theories are put to the test by the use of a framework. For example, she used the IAD framework to examine theories that had been applied to explain the supposed 'tragedy of the commons'. Particular methods such as participant observation, quantitative data analysis or experiments, provide tools that can be used within the framework. Models in turn establish which parts of the framework are most relevant. She outlined these distinctions in her Nobel speech:

> A **framework** is intended to contain the most general set of variables that an institutional analyst may want to use to examine a diversity of institutional

> settings including human interactions within markets, private firms, families, community organizations, legislatures, and government agencies. It provides a metatheoretical language to enable scholars to discuss any particular theory or to compare theories.
>
> A specific **theory** is used by an analyst to specify which working parts of a framework are considered useful to explain diverse outcomes and how they relate to one another.... **Models** make precise assumptions about a limited number of variables in a theory that scholars use to examine the formal consequences of these specific assumptions about the motivation of actors and the structure of the situation they face.
>
> (Ostrom 2010b: 646)

The IAD framework identifies an action situation, patterns of interaction within this action situation and outcomes. The outcomes that occur are evaluated and such evaluation may be used to inform the participants and help with problem-solving. The management of a common pool resource is one action situation but the term covers a diversity of other institutional settings. For example, Elinor Ostrom studied police authorities as action situations. The patterns of interaction can be mapped and are likely to include forms of action mediated by institutions including sets of culturally shaped norms. Peer-to-peer software production can be understood as an action situation and the rules that determine such production are studied as rules influencing interaction. Outcomes, of course, depend on particular criteria. These vary according to circumstances; a single universal criteria is inappropriate because different measures will have value to different groups in diverse situations. If a business situation was being analysed, profit, costs and other monetary criteria used by economists and accountants might be relevant. Such measures of efficiency are normally seen as 'objective' by economists but reliance on such ways of measuring outcome are challenged in the IAD framework. Other criteria such as sustainability might be more relevant. For a common pool resource or wider social-ecological system, sustainability is likely to be of great importance but may be assessed in different ways by different communities or user groups.

It has been suggested that an action situation is structured by seven broad attributes. These include:

(1) the set of relevant participants; (2) the roles or positions that may be taken by the participants; (3) the set of actions that can be potentially taken by participants; (4) the control each participant, whether an individual or institution, has within the action situation; (5) the potential outcomes associated with varied combinations of actions undertaken; (6) the information held by participants, and finally (7) costs and benefits produced by different actions and different outcomes (adapted from Poteete, Janssen and Ostrom 2010: 40).

Relevant participants might include users of a common pool resource. Their roles such as that of a leisure user walking their dog or an official or farmer, would be outlined in an IAD exercise. The actions they undertake and the level of power to influence events within the commons could be assessed. A 'tragedy of the commons' might result from their combined actions leading to over-exploitation of the common resource perhaps by overgrazing. The level of information about the environmental qualities of the commons and the likely action of other commoners, could be explored. Different potential interactions might be evaluated in terms of their effects on sustainable use.

In turn, an actor within an action situation faces four sets of variables:

> 1. the way actors acquire, process, retain, and use information and knowledge about contingencies;
> 2. the preferences of an actor related to actions and outcomes;
> 3. the conscious or unconscious processes actors use for selection of particular courses of action; and
> 4. the resources that the actor brings to the situation.
>
> (Poteete *et al.* 2010: 40)

Practical research would provide data which could be used to help understand these variables.

Elinor Ostrom noted that the IAD framework was drawn from game theory:

> Our seven broad rule classification system is based on game theoretical tools, which have provided us with a formal language to express the structure of relatively simple and unambiguous action situations, such as games [...]. Those familiar with game theorectic analyses will recognize these seven elements as the moving parts of any formal game.
>
> (Ostrom and Baurto 2010: 323)

It is useful to turn to game theory and related types of formal modelling, before examining the methods that can be used to gather the data necessary to build an IAD framework.

Game theory and formal modelling

Social scientists often seem to fall into two crude groups if divided in terms of their estimation of the methodological value of game theory. Economists and some other social scientists find it useful, but until recently have not looked carefully at the divergence between actual human behaviour and assumptions made of rationality and maximization. Many, but not all, sociologists and anthropologists dismiss it utterly. Game theory models strategic behaviour and has developed since the publication of John Von Neumann and Oskar Morgenstern's *Theory of Games and Economic Behavior* in 1944. Elinor Ostrom noted that its 'generality and precision' have grown since and social scientists across a wide range of fields use it:

> That one can use the same set of tools to analyze a game of tennis, the decision of when to run for office, predator-prey relationships, how much to

> trust a stranger, and how much to contribute to a public good makes game theory one of the most important analytical tools available to all of the social sciences.
>
> (Ostrom 2012a: 26)

James Buchanan made the useful point that any 'attempt to model a game requires a categorical separation be made between the rules, which describe the game itself, and the play within the rules.' (Buchanan 2007: 212). Ostrom suggested, as was noted previously, that rules exist in the form of political constitutions. Such rules may be unwritten and informal; they do not just relate to state structures and formal written laws may be ignored and lack explanatory power.

Games can be cooperative or non cooperative, zero sum or positive sum. 'Cooperative' means that a set of enforceable rules exits. Zero sum means that if one individual gains, another loses by the same amount. The terminology is somewhat confusing. Theorists such as Robert Axelrod (1984) have looked not just at cooperative games in the sense of games with enforceable rules but the notion that game theory can help us to understand cooperative rather than simply competitive behaviour. A positive sum situation occurs when an individual can gain without another individual losing.

Game theory has been based on the assumption that human beings are rational maximisers who want to get the most for themselves as individuals in a given situation. It has been conceptualised as providing a model of the micro foundations of mainstream economics. Individual behaviour depends on an individual's prediction of the likely behaviour of other individuals within a game situation. Individuals will try to predict how others will behave to calculate their own best 'move'. In a market with two dominant companies selling sweets, a price war might be predicted to break out. A firm would cut its prices to drive its competitor out of business. However if both firms kept their prices high they might both make gains and a positive sum situation would result. Crucially, the action of one firm depends on its prediction of the behaviour of the other.

In 1994, John Nash won the Nobel Prize in Economic Sciences, with John Harsanyi and Reinhard Selten, for his work on game theory. Nash equilibrium is a simple idea but has complex ramifications. Nash equilibrium occurs when both individuals do what will maximise their own benefit given their prediction of the most likely behaviour of the other. This can be illustrated by the prisoner's dilemma. The two prisoners are held in separate cells and both tend to defect. Each predicts that the other is likely to defect, i.e. to confess. Therefore each prisoner defects, because she or he fears that if the other confesses first, they will receive a longer sentence. While Nash equilibrium can take a number of forms, it is widely assumed that rationality and self-interest will lead to a sub-optimum situation from the point of view of the prisoners. If they both played the game by refusing to confess, they would both be better off because without the evidence of a confession they would both be likely to escape punishment or at least suffer a less severe sentence. Essentially, if in a two individual game, both participants seek to rationally maximise their benefits, the most likely outcome will lead to a loss of potential benefit for each.

In a price war situation, the two firms will both cut prices and both lose potential profit. If both raised their price by the same amount, the overall benefit to the two players would be higher, they would make more money and consumers would suffer higher prices. However if neither firm trusts the other, they both cut and both lose profit. This form of Nash equilibrium is likely in the prisoner's dilemma. The concept of Nash equilibrium in game theory has been used to suggest that given assumptions of rational maximising behaviour, cooperation is unlikely. Nash equilibrium is likely, given such assumptions, to give rise to less than 'optimal' results for 'players', meaning that the maximum benefit is not achieved. Paradoxically, rational competition leads to a reduction in total welfare. Game theorists have generally assumed that participants in the game would engage in 'backward induction' that would help explain the sub-optimal Nash equilibrium(s) that game theorists felt was most likely to occur. Backward induction is thought to occur in repeated rounds of a game; participants do not want cooperation to occur in the last round of the game, so project this back and refuse to cooperate in the first round of the game.

Elinor Ostrom noted how the assumption of Nash equilibrium related closely to Garrett Hardin's 'tragedy of the commons'. Her investigations of collective action problems made use of game theory to show that cooperation is sometimes possible. Game theory has been the basis of rational choice models of behaviour and used to draw pessimistic conclusions. James Buchanan noted that players might 'choose among strategies: the interdependence among these strategic choices generates an outcome that no player chooses or could choose' (Buchanan 2007: 213). It is assumed that none of the players achieve the outcome they wish because of interdependence.

Ostrom came to a more optimistic conclusion after many years of experimentation. She felt that under some circumstances individuals could cooperate to maximise their shared benefit. Like the 'tragedy of the commons', for all its sophistication, elements of game theory may prove metaphorical. The games assumed by theorists need not describe the potential of real life interactions between individuals or communities. A wide variety of games are studied by game theorists; although the prisoner's dilemma has been used to understand the supposed 'tragedy of the commons', other scenarios are used to explore competition, cooperation and other areas of interest to economists and others (Camerer 2003). While cooperation is possible, Ostrom assumed that it might require the conscious design of particular rules to encourage it.

The theoretical framework of IAD was based upon game theory, yet both Ostroms criticised the dominant approach to game theory. Elinor Ostrom found game theory useful but felt that it had to be used with care; on its own it did not 'explain' human behaviour. Elinor Ostrom has been seen as an unusual practioner of game theory because she tried to understand the perspectives of real life human beings. Her approach was as usual both unusual and nuanced:

> Ostrom evinces a curiosity about actors' own views that is not what one normally associates with game theory. Many game theorists impute motives to actors (e.g., 'Assume bureaucrats are budget-maximizers'), assume actors' myopic self-interest, and rarely attend to the question of how real-world actors 'see' their situation.
>
> (Schwartz-Shea 2010: 587)

Elinor Ostrom used both experimental methods and agent based modelling to investigate rather than 'inpute' such motives.

Experimental methods

Elinor Ostrom believed that experiments were most relevant to test hypotheses. Her starting point was to use them to test the findings of formal methods of game theory and to supplement the use of case studies. Given the assumptions of formal or metaphorical models such as the prisoner's dilemma, Olson's theory of collective action and Hardin's 'tragedy of the commons', collective management of property was thought to be unsustainable. Elinor Ostrom found that experiments replicating these models' assumptions broadly indicated that the models were correct. Nonetheless, further experimentation indicated that the assumptions that models used might not be universally applicable.

She rejected 'natural' experiments – where individuals were not told that they were part of a research process, so were unable to provide informed consent – as unethical. Her first experiments used university students, who were asked to take part, but while this was convenient, she found it more useful to undertake field tests with individuals who faced the challenge of managing common pool resources. Her experiments and those of her colleagues typically worked in the following way. First, the experimenter would bring together a group of volunteers who had consented to participate, in a controlled setting. The setting could be in a laboratory situation or in the field. The volunteers were told that the decisions they made would shape the results of the experiments that took place. Incentives in the form of money or tokens were generally used. The payoff for each individual who took part in the experiments was influenced, as was consistent with game theory, by the behaviour of others. Decisions were made using either paper or computers (Poteete *et al.* 2010: 142).

For example, Juan-Camilo Cardenas, a resource economist, carried out field experiments in Colombia with villagers dependent on collectively managed forests. Instead of tokens or money, which were used in most experiments, pay off was calculated in terms of how much time villagers spent gathering wood in a forest. If each individual villager spent more time in the forest, she or he would gain more wood but 'the return to all of them depended on everyone's keeping the harvesting to a very low level.' (Poteete *et al.* 2010: 160). If an individual took 'a free ride' and spent longer in the forest, this would have the effect of lowering the total collective harvest.

Cardenas's experiments challenged the formal models that suggested that cooperation was unlikely. Rather than producing a Nash equilibrium where the collective payoff was lower than the maximum; often but not always, participants developed behaviour that increased collective gains. The experiments suggested that assumptions such as lack of communication between individuals in traditional game theory might be unrealistic. If participants were able to communicate, unlike the prisoners held in separate cells in the prisoner's dilemma, they were more likely to cooperate. 'Cheap talk', by which is meant conversations and other forms of communication that were not backed up by potential sanctions, also made cooperation easier. He found that even mobile phone texts, rather than face-to-face communication, made cooperation more likely in the experiments undertaken.

A wide variety of experiments have shown that participants, whether in laboratories or in the field, whether commoners or students, were far from being consistent self-interested maximisers, assumed by mainstream economists. Yet neither were they natural self-sacrificing cooperators. A range of individuals showed a range of behaviour traits and individual behaviour was not always consistent. Individuals might make sacrifices to help others but did not like to be taken for 'suckers'. If they felt they were being exploited they would react negatively but were often prepared to assume that others would be cooperative and respond to positive actions to challenge the tragedy of the commons. As in Axelrod's work, briefly discussed in the previous chapter, tit for tat strategies often produced cooperative behaviour. Individuals rewarded each other's cooperation tit for tat, but defection would be met with defection. Thus the prisoner might help his fellow, who in turn would help him. However, defection tended to promote more defection.

In her 1997 address as President of the American Political Science Association, Elinor Ostrom outlined how experiments had challenged a number of preexisting assumptions. While the standard rational choice assumptions fitted some situations, she argued that extensive research indicated that this was not the case for 'social dilemmas' such as the governance of common pool resources. She noted that high levels of initial cooperation were found although they still gave rise to less than optimal results. Stating that behaviour was inconsistent with the assumption of backward induction, she quoted Rapoport (1997: 122) who concluded 'subjects are not involved in or capable of backward induction'. In turn, Nash equilibrium strategies were poor predictors of individual behaviour and individuals did not learn them in processes of game playing (Ostrom 1998: 5).

Ostrom felt that such experiments not only helped social scientists but could provide commoners with information that they might use to improve their governance of natural resources. The universally pessimistic conclusions of the formal model, typified by a sub-optimal Nash equilibrium were disproved, yet Ostrom and her colleagues felt that the formal models were still of theoretical value and experiments on their own did not provide a universal alternative framework for understanding economic behaviour. The formal models such as the prisoner's dilemma or the 'tragedy of the commons' of Olson's conceptions of collective choice scenarios, were often little more than metaphors. Elinor Ostrom felt that predictions of what she termed first generation rational choice theory provided a benchmark for research (Ostrom 2008: 16). She argued that it was important to describe the differences between the predicted equilibrium and observed behaviour, and then to develop and test explanations for such differences. She also noted that game theorists were developing more sophisticated accounts of human behaviour. Agent based techniques have provided another way of examining how social dilemmas and rationality, using computer programmes.

Agent based models

In *Working Together*, Amy Poteete, Marco Janssen and Elinor Ostrom also looked at how agent based models could be used to better understand collective action. Like experiments, such models can be used to test, refine and refute the assumptions of game theory. An agent based model is a computer stimulation of behaviour that can be used to show the effects of interactions between individuals and/or collective institutions. It is different from other forms of research when used in social science, such as an experiment or a case study, because it does not directly study human subjects. It provides a means of modelling how the potential decisions of such subjects might lead to particular patterns of social behaviour, using computer-generated exercises. It has been used in both social and natural science settings. The models developed can be used to illustrate the emergence of complex forms of behaviour. Axelrod (1984) was an early user of agent based modelling, showing that the prisoner's dilemma could lead to cooperative behaviour if in repeated games, cooperation was met with cooperation. He tested this 'tit for tat' scenario using this technique, to develop his cooperative challenge to game theory assumptions of universal self-interest and resulting sub-optimum social performance. Agent based modelling is also valuable in researching social-ecological systems and other complex adaptive systems which have a great number of potential variables. Different interactions of different variables can be modelled in situations which have so many variables that can interact dynamically that understanding would otherwise be impossible.

It is not seen as an adequate method if used alone to explain behaviour but it is an empirical technique that can be used to improve knowledge. It builds on formal theory and, in particular, on game theory. Whereas game theory is developed via a formal abstract model of assumed behaviour, like experiments with human subjects, agent based models can be used to partially test such assumptions. Agent based modelling has been described in the following terms:

> Agent based models consist of agents that interact within an environment. Agents are either separate computer programs or, more commonly, distinct parts of a program that are used to represent social actors – individual people, organizations such as firms, or bodies such as nation-states. They are programmed to react to the computational environment in which they

> are located, where this environment is a model of the real environment in which the social actors operate.
>
> (Gilbert 2007: 4)

Agent based modelling is not, on its own, proof or even a strong indication of the likelihood of a particular hypothesis. It might too seem strange that a technique that removes the human element can be part of a framework that seeks to promote democratic self-governance, yet it allows an understanding of complex systems and often unforeseen consequences, which would be difficult to detect with other methods. Case studies, to which we can now turn, provided another technique used by Elinor Ostrom to challenge the conventional assumptions suggested by the prisoner's dilemma.

Case studies

> Nobel laureate Elinor Ostrom reckons she has been in more police cars and jails than anyone she knows. That is because Professor Ostrom, 77, devoted 15 years to studying police departments in 80 metropolitan areas around the United States to see which were more efficient. She recalls: 'I always rode a policeman's full shift in his car, eight hours a day, and learnt a lot about what went on in which areas.'
>
> (Suk-Wai (13 September 2010))

While mainstream economics relies on mathematical modelling and statistical data, it has been suggested that the research method most associated with Elinor Ostrom is the case study (Boettke *et al.* 2013). Case studies may be seen as unscientific and alien to economic methodology, however formal models and purely statistical data can be misleading without further research contextualization. In Elinor Ostrom's methodological approach, case studies provide a vital complement to other techniques.

A case study deals with a detailed examination of a particular situation. It may involve historical work, participant observation, interviews or even quantitative data collection. Case studies, based on secondary data undertaken by other scholars provide the basis for the findings of Elinor Ostrom's best-known publication, *Governing the Commons*. She surveyed examples of both successful and failed commons. The examples were based on historical archive data that spanned many centuries. The case studies allowed her to show with some confidence that the 'tragedy of the commons' was far from universal and that common pool resources were often sustained over long periods of time. Comparison of successful and failed commons allowed her to develop a list of factors that encouraged successful management. These factors were investigated more thoroughly using a range of additional techniques. Her earlier work on policing also made significant use of case studies, which of course, saw her visiting jails and spending time in police cars.

Elinor Ostrom was interested in causal mechanism and processes that may be impossible to detect using purely quantitative techniques. After all, correlations are not in themselves explanations. Despite the development of far more sophisticated statistical techniques than simple regression, additional qualitative data may be needed to identify such mechanisms. Thus case studies are useful 'for concept and theory development as well as evaluation of hypothesized causal sequences and mechanisms' (Poteete *et al.* 2010: 12). This takes us back to the notion of 'institutional' facts; institutional structures may be easier to detect from participation in case studies than inference from statistical samples of data.

Case studies can also produce detailed information of norms, which is necessary given the emphasis on language and culture suggested by an IAD approach. 'Rich explanations of particular cases are often valuable substantively and theoretically' (Poteete *et al.* 2010: 12). Case studies undertaken patiently over a long period of time may also be necessary to examine informal institutions which might otherwise remain invisible. Likewise, if information is needed about the activities of non-elite groups, detailed, on the ground investigation is also necessary. While it is difficult to conceptualise the police as a non-elite group, Elinor Ostrom's work on policing in the 1960s and 1970s was enhanced by participant observation. She rode in police cars and observed the routines of the job – from arrests to paperwork. This work allowed her to understand nuances of the profession that might have otherwise been lost to her. Many common pool resources are managed by peasants or indigenous people who may often be socially marginalised and difficult to research without case study work on a local basis.

Case study work, like any technique, comes with costs and weaknesses. It is often time-consuming, expensive and may provide misleading results. In particular it is impossible to extrapolate meaningful conclusions if based upon the small samples that case studies tend to produce. On their own case studies do not provide findings that can be easily generalised but at least illuminate possibilities that can be investigated more thoroughly (Poteete *et al.* 2010: 12).

There are a number of different ways of collecting the qualitative data necessary for case studies, including participant observation, oral history, archival research and other techniques associated with anthropology and sociology. To use any one of these effectively, a researcher needs to understand the method well and to be able to address potential technique-specific problems. Participant observation, where a researcher joins and participates with the group she or he is studying, for example, gives rise to a range of practical, ethical and theoretical dilemmas. Whichever technique is used, researchers must have a good understanding of informal and thus often largely invisible institutions. This involves good detailed knowledge of the local context to gain access to such institutions and understand often subtle cultural distinctions, so as to 'accurately interpret culturally coded observation' (Poteete *et al.* 2010: 16).

Comparisons between different case studies can be a way of combining the benefits of detailed qualitative research with findings that are easier to generalise. Yet, as research may be undertaken by scholars in different disciplines, using different techniques and asking different questions, this may be difficult. One of the particular challenges Elinor Ostrom found was that the urban police authorities, commons and social-ecological systems she researched had been studied from within different disciplines including anthropology, sociology, economics and political science. This made it difficult to compare previous research work; typically, individual case studies of common pool resources had to be recoded to allow comparison of relevant data across disciplines. Qualitative case study research for even a limited number of studies, in the same discipline or even from the same research team, can also produce large volumes of data that may be time-consuming to code. Comparison of numerous case studies from researchers with different theoretical questions, is at worst impossible and at best daunting.

Ostrom and her colleagues have suggested that qualitative data analysis demands considerable discussion before undertaking case studies. Clear theoretical research questions are needed before undertaking case study work to focus the work undertaken and to prevent the volume of data collected swamping the research project.

Historical data is particularly useful as it can show the development of an institution, but its use provokes new questions. Methodological debates remain fierce within history, actual practical methods demand discussion and until recently, with the development of environmental history, historians have often marginalised the significance of ecological factors.

While Elinor Ostrom made rich use of secondary case study data including historical work, she remained aware of such challenges. Case study work allowed her to challenge the universal existence of the tragedy of the commons and to develop an initial framework to study common pool resource governance. In summary, case studies are useful for 'counterfactual analysis, process tracing, structured comparisons, and analysis of deviant cases' (Poteete *et al.* 2010: 16). Case studies are, of course, just one technique in the tool kit; they work best when combined with a variety of other methods.

Large scale quantitative techniques

Economists use quantitative techniques virtually to the exclusion of all other research practices. The discipline is, in the twenty-first century, defined by mathematics. It is sometimes supposed that Elinor Ostrom rejected large scale quantitative methods, yet while she was best known for qualitative approaches, such an assumption is misleading. While much of her work was qualitative and she was critical of an exclusively mathematical approach, she saw an important role for quantitative techniques. Reliance on a small sample cannot produce data that can be generalised; it is only through large data sets that valid explanations can be established. For this reason, qualitative methods, such as participant observation or oral history, are almost universally rejected by economists. Elinor Ostrom, nevertheless, felt that there were a number of reasons why quantitative techniques were often insufficient. Practical considerations mean that some areas in human science cannot be studied quantitatively. It may be difficult to collect large samples of data from non-elite populations, activity may be informal and, for other reasons, visibility may be low. This is a particular problem when studying many forms of common pool property because if a population is partially hidden it may be difficult to sample it accurately.

Equally, quantitative data tends to generate correlations that do not establish relationships between factors. The explanatory mechanisms that explain such relationships cannot be established purely by quantitative techniques; other means, such as case studies are necessary.

Elinor Ostrom and her colleagues argued that quantitative techniques demand careful attention to sampling and analysis. The adequacy of quantitative techniques is influenced by practical considerations. Inadequate data and failure to apply, 'appropriate diagnostic checks and technical fixes' are potential problems (Poteete *et al.* 2010: 4).

She was also concerned that quantitative techniques could crowd out other approaches which might be seen as 'unscientific'. There is a danger that quantitative techniques are assumed to be based on 'hard data', while qualitative data is 'soft', that quantitative approaches are scientific and qualitative are not. Quantitative techniques may also dissuade researchers from thinking theoretically and of course may play down the extent to which human beings have agency rather than being products of purely rule based behaviour. Such insights are consistent with Boettke *et al.*'s defence of Elinor Ostrom's use of case studies, to promote research into governance, in the spirit of Tocqueville (Boettke *et al.* 2013).

Quantitative techniques are generally used within a positivist scientific framework but Ostrom (1982: 19) noted that there are a number of competing and more sophisticated ways of conceptualising science. For both theoretical and practical reasons, quantitative methods play an important role within economics. However, according to Ostrom, they are part of a wider tool kit in the human sciences. Elinor Ostrom, Vincent Ostrom and colleagues such as Amy Poteete were critical of researchers who use " 'the rule of the hammer' and apply a single method indiscriminately, regardless of its suitability for a given research project' (Poteete *et al.* 2010: 3–4). It is difficult to make a table using only a hammer and difficult to understand a situation using only statistical data. In summary, Elinor Ostrom argued that quantitative techniques were necessary but had to be used with care:

> It is essential for empirical researchers to learn the languages of data analysis and to learn them early in their careers. Our undergraduate programs could all be strengthened by advising students of the importance of mathematics and statistics to an undergraduate major in political science. But a central task of the coming era is to reverse this domination so that the development of theory precedes the choice of appropriate methods to test a theory.
>
> (Ostrom 1982: 19)

Satellite surveys

The varied nature of the practical methods used by Elinor Ostrom is illustrated by her enthusiasm in the first decade of the twenty-first century for satellite remote sensing. Conservationists have often argued that the most effective way of promoting conservation in sensitive areas is to create national parks administered by government authorities. These have proved controversial because they have sometimes involved displacing those living within the park areas. Conflict has often ensued and Ostrom has argued that government restrictions do not always lead to conservation. Remote sensing satellites have been used to provide a relatively swift and objective means of comparing vegetation cover for different areas. This provides a test to measure the relative conservation benefits of different systems of property ownership and resource management (Ostrom and Nagendra 2006).

Ostrom and Nagendra undertook a study of forest management for the Indian states of Maharashtra and West Bengal and the Nepalese district of Chitwan. Composite images were taken from a Landsat satellite sensitive to vegetation cover, ranging from three points of time from the mid 1970s to the beginning of the twenty-first century. Forest cover was compared to different forms of land management including private ownership, national parks and commons. The satellite surveys were complemented by a range of other techniques including experimental work. It was concluded that the formal type of property ownership was of little importance:

> [...] the official designation of a forest as government, community, or comanaged does not appear to impact forest conservation as much as the legitimacy of ownership and degree of monitoring that takes place on the ground.
>
> (Ostrom and Nagendra 2006: 19227)

While Elinor Ostrom used varied techniques, each of these techniques from participant observation to satellite surveys provided complementary data. Such data was used within an IAD framework to understand given situations. At the heart of her work was an assumption that individuals were the centre of analytical concern. Such apparent methodological individualism is a controversial assumption to some social scientists and demands discussion if we are to further assess Elinor Ostrom's approach to practical research.

Methodological individualism

> Without denying the reality of individual choice, can we not employ other levels of explanation whenever they are more efficacious? For instance, does it really advance our understanding of social phenomena to insist that 'the German army invaded Poland' is somehow an unsatisfactory explanation of the events of September, 1939, and to demand that a 'real' explanation must be put in terms of why a vast number of German-speaking individuals wearing very similar clothing just happened, at the same time, to rush eastward and begin shooting at a large number of Polish-speaking individuals who all were wearing a different sort of clothing?
>
> (Callahan (24 March 2010))

Social scientists exist on a continuum from those committed to structuralism at one end, to those advocating methodological individualism at the other. Much social science research, explicitly or implicitly, lies between these two extreme points, yet economics as a discipline is defined almost universally by its commitment to individualism. The Ostroms and their co-workers often noted that methodological individualism was an important element of the IAD approach. Typically, Elinor Ostrom's colleague Michael McGinnis noted:

> Like other forms of modern political economy, institutional analysis builds on the basic principles of methodological individualism. The individual is taken to be the foundation of analysis, since individual choice is crucial to all social outcomes. Still, it is equally important to understand the institutional context within which individual choices occur, as well as the ways in which individual choices shape these institutional contexts. Institutions matter in many different ways but, ultimately, their impacts are filtered through choices made by individuals.
>
> (McGinnis 2000: 8–9)

The economist Kenneth Arrow, who eventually came to criticise methodological individualism, summarised, the case for such an approach:

> The starting point for the individualist paradigm is the simple fact all social interactions are after all interactions among individuals. The individual in the economy or in the society is like the atom in chemistry; whatever happens can ultimately be described exhaustively in terms of the individuals involved. Of course, the individuals do not act separately. They respond to each other, but each acts within a range limited by the behaviour of others as well as by constraints personal to the individual.
>
> (Arrow 1994: 3)

Structuralists, who might include many Marxists and functionalist sociologists amongst others, believe that individual behaviour is, instead, determined by larger social processes. The phrase 'the prison house of language' captures this approach; particular social institutions control what we do (Jameson 1972). Structuralism is also holistic; various social processes come together to shape society and within this the individual. Social research involves identifying such determining structures. Structuralism is thus deterministic, giving little or no role for the individual. Individual behaviour is controlled to a large extent by collective entities such as classes or nations. Structuralism can be seen along with positivist approaches to reduce human beings to mere things and may even be associated with totalitarian political systems.

Individualism is an approach favoured by economists. Social structures are seen as illusory; individuals make decisions, while collective entities such as classes or ethnic groups do not. Human beings have desires, human institutions and organisations, whether parish councils, corporations or languages desire nothing. The whole is never greater than the parts. Indeed, in this context, the right wing British Prime Minister Mrs Margaret Thatcher observed 'there is no such thing as society. There are individual men and women, and there are families' (Brittan 1996: 89).

Individualism has been criticised on methodological grounds. The institutional economist Geoffrey Hodgson has argued that it is impossible to undertake research in the social sciences from an exclusively individualistic orientation. To take a basic example, in our interactions with others we use language and language shapes how we can communicate. We cannot, as in *Alice in Wonderland* use words exactly as we so wish; meaning is shaped by use and we make use of meanings that, while far from being totally fixed, are never determined by an individual alone (Hodgson 2007). Individualism seems an oxymoronic concept in relation to social sciences. Where 'rules' are established, a structure exists that constrains individual and indeed enables individual behaviour. In recognizing this assumption, Udehn (2002) has distinguished between 'strong' and 'weak' forms of methodological individualism. Adam Smith, it can be argued, was closer to the 'weak' form of individualism than the strong form utilised by modern mainstream economists. Even Hayek and other Austrian economists might also be thought of as 'weak' in this respect because they acknowledge wider interactions and relevant institutions.

Agassi, a student of Joseph Schumpeter, coined the term 'institutional individualist' to express the notion that both individuals and institutions are significant (Rutherford 1996: 178). This description appears to be more fitting for Ostrom's work than the term 'methodological individualist', because she studied how institutions via rules help shape human behaviour. Ostrom's work cannot be seen as purely 'individualist' like that of mainstream economics because the role of institutions is seen as influencing economic and social action. Yet while institutions are collective and often impersonal, she cannot be seen as a strongly structuralist thinker. Humans construct institutions but are both constrained and helped by them. Her research into social-ecological systems influenced her consideration of such questions and the notion of complex adaptive systems was significant to her evolving thought in this area.

It might be mischievous to point out that Marx argued 'Men (*sic*) make history but not under circumstances of their own choosing' but this also seems to describe Elinor Ostrom's approach. By making us more conscious of the circumstances that shape what we do, theory makes it easier for us to disassemble and build new structures where necessary. Thus methodological individualism, for both Elinor and Vincent Ostrom, was about humans being able to make change. Paradoxically, or not, this meant a close attention to circumstances that shape human action. In turn, human social interactions cannot be reduced to simple causes. According to Elinor Ostrom, events are often multi causal in nature and individuals have the creativity to make choices. Much of social science seeks simple 'parsimonious' answers but this is rejected by Ostrom if such answers prove instead to be only simplistic. The debate around methodological individualism, structures and change has profound political implications and, as such, is developed further in Chapter 8 under the title of 'Politics without Romance'.

Multiple methods, plural practices

From participant observation of police practices in the 1960s to an interest in satellite surveys and agent based modelling in the early 2000s, Elinor Ostrom embraced an astonishingly wide variety of research methods. Yet her framework for research while evolving showed a number of constant features. Elinor Ostrom's starting point was practical. She wanted to explore particular problems, so she was attracted to the idea of economics and politics as 'scientific' in the sense that a range of techniques, including experiments, might be used to generate conclusions that could help to tackle collective action and other human dilemmas. It might be thought that a deductive approach would best describe her methodological work. Deductive research methods are used to find and test law-like behaviour, thus useful conclusions can be drawn and applied in new situations. Yet she was also aware that if human beings are studied scientifically, this ignores the fact that human behaviour is far from predictable. If we have agency, we can act creatively and change our behaviour. Indeed, the purpose of research in the 'human sciences' for her was largely about generating data that could be used by individuals and communities as a resource for them to deal with real life governance problems and puzzles. Elinor Ostrom understood research as a craft. Boldly crossing a research divide, she and Vincent saw human beings as creative but acknowledged that practical information might be used to enhance such human creativity.

Her methodology was polycentric and her methods multiple. Different methods, often associated with very different assumptions about the meaning of social science, were used. For example, she carried out participant observation and valued interpretivist approaches which see human beings as subjective and complex. While Ostrom was concerned with practical conclusions and rejected both scepticism and relativism, her pluralism and emphasis on language linked her work with poststructuralist and postmodern thinkers. Yet she saw a role for quantitative methods such as large scale data analysis, which are most obviously associated with positivist approaches to political science and economics. Ostrom's work was also polycentric because of its inter-disciplinary nature. For example, social-ecological systems had to be studied by both natural and social scientists. As a political economist, her concern with institutions meant that virtually all her work was a form of both political science and economics. Disciplines as varied as biology, law, anthropology and sociology informed her practical research. She wanted to use rigorously applied methods to pursue institutional knowledge. She observed 'it is important to me that research consists of a well-developed theory, a tested, accurate instrument, and good, tight measurements.' (Toonen 2010: 197).

The IAD framework she developed with Vincent Ostrom assumed that human beings are meaning making subjects, therefore language and symbolic resources had to be investigated to undertake social science research. Ostrom's work was methodologically close to that of Austrian thinkers like Buchanan and Hayek as we have seen. It also parallels the critical realism of both Rom Harré, who she occasionally cited in reference to rule making, and Roy Bhaskar (Bhaskar 1989). Both Ostrom and critical realists wished to move beyond positivist research but felt the scepticism of postmodernism prevents research into real life problems. Both approaches seek to link social and natural sciences but recognise that research tools are likely to be different within different sciences and precise areas of study.

Above all, Ostrom's work was modest. Conclusions were provisional, change was possible and evidence did not account for all cases. Universal explanations tended to be rejected but the idea that it was impossible to understand human action was also challenged. Such pluralism and modesty is an excellent basis for overcoming divisions within the social sciences:

> If social science were viewed less as a prizefight between competing theoretical perspectives, only one of which may prevail, and more as a joint venture in which explanations condition and augment one another, the partisan impulses that give rise to methodologically deficient research might be held in check. The question would change from 'Whether or not rational choice theory?' to something more fruitful: 'How does rationality interact with other facets of human nature and organization to produce the politics that we seek to understand?'
>
> (Green and Shapiro 1994: 204)

Extended to the areas she studied this seems a good description of Elinor Ostrom's methodological approach.

In a sense her work was a form of action research. Drawing on the tradition of Tocqueville, she believed that human beings could and should create their own means of governance. Spontaneity could not be assumed, research could provide individuals with better tools for political problem-solving. This provides important and unavoidable tension within her work. Individualism would suggest that social structures do not exist and social scientific investigation is virtually pointless. In contrast, deterministic and scientistic approaches that seek to describe structures might suggest that human life is governed by extra human forces. Yet research into the structures including institutions is important because we are able to change such structures if necessary. This is why practical research is so important. Methodological discussion, while often fascinating, should help rather than obscure such work:

> Without the careful development of a rigorous and empirically verifiable set of theories of social organization, we cannot do a very good job of fixing problems through institutional change. And, if we cannot link the theoretical results into a coherent overall approach, we cannot cumulate knowledge.
>
> (Ostrom 2005: 30–1)

This desire to cumulate knowledge was very important to her work. She noted discussion of political philosophy often 'related the lives, loves and miscellaneous thoughts' of important figures in political thought (Ostrom 2004: 44). She felt that there was often no sense of how political science grew as a body of knowledge with an accumulation of new insights that might make the puzzles of governance less mysterious. It was important, she felt, to understand how theorists 'grappled with existing theory, changed some basic assumptions, challenged others and how theories of political behaviour changed over time' (Ostrom 2004: 44). In the next chapter we shall discuss how Ostrom's sophisticated approach to methodology and practical research helped her better understand common pool resources and common pool property. This was an area where she certainly grappled with existing theory, changed basic assumptions and transformed understanding.

4 Au contraire, Monsieur Hardin!

> Whether studying California groundwater basins, North Atlantic fisheries, African community forests, or Nepalese irrigation systems, scientific case studies frequently seem to answer: Au contraire, Monsieur Hardin! There may be situations where this model can be applied, but many groups can effectively manage and sustain common resources if they have suitable conditions, such as appropriate rules, good conflict-resolution mechanisms, and well-defined group boundaries.
>
> (Hess and Ostrom 2011: 11)

Elinor Ostrom is best known for her work on the commons. It sometimes seems that commons, both in the form of resources and property rights, were almost invisible before her investigations. Typically, perhaps, the human ecologist Bonnie McCay, who later became president of the International Association for the Study of Common Property, found it difficult initially to research the subject:

> One day, back in the mid-1980s, I went to my university library and found that there were no subject entries for 'commons' except those that referred to the English House of Commons and a scattered few about the open-field farming systems of England. [...] But there was nothing in the broader sense of 'commons' or 'common property' as a particular facet of how human beings and their social institutions relate to the natural world.
>
> (McCay 2003: xv)

McCay's experience is a good illustration that until relatively recently the study of common pool property and common pool resources was obscure. To the extent that such topics were discussed at all, they were understood generally as areas of absence rather than active human management. Even before the 1968 publication of Garrett Hardin's 'Tragedy of the Commons' paper in the journal *Science*, it was generally assumed by academics that collective management of a resource would lead to chaos. Property was either private or state owned. Commons was non-property and, as such, open to all it would be abused and degraded. In contrast, Elinor Ostrom found that far from being a free for all, commons were often sustainably managed. Drawing on numerous case studies, she published *Governing the Commons* which examined why some commons succeed while others fail (Ostrom 1990). Between 1990 and her death in 2012 she collaborated with other researchers, using the wide variety of methods discussed in Chapter 3, to find out more about the commons. Her earliest research and indeed that of her husband Vincent Ostrom dealt with common pool resources. Vincent studied ranching in Wyoming on communal land and they both studied water management in California. However, at this point, they had not considered that they were studying something called the commons (Annual Reviews Conversations (2010: 8)).

This chapter introduces the concept of commons and includes a discussion of terminology. The case against the commons is examined. The initial case studies discussed by Elinor in *Governing the Commons* are outlined. Her eight key design principles for sustaining the commons are discussed in further detail, along with some of the factors she believed threatened common pool resource management.

Classifying the commons

The terminology for classifying commons can be confusing and Elinor Ostrom worked hard to bring some clarity towards the vocabulary used. She noted that researchers from a wide variety of disciplines including anthropology, economics, geography, history, law, political science and sociology had studied the topic. To bring together findings from such diverse practitioners, a precise shared terminology was needed. Commons is a word that gives rise to a number of misconceptions. While we may talk of common pool property systems or regimes as a form of governance, Ostrom's starting point was common pool resources. She noted in her Nobel Prize lecture that while economists had generally defined two types of good, 'private' and 'public', there were in fact four. Paul Samuelson had created a two-good classification for economists of 'private' and 'public' goods. A private good is one that can be bought and sold. One person's possession of the good usually excludes another person from owning and using it. A slice of pizza is a private good because if I eat it you cannot. Public goods, in contrast, can be used by more than one person. If one person uses the light from a street lamp that does not normally prevent others from benefiting from it as well. Public goods that include lighthouses, policing, defence and streetlights are hard for private companies to provide, as it is difficult to make a profit from them. The producer of a public good cannot exclude those who do not pay for their use, so may find it tough to raise revenue to set against potential costs to make a profit. In short, economists argued that private goods could be produced by the market but the state needs to intervene to provide public goods, paying for them with money raised from general taxation.

James Buchanan (1965) defined a third category of goods – 'club goods' or 'toll goods' which were non rival, i.e. similar to public goods but provided by small scale community associations rather than the state. He used the example of a swimming pool that might be built and maintained by a community group.

Club goods were owned neither by a private individual nor by the state. The notion of common property is perhaps only a step away from that of club property, in that a collective group owns both. However, Vincent and Elinor Ostrom argued that 'subtractability' was an important classification category that might distinguish different forms of property. In particular, it can be used to distinguish club goods from common goods. Subtractability refers to how much one person's use of a resource reduces the amount available to others (Ostrom 1990: 32). Each person may keep consuming a resource, subtracting from it until there is nothing left. Eating a pizza, which is of course a private good, would involve obvious subtraction. Elinor Ostrom also argued that rather than subtractability varying from zero for street lighting and other public goods to 100 per cent for a pizza slice, which would presumably be totally subtracted by a hungry buyer, subtractability could range in magnitude. Computers are a good example of a private good with less than 100 per cent subtractability, because one owner is unlikely to use the computer all the time and others may make use of it. The processing capacity of a personal computer also often exceeds the likely needs of any single user. Club goods up to the point of gross congestion are largely non-subtractable; if another person gets in to swim, this does not generally prevent others from enjoying the pool.

Elinor Ostrom distinguished a fourth kind of good, which of course was classified by the term 'common pool' (Ostrom 2005: 24). A common pool item is subtractable like a private good but users cannot easily be excluded. This gives rise to a potential problem of overuse. The Digital Library of the Commons defines common pool resources in the following terms:

> Common-pool resources (CPRs) are natural or human-made resources where one person's use subtracts from another's use and where it is often necessary, but difficult and costly, to exclude other users outside the group from using the resource. The majority of the CPR research to date has been in the areas of fisheries, forests, grazing systems, wildlife, water resources, irrigation systems, agriculture, land tenure and use, social organization, theory (social dilemmas, game theory, experimental economics, etc.), and global commons (climate change, air pollution, transboundary disputes, etc.). There is a growing corpus of work on 'new' or 'nontraditional' commons, which focuses on urban commons (apartment buildings, parking spaces, playgrounds, etc.), the Internet, electro-magnetic spectrum, genetic data, budgets, etc.
>
> (Digital Library of the Commons (2009))

Elinor Ostrom noted:

> The term 'common pool resources' is not something that most people have in their everyday language, so let me explain. It's any kind of resource that's bigger than a family backyard pool where it's difficult to keep people out – [because keeping them out is] costly. Anyone who enters may subtract

> something. So a fishery is pretty obvious. Sometimes it's difficult to figure out who can enter and what the boundaries are, but if I take fish out, that fish isn't available to anyone else.
>
> (Sullivan (2009))

An important distinction that Elinor Ostrom made is the difference between a common pool resource, which is subtractable but difficult to exclude people from using, and a common pool property system. It is easy to forget this distinction but it is vital to understanding her work. Many fisheries, forests, irrigation systems, lakes and rivers can be seen as common pool resources. However, common pool property resources can be distinguished from common pool property. Different forms of ownership can be applied to common pool resources. For example, a lake can be owned by a community, an individual, a state or may be unowned.

The legal theorist Yochai Benkler, who is one of the foremost experts on digital commons, has argued that commons can be contrasted with traditional forms of private property. He implies that commons are a form of non-property, presumably because he understands property to denote a form of exclusive ownership. While unlike Benkler, Elinor Ostrom explicitly recognizes common pool property, his understanding of commons as a legal category, illustrates her own thinking:

> 'Commons' refers to a particular institutional form of structuring the rights to access, use, and control resources. [...] The salient characteristic of commons, as opposed to property, is that no single person has exclusive control over the use and disposition of any particular resource in the commons.
>
> Instead, resources governed by commons may be used or disposed of by anyone among some (more or less well-defined) number of persons, under rules that may range from 'anything goes' to quite crisply articulated formal rules that are effectively enforced.
>
> (Benkler 2006: 60–1)

In turn, Benkler argues that commons can be divided into different types according to whether they are open to all or only to a particular group. The seas, atmosphere and many roads are examples of open commons but he notes the existence of 'limited-access common resources [...] where access is limited only to members of the village or association that collectively "owns" some defined pasturelands or irrigation systems' (Benkler 2006: 61). He also notes that commons can be regulated or unregulated, discussing whether rules of use and access are agreed and enforced.

Elinor Ostrom argued that whereas Garrett Hardin described unowned property, which was unregulated, in reality most commons are carefully managed. She noted that common pool resources are generally bounded, or enclosed in some way, so that those outside the community cannot abuse them. The members of the community who are allowed to exploit the resources can do so only within rules that are used to ration the resource so it is not degraded. However, such management requires the creation of particular property rights. The International Digital Library of the Commons describes common property as 'a formal or informal property regime that allocates a bundle of rights to a group. Such rights may include ownership, management, use, exclusion, access of a shared resource' (Digital Library of the Commons (2009)).

The tragedy of the commons?

The commons had been criticised as unsustainable long before Garrett Hardin discussed this apparent tragedy. The economist Gordon Scott (1954) argued that commons tend to lead to over-fishing because individuals had an incentive to fish as much as they could, resulting in lower catches for all, but concern about the commons can be traced back to Aristotle (Ostrom 1990: 2).

Elinor Ostrom described three models that had been used to suggest that 'commons' would fail and would therefore need to be turned into state or private property. These included 'the tragedy of the commons', prisoner's dilemma and Olson's understanding of the logic of collective action. The prisoner's dilemma, as we have seen, suggests that the most likely outcome will involve the prisoners betraying each other. Their likely defection is linked to the idea of free riding in the commons. One commoner assumes that another will get a free ride, so they refuse to take action for the common good. Thus if one commoner considers grazing his or her cattle less or fishing less to sustain the commons, they will think again and refuse to do so. Each commoner assumes that if they reduce their exploitation of the commons, other commoners will 'play them for suckers' and use the commons more. The prisoner's dilemma can be seen as a way of formally modelling Hardin's tragedy (Ostrom 1990: 3). However, as experiments have shown, cooperation may be a possibility, especially as commoners are not prisoners in separate cells but can communicate.

Elinor Ostrom also noted that Mancur Olson's book *The Logic of Collective Action* (1965) indicated that effective collective management was unlikely. Olson did not directly study the commons but was concerned with social movement and pressure group activity. He challenged the assumption of political scientists that individuals would form associations and work together for their collective ends in pressure groups, trade unions and political parties. He argued that this was unlikely because of a collective action problem caused, once again, by the free rider effect. Political activism is expensive; it takes time and often money and can have negative effects on an individual's career. Successful political activism can bring gains for an individual activist but these are shared with others in a group. For example, if you join a trade union this means paying a membership fee and may involve attending meetings. If the trade union succeeds in improving your pay or reducing working hours then you gain. However, everyone else in your group gains as well. Therefore, as with the prisoner's dilemma and the tragedy of the commons, there is an incentive to defect. If you refuse to join the union, you can get a free ride on the collective gains made by others. Such an awareness of free rides means that it will be difficult to organise collective action.

While less central to Ostrom's work, it is also worth briefly noting Harold Demsetz's criticism of communal land rights. He argued that to have more than one property owner would multiply the difficulty of agreeing questions of resource use. He illustrates this with the example of a farmer on one piece of communal land who, while ploughing, sees an engineer on adjacent land, damning a stream. The farmer wants to keep his source of water, which will be lost if the dam is completed. However, any agreement has to be made not just with the engineer but the other commoners who own the resource collectively:

> The farmer prefers to have the stream as it is, and so he asks the engineer to stop his construction. The engineer says, 'Pay me to stop.' The farmer replies, 'I will be happy to pay you, but what can you guarantee in return?' The engineer answers, 'I can guarantee you that I will not continue constructing the dam, but I cannot guarantee that another engineer will not take up the task because this is communal property; I have no right to exclude him [*sic*].' What would be a simple negotiation between two persons under a private property arrangement turns out to be a rather complex negotiation between the farmer and everyone else. This is the basic explanation, I believe, for the preponderance of single rather than multiple owners of property. Indeed, an increase in the number of owners is an increase in the communality of property and leads, generally, to an increase in the cost of internalizing.
>
> (Demsetz 1967: 357)

Demsetz recognised that collective property ownership was possible and argued that for many nomadic peoples, where population density was low, common property was an attractive option. Nonetheless, he argued that in many situations it led to cumbersome and costly negotiations. While for him commons were not tragic, common pool property was often inefficient. Institutional economists often use transaction costs to explain the emergence of particular property rights. Demsetz's explanation is based on such an approach. Plausible as it is, like Hardin's work, metaphor and narrative are mobilised rather than empirical research to explore the supposed effect of expensive transactions that make common property ownership allegedly inefficient.

With the exception of Demsetz's account, which merely says commons are likely to be inefficient but not universally unsustainable, these formal models or metaphorical scenarios are different ways of restating the same assumption. The 'tragedy of the commons', the prisoner's dilemma and Olson's model, are each based on rational choice assumptions that suggest collective action is unlikely and the commons will therefore fail. Yet the commons did not always fail. By 1990 when Elinor Ostrom published *Governing the Commons*, many case studies of long-term sustainable common pool property systems had been identified by a range of researchers. The commons had apparently ceased being inevitably tragic.

The triumph of the commons?

Ironically, perhaps, given that Demsetz's argument rested on a hypothetical problem of sharing water, the Ostroms' work began with water commons. They examined how collective, state and private institutions managed the water resources surrounding Los Angeles (Ostrom 1990: 1). Irrigation is often organised as a commons and water systems almost inevitably involve some collective management agreement. If the owner of the land at one point in a system takes too much water, other users will suffer. Water systems tend to be 'subtractable' but it is difficult to exclude users who might subtract too much. The starting point for the Ostroms was not that communal property might fail, but that, instead some resources were common resources and so presented a potential problem. Individual private ownership might be possible but it would not solve the problem of resource overuse, unless private owners were able to cooperate effectively. She noted that the question of the commons was a puzzle with practical implications in many contexts, observing that the economist John H. Dales (1968: 62) had identified 'the perplexing problems related to resources "owned in common because there is no alternative!" (Ostrom 1990: 3).

Dale's contention was illustrated by the water crisis in West Basin, California. West Basin is a water system near Los Angeles, which Elinor Ostrom studied for her PhD (Ostrom 1965). Vincent Ostrom also researched shared systems of water use in the area (V. Ostrom 1950). Users in the early twentieth century had the right to pump as much water as they wanted, which in the arid Californian landscape eventually led to near catastrophe. The water level fell, leading to a risk that salt water from the Pacific Ocean would be sucked into the system, potentially leading to contamination. This, indeed, would have been a 'tragedy of the commons.' Property owners were subtracting too much water; this threatened to destroy the value of water for irrigation, and an individual who used less water was likely to be exploited by free riders who would continue to use too much. Privatisation was impossible because individual users could not own the water, so the common resource had to be managed communally. While this involved difficult negotiations, because of conflict between water users, disaster was averted. The users established a West Basin Water Association and a survey was undertaken, which confirmed the severity of the problem. In October 1945, 'two private water companies and a city filed a suit in Superior Court against a long list of known water producers in West Basin (Ostrom 1965: 30). It was suggested that water users had to reduce their water subtractions by two thirds. Water Association members and other users felt this was too great a cut to sustain farming and other economic activities, yet they agreed to reduce their consumption, created a collective agreement and appointed a 'watermaster' to make sure users kept to it. While the story is a complex one, it illustrated to the Ostroms that users could solve collective problems of resource use.

Elinor and Vincent Ostrom moved into new areas of research such as policing and local government but by the 1980s, scholars began to compare notes and research into the commons advanced. The US National Research Council established a panel to research common pool resource management and the political scientist Ronald Oakerson developed a framework for studying common pool resources (Oakerson 1986). In 1989, Elinor Ostrom helped found the International Association for the Study of Common Pool Property. In 2006, reflecting the importance of both common pool resources and common pool property, along with the growth of new commons in cyberspace, the name of the association was simplified to the International Association for the Study of Commons. Scholars from the Ostroms' workshop in Indiana University created a database to compare case study research into common pool resources from around the world and from many different disciplines.

In 1990, Elinor Ostrom published *Governing the Commons*, which brought together many case study examples of commons from a variety of sources. *Governing the Commons* showed that something theoretically unlikely, according to prevailing academic wisdom, was both possible and surprisingly widespread. It was relatively easy to show the flaws in a universal tragedy of the commons by pointing to examples of successful sustainable commons. Elinor analysed both successful and failed commons to understand better how commons worked. She focussed on case studies that were backed by rich empirical data, and covered many centuries of management. These were supplemented analysis of the workings of the ground water basin around Los Angeles including West Basin that she had investigated.

One of the case studies she noted was that of Törbel in Switzerland that had been investigated by the human ecologist Robert Netting. He noted that 'communal control, equitable division, and careful conservation measures preserve necessary resources from reckless or selfish exploitation and avoid the "tragedy of the commons" often envisaged' (Netting 1981: 82). Törbel is a village of about six hundred people high in the Swiss Alps. Privately owned plots to grow fruit and vegetables are part of a mosaic of land ownership with a large common pool element including cattle pastured on communally owned land. Historical research is possible because of a rich source of local archives:

> Written legal documents dating back to 1224 provide information regarding the types of land tenure and transfers that have occurred in the village and rules used by the villages to regulate the five types of communally owned property: the alpine grazing meadows, the forests, the 'waste' lands, the irrigation systems, and the paths and roads connecting privately and communally owned properties.
>
> (Ostrom 1990: 62)

In February 1483, citizens signed an agreement to form an association with formal rules to manage the use of their communally owned properties. Existing commoners had the power to allow outsiders to join their community. The commons were strictly regulated; Netting (1981: 139) observed 'no citizen could send more cows to the Alps than he could feed during the winter.' Rules which are still in existence in the twenty-first century, imposed substantial fines on commoners who overgrazed pastures. The overgrazing rule was easy to monitor and enforce; it simply involved counting cattle and disciplining those who overgrazed. All citizens who owned cattle agreed the rules, democratically. Their association met once a year to discuss such rules and elect officials. Officials monitored the commons, imposed fines, arranged manure distribution and organised the rebuilding of huts, if avalanches had damaged them. The harvesting of trees in the communally owned forest area was also carefully regulated. Meadows, gardens and grain fields were owned privately but shared between citizens on an equal basis. For much of the period, population was regulated by late marriages, celibacy, long birth spacing and 'considerable emigration' (Ostrom 1990: 63). Netting argued that these arrangements maintained the productivity of the land around Törbel for many centuries; he believed that clear rules and community involvement created an ecologically sustainable system of land management.

Ostrom's second example of historical commons comes from the work of the political scientist Margaret McKean who studied three Japanese villages: Hirano, Nagaike and Yamanaka. The villages are located in a similar environment to that of Törbel, established on steep mountains with individually owned gardens as well as communal land. 'Waste' produced timber, thatch for roofing and animal fodder along with fertilizer, charcoal and firewood. While the Törbel villagers lacked an overlord, the Japanese commoners lived within a feudal system where elite landowners could regulate some access to communal land and resources. Landowners appointed agents to regulate land use in the commons, but peasants over time asserted their right to establish their own rules for management.

As in other communal systems, collective labour was necessary to maintain some features of the commons. Each household was obliged to help with a number of tasks to maintain the commons, which included:

> [...] annual burning (which involved cutting nine-foot firebreaks ahead of time, carefully monitoring the blaze, and occasional fire-fighting when the flames jumped the fire break), to report to harvest on mountain-opening days, or to do a specific cutting of timber or thatch. Accounts were kept about who contributed what to make sure that no household evaded its responsibilities unnoticed. Only illness, family tragedy, or the absence of able-bodied adults [...] were recognized as excuses for getting out of collective labor [...]. But, if there was no excuse, punishment was in order.
>
> (McKean 1986: 559)

Monitoring to assess if regulations were broken and the imposition of punishment if they had were of course also needed. Monitoring, while important, varied between villages but commoners often hired 'detectives' who would patrol the commons on horseback, arresting those in breach of the rules. Sanctions were graduated, according to McKean, from minor infractions, which would be met by demands for saké and cash. At the top of the scale, ostracisation or even exile might result. Nevertheless, rules were broken; commoners might disagree as to the relevance of rules or become impatient to harvest plants outside of the determined season. The success of regulation, argued McKean, depended upon the rules being agreed by the commoners rather than imposed from outside.

A third case study of a long-term and environmentally sustainable commons comes from the Spanish irrigation systems known as *huerta*. Some of these persisted for nearly 1,000 years. Ostrom noted the existence of a commons agreement between 84 irrigators signed on 29 May 1435 at the monastery of St Francis near Valencia to regulate the use and maintenance of the Benacher and Faitanar canals. In the arid regions of Spain, farming would have been difficult without sophisticated systems of irrigation. Vincent Ostrom studied communal management of water systems in California influenced by such Spanish water commons (V. Ostrom 1950).

Elinor Ostrom discussed several different examples of *huerta*; all involved locally determined rules, effective monitoring and a scale of gradually increasing punishments for rule breaking. The farmers in the Valencia irrigation system met every two or three years to elect an official known as the syndic, whose responsibilities included enforcing the rationing of canal water:

> The basic rules for allocating water are dependent on the decisions made by the officials of the irrigation community concerning three environmental conditions: abundance, seasonal low water, and extraordinary drought [...]. The most frequent condition under which the canals operate is that of seasonal low water. When the low-water condition is in effect, water is distributed to specific farmers through a complex, rule-driven hydraulic system.
>
> (Ostrom 1990: 73)

Finally, she looked at the *zanjera* irrigation communities in the Philippines. Their origins are clouded but they may have evolved from *huerta*s during the Spanish occupation of the islands, either directly from Spain or via Mexico. They are at least two hundred years old. A recent research report from the UN Food and Agriculture Organization (FAO) outlines that the *zanjera* continue to provide a means of managing water collectively and sustainably:

> Water-sharing arrangements within the *zanjera* as well as with other *zanjeras* are governed by certain rules which involve specific schedules for water delivery, labor assignments and a penalty structure for violation of *zanjera* rules. Most of the *zanjeras* observe rotational (*squadra* or *cuadra*) irrigation during dry season when water is scarce.
>
> Other *zanjeras* do not see any need to allocate water on a rotation basis because of perennial supply of water from springs or drainage.
>
> In cases of conflict within or between *zanjeras*, mediation facilitated by the officers is employed, and recourse to litigation is avoided as much as

> possible. Penalties imposed for violation of a *zanjera* rule comes in the form of fines (*multa*), and are enforced for offences such as absence from required *zanjera* activities and water stealing. The latter offence carries a relatively heavy fine, reflecting the high value accorded to irrigation water.
>
> (Kho and Agsaoay-Saño 2005: 9)

Elinor Ostrom used these case studies as the basis of *Governing the Commons*, but she combined such secondary case study work with a wide variety of techniques including statistical analysis, game theory and experiments to enhance her knowledge of sustainable management of the commons, during her decades of work on the topic. While she discovered that sustainable commons were extremely diverse in nature, she postulated a number of design features that helped to make community management of resources work. It is to these that I shall now turn.

Designing successful commons

Elinor Ostrom sought to discover what made commons more 'robust'. The phrase 'institutional robustness' was taken from the political scientist Kenneth Shepsle (1989) who used it to denote a long-lasting institution whose rules were modified, where necessary, over time to ensure such longevity. She further suggested that 'robust' could be defined as applying to an institution that was adaptable so that it could maintain a set of desired characteristics over the long-term despite disruption (Ostrom 2005: 258). She found that the characteristics of long lived common pool property systems were extremely diverse; so diverse, in fact, that initially she found it difficult to identify any universal features that could be applied to sustainable systems. This did not surprise her because diverse features are likely given the diversity of both human societies and the environments under consideration.

Nonetheless, after much thought and research, she identified eight broad design principles that tend to create successful robust commons. She often stressed that these principles were not a blueprint or a set of rules but described broad structural features often found in commons that succeeded and were absent in case studies of commons that failed.

These included:

1 Clearly defined boundaries (effective exclusion of external unentitled parties);
2 Rules regarding the appropriation and provision of common resources are adapted to local conditions;
3 Collective-choice arrangements allow most resource appropriators to participate in the decision-making process;
4 Effective monitoring by monitors who are part of or accountable to the appropriators;
5 The existence of a scale of graduated sanctions for resource appropriators who violate community rules;

6 Easy and low cost access to conflict resolution mechanisms;
7 Self-determination of the community is recognized by higher-level authorities;
8 Organization in the form of multiple layers of nested enterprises, with small local CPRs at the base level.

These were suggested in *Governing the Commons* and refined with further research. In her 2005 book *Understanding Institutional Diversity*, she rephrased the second design principle as one of cost and benefit equivalence rather than local rule adaption alone. In turn, Cox *et al.* (2010) analysed over ninety other academic studies that sought to apply her design principles to the commons. Most of these broadly supported her findings, although a number stressed the importance of broader macro social and economic factors or emphasised that community trust was the key variable. The interaction between macro social, economic and particularly ecological factors is discussed in subsequent chapters. In line with her collaborative and cooperative approach, Ostrom amended some of her design principles in the light of Cox *et al.*'s work, as will be discussed below.

She argued that it is impossible to 'design' a complete system, noting that her colleague Michael McGinnis had gained an insight from Herbert Simon's book *The Science of the Artificial* to this effect. Simon (1996) argued that no humanly designed system could be designed to produce optimal performance. However, Simon noted that complex systems were constructed out of simpler components and that the starting point for construction was important (Ostrom 2005: 270). Thus, the design principles were a good way of investigating the building blocks of a sustainable commons system but she felt strongly that they should not be seen as deterministic or inevitable. Elinor Ostrom also argued that her design principles could be rephrased as questions that might help communities to improve their systems of resource management. The design principles could provide a better beginning and reduce the search costs for developing sets of relevant rules for specific common pool resource governance.

Elinor Ostrom also outlined five forces that tended to degrade and disrupt commons. These included rapid exogenous change, corruption and rent seeking behavior, blueprint thinking, transmission failure and lack of supportive external structures. In *Understanding Institutional Diversity*, she used these design principles and potential disrupters to analyse sustainable resource use more generally. The rest of this chapter discusses these categories in detail to understand how they might lead to better collective management of common pool resources.

Clearly defined boundaries

Ostrom believed that conservation zones which are imposed by central government or a conservation body might be 'paper parks' and as such ineffective at protecting the environment. While she acknowledged that this was not always the case and some national parks and reserves worked well, often they did not take into account local circumstances. In particular, communities living within such areas might not be aware of their boundaries. In turn, a well-managed commons needs to have a clearly defined territory to avoid the problem of free riding. While much effort is put in to prevent free rides in a working commons by community members, it is just as important to be able to stop non-community members from subtracting from the resource. Unless users and potential users know the extent of the commons, it will be open to abuse. Elinor Ostrom cited the example of forest commons in Uganda, which had been investigated by political scientist Nathan Vogt (Ostrom 2005: 262). Vogt and his associates used archives and interviews with older commoners and officials to investigate how some forest reserves in the country had remained resistant to deforestation. They found that boundaries had been established in 1900 as a result of an agreement between the Regents of the Buganda Kingdom and the British colonial authorities. They had survived for more than a century and were shown by cairns of stone, which were marked symbolically by planting trees at their centre. Rather than being imposed by a top-down central authority, the boundaries were agreed with local clan elders and other traditional administrators. Strong and agreed boundaries make for a commons that is more likely to be conserved. Poor boundaries lead to outsiders being more likely to abuse the resource. However, it is clear that for many indigenous North American groups, boundaries were vague and shifting (Cronon 1983). Yet while access to land might overlap, usufruct rights to hunt or gather plants were usually defined clearly for them. As Ostrom observed, commons will tend to work best when they are within wider and deeper nested systems. Where there is a boundary, it needs to be effective. She agreed with Morrow and Hull (1996) who had felt that the first design principle should be rephrased after studying a forest conservation project. They suggested that not only was a clear boundary necessary but that 'the appropriators are able to effectively defend the resource from outsiders' (Ostrom 2005: 262). A boundary that could not be maintained to prevent others from eroding the commons was largely useless. She also acknowledged that Cox *et al.* (2010) had found that both user boundaries and resource boundaries had to be considered. A user boundary separated a commons community from non-users, while the resource boundary separated 'a specific common-pool resource from a larger social-ecological system' (Ostrom 2010b: 653). A lake or a forest might, for example, be considered as a common pool resource, the political community that governed use might have different borders to such a resource.

Cost benefit equivalence

Elinor Ostrom observed that 'fairness is a crucial attribute of the rules of robust systems' (Ostrom 2005: 263). She argued that for the rules in a commons to work, the resources gained from a commons had to be distributed so that inputs balanced outputs. She believed that it was important to relate user inputs to benefits; if some individuals made little contribution but gained large benefits, this would tend to mean the system would break down. If a small group gained most of the benefit from a commons, other users would be unwilling to abide by the rules. She noted the example of the Chisasibi Cree who constructed a complex set of rules to manage both fish and beaver stocks. The success of the systems of environmental management worked and survived over a long period because rewards, according to her understanding, were distributed evenly. The community supported the rules because they generated mutual benefit. Those who broke the rules lost favour with the animals, which in the Cree cultural system meant that they would find hunting difficult. Those who broke the rules also suffered social disgrace.

'Fairness' though is difficult to define. Political philosophers have mused over it for centuries. In turn, some forms of common pool property are highly informal. For example, in many parts of the world, people still have the right to enter a forest and pick mushrooms. Such procedures are unlikely to be regulated, although individuals who take too much may be subject to sanctions. Caste and class may also disrupt such 'fairness'. In feudal England, commons were a pressure valve and means of social reproduction in an institutionally unfair system. Commoners who worked the land as serfs were provided with commons, so they could survive and raise new generations of serfs to work for the social elite. Access to common land may also have functioned a means of reducing social tension and making revolt less likely. Nonetheless, numerous empirical studies have provided strong evidence that an approximate equivalence of input and output factors is an important design feature of a sustainable and robust commons system (Cox *et al.* 2003; Trawick 2001).

Locally adapted rules for collective governance

The third design principle is that the individuals who use a commons need to be authorised to participate in rule making and modification. Rules need to be adapted to local circumstances and constructed by the community of commoners in particular localities. It is necessary for rules to be adapted to local circumstances rather than for a universal set of rules to be externally imposed. From a theoretical perspective, this reflects the insights of Friedrich Hayek, Michael Polanyi and Jane Jacobs. Knowledge may be spread thinly through a society and one central body will lack access to accurate knowledge and may, in turn, risk policy failure if it imposes measures from above. Knowledge may be tacit so it is difficult to transmit. Ostrom found that case study examples showed that the exact rules used to manage commons sustainably varied enormously. At first, this confused her but she came to understand that because commons are so varied, varied rules would most likely be appropriate. Common resources are differentiated by different environmental factors and are used by social groups that are also varied. It would be unrealistic to expect that one set of universal rules would work. The more locally rules are adapted, the more likely they are to harness local knowledge and to be flexible enough to deal with varied environments and societies. Ostrom felt that this was particularly important because of possible environmental change. Such change would challenge existing practices that might need to be altered to maintain sustainability. Local people would notice such changes, unlike officials who might be based far away, so adaption to change is much more likely if local knowledge is harnessed instead of ignored.

It is important to ration access to a common resource to avoid overuse and subsequent potential degradation. Such rationing will involve sacrifice but sacrifice, agreed by members of the community, is more likely to be supported, than a sacrifice determined by an external body. We still may break rules that we have agreed to but we are less likely to break them, than rules imposed by an external authority. While Demsetz suggested that negotiation is likely to be costly, once a governance system is in place, it can cut such costs (1967). Governance systems can also be seen as ways of transmitting information over time and in some of Ostrom's case study examples worked over many centuries. The initial work in design may take much effort but once a system of governance is in place it can be adapted and fine-tuned over time.

Elinor Ostrom noted that the political scientist Madhushre Sekher, found from a study of villages in Orissa in India that the 'wider the representation of the community in the organization, the better are its chances of securing local cooperation and rule confirmation for managing and preserving the resource' (Ostrom 2005: 264).

Local design input, to a greater or lesser extent, equals self-governance. Both Elinor and Vincent Ostrom were, as I have noted, strong advocates of self-governance. They believed that democracy was most democratic when constitutional systems were designed by participants. Democratic constitutions covered not just the state but also potentially all forms of governance. As a political economist, Elinor Ostrom's economic principles cannot be separated from her emphasis on governance.

Monitoring

Strong boundaries and effective rules will only work if they are policed in some way. Norms of good behaviour while useful are unlikely to be sufficient in protecting a commons. The first step to effective policing is via effective monitoring. An individual or individuals need to record any infractions of the rules. Thus in the Japanese examples discussed by McKean, a constable might be hired. The West Basin water users employed a watermaster. In medieval Europe, a number of different officials were put in place to monitor the use of the commons. For example, the hayward has been described as:

> One who keeps a common herd of cattle of a town; and the reason of his being so called may be because part of his office is to see that they neither break nor cross the hedges of the enclosed lands; or because he keeps the grasses from hurt and destruction.
>
> (Rapalje and Lawrence 1888: 595)

Monitoring is a way of making sure that the free rider problem is overcome by identifying those who ignore the rules and exploit a resource. Elinor Ostrom saw a danger that 'comanaged paper parks' might exist if monitoring was not carried out on a local basis. Central authorities might cooperate with local owners of a commons, but unless monitoring was organised locally it might fail to have any real existence other than on paper.

She noted that many local communities created an official monitoring post. She observed that in some systems the position rotated so that every member of the community would take the role at some point. She found that in government-controlled forests, the use of local monitors, also helped conservation. In Brazil, for example, forest conservation had been improved by using the local rubber tappers to monitor the forests to prevent damage (Ostrom 2005: 266).

Graduated sanctions

Sanctions are necessary as it is unlikely that goodwill alone will prevent abuse of the commons. Free riders need to be sanctioned or else they will abuse the commons and tragedy will occur. Nevertheless, Ostrom's research suggested that sanctions should be carefully graded from soft to more severe. In many cases, users might break a rule without being conscious of doing so; a simple warning will remind them of the rules. To use strong punishment for a first offense might be costly and cause resentment, which could make the system more difficult to sustain. The Japanese example where commoners might be fined in saké by the detectives hired by the community is indicative (Ostrom 2005: 68). Informal and gentle sanctions are also likely at first. A fisher who broke commons rules, perhaps going out to sea on fallow days, might wait a long time before being served a beer in the village bar. Such graduated sanctions are also often part of indigenous justice systems. The notion of a 'grim trigger' suggested by games theorists, where after one infraction all cooperation is removed and the individual who breaks a rule is expelled from the game, was not found by Ostrom or other researchers into commons (Ostrom 2010b: 650). While the threat might be thought to be so severe as to prevent rule breaking, other commoners who would lose the work input of the violator, after a single offence, might see it as too costly. Commons often require collective work input to build fences or maintain buildings or ditches; loss of a commoner can reduce such capacity.

Drawing upon the work of the political scientist Margaret Levi (1988), Elinor Ostrom observed a number of precise advantages of a system of graduated sanctions. Without early sanctions, mistakes can increase and if there is no correction, however mild, faith in the system will decline. This will have a positive feedback effect and a cascade of infractions may occur until the management of the commons breaks down and tragedy occurs. Levi argues that self-organised systems often rely on 'semi-voluntary' cooperation rather than complete cooperation or coercion. Graduated sanctions promote such low cost semi-cooperation by increasing confidence that free riding is less likely. If individuals continue to break the rules, they can be warned that sanctions will become more severe. At worst, they may be exiled from the community.

Conflict resolution mechanisms

Conflict is perhaps inevitable. Economics involves access to scarce resources and such scarcity leads to disputes between different social groups and different individuals. The previous design principles tend to reduce the possibility of free riding and to prevent open conflict from breaking out. Yet disputes are likely and low cost conflict resolution mechanisms are necessary. The court leet system, which was in existence from the Anglo-Saxon period, was used to attempt to resolve such disputes. For example, Cricklade water meadow in Wiltshire in the UK has been managed as a commons for over 1,000 years. The court leet made up of elected officials from the local community continues to exist in the twenty-first century to help conserve and sustain the water meadow, known for its richness in wild rare wildflowers (http://crickladecourtleet.com/).

Elinor Ostrom noted that rules, even if simple and agreed by participants, could be interpreted in different ways. An agreed judicial body can mediate such differences even if it is highly informal. She also suggested that such mechanisms would make it more difficult for a local elite to take control of the resource. The substitution of local manorial courts, such as the court leets, which managed the English commons by more distant and formal bodies, has been seen as one factor that led to the decline in the commons (Rodgers *et al.* 2010; Thompson 1991).

Slater and Flaherty (2009) have shown how a council of elders governed the Irish common pool property systems, the rundale, and an official called the King. They argue that this was a self-governing system with commoners electing the King and elders. Conflict was endemic to the rundales but the King and council managed disagreements. A good king had a number of precise duties and desired talents:

> Stature, strength, comeliness of person are mentioned, as are justice, wisdom and knowledge. Literary attainment is desirable; a good talker, a good story-teller, knowledge of two languages, the ability to read and write, all of these were laudable in the King. A degree of economic well-being or independence was also thought fitting. He had very positive and definite functions. The regulation, division and apportioning of fishing and shore rights and the allotment of tillage and pasture land was left to him, and in some cases, he appointed subsidiary officers such as herdsmen. He was expected to maintain traditional laws … in some instances we are told that he specifically punished wrongdoers. He was expected to speak for his community in their relations with the outside authority.
>
> (Ó Danachair 1981: 25–6 quoted in Slater and Flaherty 2009: 14–15)

They note references to Queens including one who managed the commons in Erris, Mayo (Slater and Flaherty 2009: 14).

The right of users to organize

Intervention from above may disrupt the maintenance of a commons system. More fundamentally many commons have been privatised or taken into state control. Yet Elinor Ostrom noted that despite political change at a state or regional level, commons have often been ignored and allowed to continue. Some common pool property systems are largely invisible to external authorities. For example, a group of fishers in Bengal, who saw themselves as illicit, enforced a commons system without any recognition by government authority (Ostrom 2005: 268). Yet if a commons system is unrecognised by higher authorities, any individual who becomes unhappy with the system can then complain to the authorities, who may intervene to the detriment of the collective owners. Paternalistic regulation from external authorities can also be damaging; while such regulation may be well meaning, it is often insensitive to local conditions. External regulation also reduces the possibility of self-governance that is necessary, according to Ostrom, for a commons to work well.

External authorities have often taken over and destroyed commons. This is the history of much of the indigenous commons that dominated North America and continues to be repeated. The political factors eroding commons are important to understand and can nullify well-designed and maintained local systems of governance.

Nested structures

Commons need to work within wider systems. Environments are not discrete islands and even islands are influenced by weather systems and oceans. Despite Ostrom's emphasis on boundaries, common property systems may overlap with inter-commoning occurring between different communities. There must, therefore, be ways of negotiating the links between inter-locking commons. Irrigation is one good example of this design feature. A local irrigation system, which is run as a commons, may well be part of a wider water network. Unless local commons can work with other systems, failure will be likely. Also within an irrigation system, rules may differ from one location to the next. Ostrom noted that the rules for allocating water to farmers along a single distribution channel would be different from other parts of an irrigation system. She believed that research indicates that purely localised systems are as likely to fail as centralised systems that do not recognize local knowledge. Ostrom felt that far from 'small is beautiful' acting as an automatic rule, a variety of scales of management might be necessary, thus the principle of polycentricism discussed in earlier chapters is relevant. Commons need to be nested into larger systems but this insight is perhaps best discussed in detail in Chapter 5 where Ostrom's work on social-ecological systems is outlined.

Rapid exogenous change

Elinor Ostrom also identified a number of threats to the commons. The first was pressure created by fast external change. She noted that rapid changes in a number of factors were particularly dangerous to collective sustainable governance of resources. Technological innovation by, for example, improving harvesting that made it far easier to extract resource units, such as fish, from a commons could be dangerous. She also identified rapid changes in human, animal or plant populations as threats. Either sudden population increase or decrease could change ecological characteristics that might make existing systems of management irrelevant or even damaging. Out-migration of commoners might lead to a loss of those who maintained the commons. In particular, with economic change, younger people might leave an area and traditions of good management might fail to be transmitted to a new generation. Equally, sudden and rapid in-migration might bring in new participants who are less likely to trust each other and learn the appropriate social norms. She noted that collective action is based largely on mutual trust and reciprocity and that some studies have indicated that areas of rapid settlement have seen commons management collapse quite quickly.

She also noted the 'substitution of relative importance of monetary transactions in the national governance system' (Ostrom 2005: 272). I am assuming this refers to both taxation and commodification. Many colonial regimes in Africa imposed taxation on local communities, where both monetary exchange and taxation had been low or unknown. Community members had to raise revenue to pay taxation. This meant accelerated commodification of economies based on subsistence with greater integration into monetised systems. This in turn could lead to increased resources extraction that might degrade the commons.

Increasing 'heterogeneity' of participants is yet another danger identified which might make management more difficult. None of these changes is necessarily catastrophic. She believed that a commons system might adapt to relatively slow change. Even moderately fast change can be dealt with but rapid change tends to destroy the governance framework. Many writers on the environment and society have risked, perhaps, being deterministic by identifying a single external factor that threatens sustainability. Cultural change, rising populations or economic growth can be seen as inevitably destructive and unmediated. Elinor Ostrom, in contrast, noted the existence of such potential external threats but did not view them as inevitably catastrophic. She believed that human beings had agency and could come together to manage such threats. Nonetheless, rapid change in a wide variety of variables was potentially dangerous.

She noted the example of the northern Norwegian fisheries where technology and population density changed fast, along with other factors, and led to the destruction of the system of communal management (Ostrom 2005: 273). The fisheries were originally seasonal, as they only took the fish for part of the year. This helped to preserve stocks. Their technology was limited, which restricted their boats to coastal areas. Even without particularly sophisticated management, it was almost impossible to degrade the fish stocks. A number of factors changed rapidly and put immense pressure on fish stocks. After the Second World War, fishermen from other countries started to use the waters. Technology improved. The local population increased. The Norwegian Raw Fish Act of 1938 allowed fishermen to negotiate and set an enforceable landing price for their fish. John R. Commons would no doubt have seen this as an example of how institutional change can be used to empower a previously less powerful group within a market. Good intentions contributed to a negative outcome. Fishing became more lucrative and incomes initially rose and became more predictable. The Act provided a greater incentive for increased exploitation, which damaged fish stocks. Any one of these factors was not necessarily threatening, Ostrom assumed, because fishermen could discuss and eventually implement new rules for sustainability. Yet because the changes were multiple and rapid, the consequences were severe.

Transmission failure

Rapid exogenous change was also likely to lead to transmission failure (Ostrom 2005: 273–4). Successful commons regimes have survived over many centuries and some have no doubt continued for thousands of years. Commons systems are not static but if management rules are not transmitted from one generation to another they will fail. Institutional economics, in its varied manifestations, is related, consciously or not, to the notion that access to knowledge is economically vital. Economists generally accept that the closer to perfect knowledge, the more efficient the decisions undertaken will be. Perfect knowledge is impossible so perfect systems are unattainable; however, better access to better knowledge is likely to lead to better decision making. Institutions make it possible to gather and transmit relevant knowledge. Demsetz (1967) suggested that individuals would find it costly to make decisions in a communal system, yet within communal systems social learning over many generations apparently makes negotiation easier than he had imagined. The design principles of a working commons lead to the creation of institutions that transmit knowledge of best practice. Such institutional transmission may be informal or even tacit. If transmission is broken, then it will be difficult to relearn such institutional knowledge.

Ostrom argued that with rapid change, rules might, if they survive, become formalised and therefore brittle and hollow. Written rules will be adhered to and even unwritten assumptions may be recognised, yet subtle but often vital nuances may be lost. Formal adherence may lead to a chain of consequences that erodes the system. Implicit in her analysis of the commons is the assumption that shared norms and consensus help lead to mutual cooperation. Commons systems demand cooperation, while sanctions are necessary; the commoners rarely have the coercive force that belongs to the state. This means that informal norms and a commitment to cooperation are necessary. If individuals within a commons system agree to the constitutional design of the system, they are likely to have faith in the system.

Rapid changes in culture or population mean that underlying constitutional acceptance may be lost. Elinor Ostrom argued that people might adhere to the formal rules but forget the reasons for such rules. The rules are kept to the letter but their spirit and rationale is forgotten. She speculated that a system might, for example, have a simple majority rule to ease decision-making but that to work well the system needed broad consensus. If transmission failure occurred, more and more decisions might be made on narrow majority votes. Thus, the simple majority rule would be met but the importance of gaining greater acceptance might be forgotten. In the past, major changes might not be introduced if they only had a minimal working majority in their favour. If winning became more important than attempting to gain broader support, ultimately the system might fall apart because of factionalism, manipulation and growing mistrust. The rules might become hollow and the system fragile. Such fragility would lead to further erosion. To gain a majority, greater horse-trading and deal making might become necessary. Rules might be manipulated to achieve decisions. Rent seeking behaviour would also grow because increased access to powerful resources would help build winning coalitions. Manipulative politics would further reduce faith in the system and participation would fall. Falling participation would challenge the independence of the system by increasing the need for external support. Elite external donors could manipulate the internal politics of the commons more easily and resistance to the removal of the system might lead to its absorption by others. Ostrom noted leaders who rely on coalitions to win close votes rather than wider agreement will be driven to rely on coercion, corruption and patronage.

She noted that if participants view the rules as obstacles rather than useful enabling devices, they would attempt to bend the rules, ignore them or push for reinterpretation. Each household might try to find ways of minimizing the labour they contribute, leading to further weakening of the system. As has been noted, many commons need donations of labour to work, so that irrigation channels can be maintained, boundary fences mended or in some systems communal production of crops continued. It is also likely that to make monitoring effective, either resources are provided to employ an official or individuals take on the role on the basis of a rota. If the rules of the system decay, motivation is eroded and individuals opt out until the system collapses.

Blueprint thinking

Elinor Ostrom found that rules used to govern commons varied dramatically, this was because environmental and social conditions tend to vary too, and so one set of rules was unlikely to fit all situations. Her tentative design principles generally applied but within successful systems were on occasions contradicted. A blueprint approach would, based even on the best empirical research, be likely to lead to failure. Such an insight is in sharp opposition to Hardin's assumption that a blueprint imposed from outside would protect users and promote sustainability (Ostrom 2005: 274).

Ostrom was concerned that even well-meaning external authorities who sought to promote local governance of resources could create damage if they used blueprint thinking. Ostrom took the term 'blueprint thinking' from David Korten and it was the core of her critique of much institutional aid giving in a development context. Aid from rich to poorer countries could cause harm if it was applied in an unsophisticated way. She defined 'blueprint thinking' as when academics, policy makers or NGOs proposed uniform solutions to complex problems. Rather than using sweeping policies based often on sloganistic proposals, local realities had to be assumed to be complex. Detail was everything if solutions were to work. Often policymakers would find that their projects failed and swiftly change them. Such change was based often on intellectual trends that might be fleeting rather than an understanding that blueprint thinking was intrinsically flawed.

She argued, 'tragically, advocates of community governance have sometimes fallen into this trap' (Ostrom 2005: 275). For example, she argued that the World Bank introduced a community-driven development process, yet while this funded infrastructure projects that were proposed by local individuals, she noted that empirical work showed that beyond a local individual, typically a politician making a proposal, community involvement did not occur. She noted that elite capture and fraud were serious risks.

External funding seemed to invite the suggestion that local solutions drawing upon community knowledge, often gained over centuries, were valueless. Often this meant that existing institutional arrangements went unrecognised. She observed that this had a number of negative consequences. Property rights developed over long periods of time might be swept away and poorer or more marginalised groups might lose access to assets. Those who had invested time and expertise in existing systems of management felt that such investment was lost and became discouraged from future participation. There was also a downgrading of indigenous institutions and knowledge. Typically in Latin America, she noted, efforts to promote community forestry – because they drew upon a 'blueprint approach' – ignored existing collective institutions to manage forestry.

Corruption and rent seeking behaviour

Corruption would also erode the sustainable management of the commons. External donations may promote the opportunistic forms of behaviour within communities. In turn, local management is eroded as local elites can either emerge or become stronger because of donations from external authorities. Politics becomes increasingly undemocratic because politicians are tempted to extract resources and gain rent. Such rent allows them to buy support and a cycle emerges that erodes local governance and management of resources. Community ownership is destroyed as a consequence. In any system, rent seeking behaviour – when individuals try to gain resources without working for them – is possible. So too is corruption but well-designed community governance tends to reduce the problem. Centralised control, in her view, often makes it worse.

Elinor Ostrom's work on common pool resource management gained her a Nobel Prize and was a magnificent achievement. Nonetheless, it is just one part of her wider body of work. Her analysis built on the concern with democratic governance and ecological sustainability that had marked her and Vincent's life-long quest into sustainable and democratic governance. It is difficult to understand her approach without reference to the wider body of theory she drew upon. Thinkers like Herbert Simon, James Buchanan and John R. Commons informed her work. Simon's work indicated that institutional design was both essential because of the limited nature of our access to knowledge but noted that any science of the artificial would be incomplete. Simon's work focussed upon the necessity of design and this included the design of governance systems. Implicit in much of her work on the commons is the shadow of James Buchanan's thinking on constitutional rule-making, especially the need for broad agreement over governance structures. John R. Commons' work which examined how markets were shaped by institutional power and, above all, his notion that property was diverse rather than a binary between individual and state was equally important. Game theory, of course, also shaped Elinor Ostrom's practical investigation of the commons. Concepts and intellectual tools were mobilised by her, sensitively, in a new area of research into common pool property. Her analysis built on the empirical work of others, refined theoretical understanding from it and this was then feedback into further research. Her work on the commons from one point of view was uniquely her own product but from another perspective, it was utterly collective and peer-to-peer.

Any common pool resource is likely to be embedded in a wider system of governance. Common pool property regimes, in turn, cannot be seen in isolation. Elinor Ostrom's concern with environmental sustainability, and problems such as climate change, brought her to focus increasingly on the concept of social-ecological systems. Social-ecological systems can be seen as an example of the nested nature of resource systems, with local commons sitting within such wider structures, and as such will be discussed in Chapter 5.

5 Green from the grassroots

Social-ecological systems

> Sustainability at local and national levels must add up to global sustainability. This idea must form the bedrock of national economies and constitute the fabric of our societies.
>
> The goal now must be to build sustainability into the DNA of our globally interconnected society. Time is the natural resource in shortest supply [...]
>
> Setting goals can overcome inertia, but everyone must have a stake in establishing them: countries, states, cities, organizations, companies, and people everywhere. Success will hinge on developing many overlapping policies to achieve the goals.
>
> We have a decade to act before the economic cost of current viable solutions becomes too high. Without action, we risk catastrophic and perhaps irreversible changes to our life-support system.
>
> Our primary goal must be to take planetary responsibility for this risk, rather than placing in jeopardy the welfare of future generations.
>
> (Ostrom 2012c)

When I met Elinor Ostrom in March 2012 she was enthusiastic about the solar panels she had fitted at home. She was often highly sceptical of government policy and never believed, to maim a metaphor, that the state would unproblematically act as the knight who would come and kill the dragon of market failure. She saw grants for solar energy as a good piece of policymaking initiated by local government to make it easier to be green. Elinor Ostrom argued that sustainability was vital. She believed that human interactions with the wider environment had to be sustainable in the sense that economic activity should not threaten future human prosperity. However, as we have seen, she was interested in practical problem-solving rather than sweeping ideological statements. She worked hard to investigate how sustainability could be achieved. The concept of social-ecological systems became of increasing importance to her work during the twenty-first century. She felt that the concept allowed the development of inter-disciplinary research into environmental sustainability by linking both natural and social sciences. At its simplest, a social-ecological system (SES) is a system that links human action with that of other species and the wider environment. Ecologists try to understand the inter-relationships between different species in an ecosystem, while social scientists investigate human interactions. Social-ecological systems were understood by Ostrom from both perspectives. Analysis of a SES combines the natural science of ecology, supported by other disciplines such as biology, with social sciences such as economics, geography, law, political science and anthropology.

It is easy to forget that Elinor Ostrom was a political ecologist as well as a political economist. She joined the Ecological Society of America and worked to integrate ecological factors into her analysis (ESA 2013). Her contribution to ecology was recognised in 2005 when she shared the ESA's Sustainability Science Award in 2005 with Thomas Dietz and Paul Stern for a paper entitled *The Struggle to Govern the Commons* (Dietz *et al.* 2003).

Practical action to tackle climate change became one of her key concerns, indicating a movement from local problems of sustainability to global threats within her academic work. She wrote *A Polycentric Approach for Coping with Climate Change* for the World Bank (Ostrom 2009a) outlining her perspectives on climate action and on the day she died, 12 June 2012, one of her final pieces of writing 'Green from the grassroots', which set out her analysis of the upcoming United Nations Rio+20 summit, was published (Ostrom 2012c).

This chapter outlines Elinor Ostrom's understanding of the global environmental crisis and examines her critique of 'panaceas' and other reasons for environmental policy failure, before moving on to discuss social-ecological systems and her approach to climate change policy in more detail.

Global environmental crisis

The term 'global environmental crisis' is perhaps misleading. Elinor Ostrom felt that different environmental problems had different causes and varied potential solutions, yet she was aware that environmental degradation was increasingly globalised. She and Vincent Ostrom had long argued that economic and political systems are embedded within ecosystems. By the beginning of the twenty-first century, a number of global environmental problems were becoming more significant including loss of biodiversity, various forms of pollution and deforestation. Ostrom identified climate change as one of the most serious challenges facing humanity in the twenty-first century (Ostrom 2012c). The devastation of the world's ocean was one major concern and she was aware that rising levels of CO_2 were leading to the ocean acidification. When asked by the German news magazine *Der Spiegel* what she saw as the biggest environmental challenge beyond climate change she replied:

> The oceans! They are being threatened to an ever greater degree. It is a disaster, a very difficult situation. The fish resources are overexploited and waste, including CO_2, is dumped in huge quantities into the ocean. The law of the sea has not been effective at all. A lot of fishing ships act like roving bandits. That's why better ocean governance is one of the top priorities for safeguarding the future.
>
> (*Der Spiegel* Online (16 December 2009))

Elinor Ostrom was critical of much of the policy that had been developed to mitigate environmental problems. She was aware that environmental problems are often complex and that there is an important distinction between an ecological approach and a purely environmental one. Ecology is the study of relationships between species within a wider environment. Inter-relationships are often complex and nearly always dynamic. Policy measures that are not based on detailed local knowledge are often too crude to be effective and good intentions can often lead to damaging unintended consequences. Local knowledge of ecosystems amongst those who have used them can be more useful than apparent 'expertise' from trained scientists. For example, she and Marco Janssen noted the contrast between indigenous and Canadian government attempts to manage caribou stocks:

> Users of the aboriginal system do not search for a way of controlling the caribou by developing a self-conscious estimate of herd size and hunting limits. Rather, the hunters pay close attention to the fat content of the caribou they harvest. This provides them with a reliable, qualitative model of the trends – increasing or decreasing – of caribou health over time. When the caribou are seen as less healthy, the normative system of the hunters is to reduce hunting until the fat content of the caribou appears to rise. By using this qualitative model, the hunters learn the direction of change in which a population of wild animals is headed and can respond accordingly (see also Berkes 1999). Furthermore, the cost of this method is dramatically less than the cost of conducting a head count of a widely dispersed population.
>
> (Ostrom and Janssen 2004: 245)

Of course, indigenous knowledge might be flawed or inadequate but automatically assuming that it is of no value can lead to policy failure. Centrally imposed policies, even where well designed, need to be implemented and decreeing them from above is no guarantee that such implementation will be effective. Conservation policies can create paper parks, where lines drawn on administrative maps are ignored by local people. Even when the 'parks' are real, individuals are most likely to support policies if they feel that they have been involved in their creation. Elinor Ostrom was concerned that local people could and should be involved in practical policymaking rather than just a minority of politicians or civil servants. A global agreement is unlikely to involve meaningful democratic agreement so discourages active involvement and support. While Elinor Ostrom did not research climate scepticism, her emphasis on self-governance may explain why it has grown. For example, while much of the opposition to climate change policies has come from professional lobbyists attached to fossil fuel extraction, it may have gained traction amongst many voters in countries like the US and UK because climate policies seem to be the product of elite groups rather than any active grassroots. In contrast, locally developed policies can harness the creativity and tacit knowledge of local peoples.

She also criticised the tendency for policy makers to advocate 'panaceas by which she meant approaches based on one solution alone. She rejected the idea that one solution would be appropriate to all environmental problems. As we have seen in her work on common pool resources, she felt that diverse systems of property ownership combined with diverse forms of governance were appropriate. She certainly never argued that collective property rights would always work or government control or private ownership would always fail. Her view is captured in the writer H.L. Mencken's phrase 'For every complex problem, there is a solution that is simple, neat, and wrong.' Successful governance practices to promote sustainability would vary with many factors both ecological and social. In summary, she argued policymaking should be polycentric and ecologically sophisticated.

> Those researchers and practitioners who propose panaceas for solving complex environmental problems make two false assumptions. First they assume that *all* problems of a general type, such as air pollution or maintaining species diversity, are similar; and second, all of the people involved have the same preferences, information, and authority to act. Neither is true. For air pollution, the problem of controlling CO_2 which spreads evenly in the atmosphere is entirely different from the control of mercury, which falls near the source. The consequence of eliminating a species that is the only species at a trophic level in an ecosystem is catastrophic to ecosystem functionality as contrasted to the elimination of a species in an ecosystem characterized by many species at that trophic level.
>
> (Ostrom 2007: 3)

To improve the sophistication of ecological policymaking and to integrate both human and extra-human systems it was essential to bring together researchers from both the natural and social sciences, therefore the concept of social-ecological systems became a key focus for her later work.

Social-ecological systems

Elinor Ostrom believed that both social science and natural science were necessary to analyse environmental problems. Environmental issues cannot be understood without chemistry, biology and physics; yet environmental problems such as climate change are also a product of human action. Human action examined from the perspective of the social sciences. Political systems, economies and sets of values all shape how our species interacts with the wider environment, so they, along with other social factors, need to be accounted for. It is vital to bring both diverse fields of the ecological and social into play using the concept of a social-ecological system (SES). Even within the social sciences alone, knowledge is increasingly fragmented, so linking a number of social sciences and a number of natural sciences is challenging. Ostrom was also concerned that a common language based on shared concepts could be developed. She argued that it was difficult to aggregate research findings from different disciplines without shared terminology.

To develop these insights more fully she worked to deepen the concept of social-ecological systems. Elinor Ostrom was keen to learn from theoretical ecology how to understand the complexity of ecological systems. Ecological systems in the absence of human intervention, by definition are systems of relationships between different species within a physical environment, which is also shaped by geological and other factors. Different species are combined in ecosystems. Ecosystems can be studied only by understanding the relationships between different species and their wider environment. Economists and politicians are generally only dimly aware of the importance of ecosystems to the detriment of the environmental policies that they propose. Ecosystems are vital to human life and prosperity, their degradation is a threat to the future well-being of our species. Folke *et al.* note:

> Ecological systems play a fundamental role in supporting life on Earth at all hierarchical scales. They are essential in global material cycles like the carbon and water cycles. Ecosystems produce renewable resources (food, fiber, timber, etc.) and ecological services. For example, a fish in the sea is produced by a marine food web of plants, animals, and microorganisms. The fish is a part of the ecological system in which it is produced, and the interactions that produce and sustain the fish are inherently complex. Ecological services are also generated by ecosystems; these include maintenance of the composition of the atmosphere, amelioration of climate variability, flood control and drinking water supply, waste assimilation, nutrient recycling, soil generation, crop pollination, pest regulation, food provision, biodiversity maintenance, and also maintenance of the scenery of the landscape, recreational sites, and aesthetic and amenity values.
>
> (Folke *et al.* 2007)

Scientific understanding of how ecosystems develop has changed radically in recent decades. In the nineteenth and early twentieth centuries, ecologists believed that environmental change would tend to lead to a particular local or regional environment (Clements 1916). It was assumed that an ecosystem would move through a number of successive 'seres' or stages. Eventually a final seral community of climax species would be achieved. It was thought that feedback mechanisms would then tend to preserve this apparently 'natural' ecosystem. For example, after the British Isles were transformed by the last glaciation, which ended approximately 12,000 years ago, much of the land surface had been scraped back to bedrock. Initially grasses colonised the rock, this led to the creation of thin soils that allowed the next seral stage to occur with stronger vegetation, a later stage involved light woodland with birch trees (Perrins 2010: 3). Ecologists in the early part of the twentieth century assumed that finally after several centuries, a mixed deciduous woodland would result. Such climax vegetation would be the equilibrium which the ecosystem would maintain in the absence of external shocks. Ecologists in recent decades have become sceptical of the notion of a series of stable seral stages leading to climax ecosystems that are largely unchanging. Human action can lead to different ecosystems, although even in the absence of human beings ecosystems may evolve in varied directions. Thus while human action involves a variety of political, economic and cultural factors, human beings act as another species within an ecosystem. This assumption was implicit in Elinor Ostrom's study of common pool resources, rather than seeking to exclude humans from a supposed wilderness, the human element was seen as part of an ecological system (Ostrom 1990). Whereas some conservationists sought to remove human influence, she recognized that humans were also part of the environment and could interact in a sustainable way.

Elinor Ostrom believed that SES models needed to be understood to place common pool and other natural resources within a wider social and ecological context to promote sustainability. SESs are complex adaptive systems. The notion of adaptivity was familiar to Elinor Ostrom via Herbert Simon and psychiatrist William Ross Ashby who used the concept to discuss brain functions in his development of cybernetics (Ashby 1960). Vincent Ostrom often cited Ashby's work (V. Ostrom 1971: 105) and had worked with him at the Palo Alto Center for Advanced Studies in the Behavioral Sciences in 1955 (Toonen 2010: 198). Adaptive systems – whether in ecology, engineering or in other fields – involve feedback that preserve the integrity of the system under examination. A SES can be understood as a particular form of complex adaptive system that is relatively 'resilient':

> Resilience, rooted in ecology, is a loosely organized cluster of concepts relating to the interplay of transformation and persistence of non-linear dynamical systems. Resilience emphasizes that ecological, and more broadly, SESs, are composed of multiple elements that interact across scales and levels of organization. These interactions generate regimes that SESs occupy, and slow changes in variables (e.g., phosphorus loading in lakes) that structure those regimes can induce rapid regime shifts (flips in lakes from oligotrophic to eutrophic states).
>
> (Anderies and Janssen 2012)

Resilience came to replace the notion of robustness in Elinor Ostrom's thought. Robust systems return to the same point if disrupted; for example, an ecosystem will return to the same form of climax vegetation. In contrast, resilient systems change but in such a way as to maintain overall sustainability. Resilient systems may change but in ways which tend to preserve diversity and productivity. 'A core idea emerging from resilience theory is that complex systems such as SESs organize around continuous change', a notion that reflects the shift in ecological assumptions over recent years (Janssen, Andries and Ostrom 2007: 309).

Elinor Ostrom noted that the social elements of such a system included human beings working with particular sets of rules. Such rules made up institutions and the institutions, which could be modelled using the IAD framework, influenced the ecological system and were, in turn, changed by it. SESs were inevitably complex but according to Elinor Ostrom could be decomposed or split into different building blocks that could be reassembled to aid understanding. Elinor Ostrom noted Herbert Simon had observed that systems were divisible:

> They are arranged in levels, the elements at each lower level being subdivisions of the elements at the level above. Molecules are composed of atoms, atoms of electrons and nuclei, electrons and nuclei of elementary particles. Multicelled organisms are composed of organs, organs of tissues, tissues of cells.
>
> (Simon 2000: 753)

Modelling a SES allowed it to be better understood and managed. While property rights are an important aspect of the social element of a SES, they are just part of a wider system or set of inter-locking systems. Elinor Ostrom argued that investigation of a SES should include a study of the relevant resource system such as a fishery, lake or grazing area. Of course, to some extent the definition of such a system is arbitrary and may overlap with other systems. SESs are decomposable so can be scaled up or down to include entire regions. The Arctic region, for example, can be studied as a SES or divided into regional or local SESs. In turn, to organise the analysis of an SES, she argued that the resource units produced such as fish, water or fodder should be defined and examined. The analysis should also include the users of that system, the governance system, patterns of interactions and the outcomes that result. She argued:

> Further use and development of this framework will hopefully enable researchers to develop cumulative, coherent, and empirically supported answers to three broad questions:
>
> 1. What patterns of interactions and outcomes—such as overuse, conflict, collapse, stability, increasing returns—are likely to result from using a particular set of rules for the governance, ownership, and use of a resource system and specific resource units in a specific technological, socioeconomic, and political environment?
> 2. What is the likely endogenous development of different governance arrangements, use patterns, and outcomes with or without external financial inducements or imposed rules?
> 3. How robust and sustainable is a particular configuration of users, resource system, resource units, and governance system to external and internal disturbances?
>
> (Ostrom 2007: 8)

SES research can be fed back to participants governing an ecosystem to aid management. The ecologists Carlsson and Berkes (2005: 65) have outlined a series of steps for conducting policy analysis of co-management systems using an SES framework:

> This kind of research approach might employ the steps of (1) defining the social-ecological system under focus; (2) mapping the essential management tasks and problems to be solved; (3) clarifying the participants in the problem-solving processes; (4) analyzing linkages in the system, in particular across levels of organization and across geographical space; (5) evaluating capacity-building needs for enhancing the skills and capabilities of people and institutions at various levels; and (6) prescribing ways to improve policy making and problem-solving.
>
> (Carlsson and Berkes 2005: 65)

An interesting example of a social-ecological system is the irrigation and agricultural complex of the Indonesian island of Bali (Lansing 1991). The system is complex because of contradictory irrigation needs. The control of pests is helped if the rice fields have the same planting schedule but the hydrologically interdependent system with long systems of canals and aqueducts makes this difficult to achieve. To allow for appropriate fallow periods in a complex system, an elaborate water calendar developed and has been in use for many centuries. Specific action, for example, the release of water into a particular dam, needs to occur on particular days. These actions are coordinated via temple offerings at a number of levels from small temples next to rice fields to temples at village level, regional level and culminating at the *Pura Ulun Swi*, the 'Head of the Rice Terraces', where the high priest known as the Jero Gde, acts as the representative of the Goddess of the Temple Crater Lake. The offerings are made in return for water from the crater lake that feeds the system. The system is both decentralised and nested. The Dutch, who had colonised Bali, sought to bureaucratize the system and promoted cash crops but did not challenge the temple rituals. However, during the 1960s the post-independence Indonesian government introduced the Green Revolution, with an emphasis on modernising rice production. New strains of rice were introduced and fertilizers subsidised. While the temple rituals were still used, different planting times meant that they no longer led to irrigation when it was most appropriate. The system became infested with pests and productivity declined. The farmers sought to return to the original system but their desire to do so was initially dismissed as being based on outdated religious prejudices. Nonetheless, detailed analysis of the system led to a return to traditional irrigation methods:

> Lansing quoted a frustrated American irrigation engineer, 'These people don't need a high priest, they need a hydrologist!' (Lansing 1991: 115). It was Lansing who unravelled the function of the water temples and was able to convince the financers of the Green Revolution project on Bali that irrigation was best coordinated at the level of the water temples. Lansing built a computer model of the artificial ecosystem and showed that for different

> levels of coordination, from the farmer level up to central control, the temple level was the scale at which decisions could best be made to maximise rice production.
>
> (Ostrom and Janssen 2004: 254)

This account nicely illustrates a number of points within Ostrom's use of SES. Indigenous knowledge is often important, yet new techniques are not automatically destructive and change can occur without catastrophe. Centralised control can lead to problems but systems are far from being anarchic or radically decentralised. Governance is necessary but is neither entirely local nor purely centralised, neither is governance a matter of state control alone. For example, religious tradition, along with other cultural systems, can act as a form of governance, although this is not always the case. Ecological factors cannot be ignored but they are mediated by social factors. Social factors are, in turn, shaped by institutions. Ostrom and Janssen cited the institutional economist Douglass North in this regard:

> Belief structures get transformed into society and economic structure by institutions – both formal rules and informal norms of behaviour. The relationship between mental models and institutions is an intimate one. Mental models are the internal representation that individual cognitive systems create to interpret the environment; institutions are the external (to the mind) mechanisms individuals create to structure and order the environment.
>
> (North 1996: 348)

Slater and Flaherty (2009) also noted that supernatural justifications were used to promote sustainable use within the Irish commons known as the rundales. There were a number of supernatural places visible only to 'local eyes':

> Especially important were the connections between the fairies and land boundaries. These boundaries were protected by the fairies, and the local people did not like to work the land too near the boundary in case they would anger the fairies [...]. Within the rundale landscape, then, there were certain spatial nodes, which were perceived not only as 'spiritual' but as also performing the role of protecting the boundaries of the commune, without the need for on-the-spot surveillance. This form of communal governance is essentially a moral code embedded in the landscape through the medium of oral culture (Slater 1993). The 'fairies' patrolled the individual plots and the communal lands while the commune's members slept.
>
> (Slater and Flaherty 2009: 14–15)

An understanding of governance is combined with an analysis of ecology when studying SES. In the same way that Elinor Ostrom was aware of more sophisticated strains of economics, rejecting a single model of a rational human being for greater diversity, she was also ecologically sophisticated. Her work on SES was not based not on a desire to protect an unchanging environment but an understanding that the resilience of diverse systems might be based on change. The ecologist Liam Hengham notes that the concept of resilience means that environmental policymaking must be based not on protecting particular species, like pandas or blue whales, but on a notion of sustaining a dynamic ecosystem within which varied species live. Like Ostrom and other proponents of an SES approach, he noted that diversity was essential to resilience and sustainability:

> Resilience thinking assumes that change and disturbance are an integral part of every system, but that some systems are more resilient to destructive change than others. This might seem a subtle point, but if we understand the processes that promote or restore resilience, we have a much better chance both of mopping up after ecological catastrophes – or of avoiding them altogether.
>
> Resilience thinking can be applied to economics (the capacity of financial markets to absorb shock), friendship (the capacity of our loved ones to tolerate our nonsense), and nature (the capacity of ecosystems to endure disruption). One of the striking findings is that diversity is crucial to success. When an ecological system is managed for just one factor (say, a single crop) or where a nation's wealth is dominated by a single economic sector (say, the housing market before the 2008 global financial crisis), the result is a loss of resilience. Resilience thinking ultimately theorises about the limits of a system's capacity to endure. Financial markets collapse, crops fail, love blanches, ecosystems unravel, and death, alas, is a part of every life.
>
> (Heneghan (9 October 2009))

The implications of a SES informed approach to environmental policymaking are extensive. The idea of preserving unchanged landscapes is unrealistic not only because climate change is likely to make this impossible but, more profoundly, because ecosystems are dynamic and change. The prevailing approach of focussing upon the conservation of a particular species is also unrealistic; instead whole ecosystems have to be managed, because degradation of an ecosystem is a great danger to individual species including the human species. The SES concept gives rise to a number of theoretical and practical dilemmas. For example, there is the question of 'fit'. Carl Folke, the science director of the Stockholm Resilience Centre, and his colleagues, addressed this question in a 2007 paper, noting that 'fit' refers to the interplay between different elements in an SES. Whether species or institutions, the elements defined do not fit together like Russian dolls or children's building blocks but interact dynamically. Because of ignorance of such dynamic interaction there is often a poor fit between environmental policies and the promotion of sustainability with SES. As such, measures aimed at maximizing particular resource outputs, are likely to fail and short-term success can lead to long-term damage:

> Examples include the initial decades of chemical control of spruce budworm in Canadian forests, where more and more control efforts seem to result in

> larger and larger infestations when they do occur, and forest fire suppression in Yellowstone National Park in the United States, where almost half of the Park burned down in one major fire in 1988, following a century of fire suppression. The very success of a well managed fishery tends to trigger its own demise by attracting additional capitalization and fishing effort until all resource rents are dissipated, a well known phenomenon in fishery economics [...]. There are many examples of apparently successful management, later leading to environmental backlash or surprise; examples range from pesticide use to the damming of major African rivers.
>
> (Folke *et al.* 2007)

Folke *et al.* felt that the social norms and rules that dominate industrialised societies perspective towards sustainability tend to disrupt resilient use. They argue that these include a faith in the use of narrow welfare indicators such as GDP, worldviews that separate humans from ecosystems and the 'assumption that it is possible to find technical substitutes for the loss of ecosystems and the services they generate' (Folke *et al.* 2007).

Elinor Ostrom championed the seven-generation rule, looking to long-term human well-being rather than exclusively short-term considerations. Policies based on the long term do not involve removing human beings from nature and recreating wilderness. Human beings are part of ecosystems and the concept of untainted wilderness is a myth (Cronon 1983). Folke *et al.* identify a number of precise policies used by indigenous and peasant communities to maintain SESs but they warn against functionalism and a blanket assumption that modernity is ecologically destructive. Traditional forms of ecological knowledge can have value but are imperfect and change over time:

> Although many of our examples of 'lack of fit' between institutions and resources are taken from industrial or commercial modern economies, we do not mean to imply that whatever is modern is maladaptive. The characteristics of institutions which do not maintain the structure and function of ecological resources are generally applicable to traditional institutions as well. We do not subscribe to belief in the 'ecologically noble savage' [...]. We do make the argument that in many cases proximity and direct dependence on the resource base make it easier to filter out and discard practices that are clearly unsustainable, and this close connection to nature is a property of many indigenous traditional systems.
>
> (Folke *et al.* 2007)

Policies that work best to promote resilient sustainability, given the dynamic complexity of social-ecological systems, are policies that promote diversity. Swift adaption to changing environmental and social circumstances is important and experimentation is also vital. Policies which are imposed by external bodies are less likely to be sensitive to ecological and social factors. The work by Folke *et al.* and other students of social-ecological systems takes us back to the

Ostroms' notion of political science as a craft. Human beings have to work to craft systems of governance sensitively. Respect for 'fairies' may be appropriate but respect for scientists is also essential. The SES concept is a powerful contribution in this regard, uniting traditional practice with natural and social science. While environmental problems cannot be solved in isolation, the SES approach informed Elinor Ostrom's perspectives on climate change. Rather than looking for a reductionist or top-down approach she pioneered a polycentric policy framework to this vitally important challenge.

Polycentric solutions to climate change

Elinor Ostrom's work focussed increasingly on climate change as a severe threat to future generations. She emphasised that mitigation was more important than adaption but adaption was becoming necessary as evidence of climate change became more apparent. In May 2010, she co-signed a letter in *Science*, along with 254 other members of the National Academy of Sciences, criticising attacks on scientists who embarked on climate research and calling:

> [...] for an end to McCarthy-like threats of criminal prosecution against our colleagues based on innuendo and guilt by association, the harassment of scientists by politicians seeking distractions to avoid taking action, and the outright lies being spread about them. Society has two choices: We can ignore the science and hide our heads in the sand and hope we are lucky, or we can act in the public interest to reduce the threat of global climate change quickly and substantively.
>
> (Gleick *et al.* 2010)

Elinor Ostrom believed that solutions to environmental problems including climate change had to work at local, regional, national and international levels. Climate change is global in nature, so cannot be solved without a global dimension, but Ostrom felt that focussing only on the global approach was inadequate. She accepted the need for international agreements and was aware that there have been examples of successful global environmental policymaking. For example, the Montreal agreement began a process of outlawing chlorofluorocarbons in a largely successful attempt to reduce the threat from a thinning ozone layer. Where the science is relatively simple, agreement is relatively easy to reach and local agreements can be integrated with global ones, international policymaking is more likely to succeed. However when it comes to climate change the science is complex, agreement on reducing emissions is difficult and where policies have been introduced they have not always been integrated at a local level. Thus while Ostrom felt that a global approach was needed, she was aware that this posed a serious challenge because it was more difficult to build trust at an international level than at a regional or local tier. She also felt that it was dangerous to wait for a global solution because this might delay essential action.

> Part of my discouragement with the international negotiations is that we have gotten riveted into battles at the very big level over who caused global change in the first place and who is responsible for correcting [it]. It will take a long time to resolve some of these conflicts. Meanwhile, if we do not take action, the increase to greenhouse gas collection at a global level gets larger and larger. While we cannot solve all aspects of this problem by cumulatively taking action at local levels, we can make a difference, and we should.
>
> (IRIN Global (25 April 2012))

She was also critical of some of the specific elements of the current global framework to combat climate change, particularly the Clean Development Mechanism (CDM) and Reducing Emissions from Deforestation and forest Degradation Schemes (REDDS). The Clean Development Mechanism (CDM) allows firms to produce more greenhouse gases if they reduce them elsewhere. In theory this is a flexible way of reducing total emissions efficiently. A British steel works might need to emit CO_2 but pay for the insulation of homes in a city or to rebuild an Indian power plant so it produces less CO_2. Yet, Elinor Ostrom noted it could be 'gamed', by which she meant the rules could be exploited to benefit industrial users without reducing emissions. A firm might claim that it was going to create more greenhouse gases and then gain a grant to pay for reducing emissions that it had had no intention of producing in the first place. She stated that a large proportion of the CDMs relate to 'HFC-23, a greenhouse gas that is not associated with transportation or power generation but is used as a refrigerant' (Ostrom 2009a: 25). She cited Sovacool and Brown (2009) who had found:

> The sale of carbon credits generated from CERs for HFC-23 has become far more valuable than its production in the first place. Manufacturers of HFC-23, responding to market demand for CERs, started producing it just to offset it. Researchers at Stanford University have calculated that, as a result, payments to refrigerant manufacturers and carbon market investors to governments and compliance buyers for HFC-23 credits have exceeded €4.7 *billion* when the costs of merely abating HFC-23 would have been about €100 *million* – a major distortion of the market.
>
> (Ostrom 2009a: 25)

REDDS aim to preserve forests because they are a carbon sink that absorb emissions to some extent and slow climate change. While Elinor Ostrom supported this principle, she was concerned that in practice it might fail. Local communities of forest users with strong institutional rules acted as a strong force for forest conservation. She was worried that REDDS might lead to the removal or erosion of such community control. Speaking at the opening plenary of the Copenhagen climate summit in December 2009, she noted, 'If local users and indigenous peoples are not recognised and given clear rights, REDDS could lead to more deforestation,' and noted, '[S]ounding good is not enough.' IU Newsroom (14 December 2009).

She also felt that climate change policy with regard to forest fires was flawed (Ostrom 2009a: 25). International climate policy has included measures to reduce forest fires, which have become more common with rising temperatures. While this sounds uncontroversial, ecologists have noted that fires are often functional to sustainability. Hunter-gatherers often use slash and burn agricultural techniques and these have been condemned for leading to deforestation. Yet, in many areas of the world the regular fires used to create temporary fields are followed by forest regeneration. Also by outlawing fires, brushwood and other detritus build up, so if a fire is caused it has a much more fundamental effect, because it has more fuel to burn. Preventing fire can lead to the build up of flammable material that leads ultimately to devastating fires and major damage. A scientific understanding of ecology indicates that policies, which are not developed with great caution, can lead to damaging, unintended consequences.

Elinor Ostrom believed that global policies needed to be linked with action at the level of the individual, the community/local government, nations and regional blocs of nations such as the European Union. Personal lifestyle change had a role in her view, especially when supported by other tiers of action. She felt that individuals taking action to reduce emissions could have a cumulative role in making a major impact, noting for example that individuals cycling instead of driving to work would, if undertaken on a large enough scale, drastically reduce emissions. She also believed that individual action to cut emissions brought benefits. Rather than seeing carbon reduction as a sacrifice, it has numerous material gains. Cycling or walking was healthier than driving and insulation or the installation of solar panels tended to reduce energy bills. At an individual level, such gains made the perception of a free ride problem less likely. Rather than refusing to take action because we felt that we could get a free ride on the action of others we might derive real personal benefits from reducing our greenhouse gas emissions:

> We have modelled the impact of individual actions on climate change incorrectly and need to change the way we think about this problem. When individuals walk a distance rather than driving it, they produce better health for themselves. At the same time they reduce the amount of greenhouse gas emissions that they are generating. There are benefits for the individual and small benefits for the globe. When a building owner re-does the way the building is insulated and the heating system, these actions can dramatically change the amount of greenhouse gas emissions made. This has an immediate impact on the neighbourhood of the building as well as on the globe.
>
> (IRIN Global (25 April 2012))

She was impressed by local action to deal with climate change in the German city of Freiburg.

SPIEGEL ONLINE: Why Freiburg of all places?

OSTROM: I spend quite a bit of time in Germany and I'm very impressed by some of the local action I see. Local action cannot do it fully, but just think about all the bicycle-paths that they have built there. That is a case where the action of individuals is reducing emissions. At the same time it is a very healthy thing. On Sundays everybody is going to the woods and has a good time on their bikes – and not in their cars. It's good for your health and for the environment. So everyone should ask himself: Why don't I bike to work and leave the damn car at home or get rid of it entirely?

(*Der Spiegel* Online (16 December 2009))

Most emissions she felt were produced by individuals living in cities, therefore action at a city level was crucial in achieving change. Global solutions might not take into account the realities on the ground but citywide policies and alliances between cities might be more effective. While she was critical of inaction on the part of the US government, she was encouraged by the action taken by US cities and local authorities to reduce emissions. Indeed her installation of solar panels with the aid of a grant from local government in Indiana (Ostrom 2012 interview with the author) was a good example of individual action supported by local government policymaking.

She felt that the regional level was important as groups of neighbouring countries could come together and act. Even if global cooperation was slow to be achieved, neighbouring countries might get together to reduce emissions. Therefore despite her criticism of some elements of carbon trading such as its panacea-like quality and the problems with CDMs, she was cautiously optimistic that the creation of an emissions trading system by the European Union would help to combat climate change. She also suggested that the problem of free rides was only partially applicable at an international level as entire countries could gain as well as lose by introducing emission cuts. The resulting development of new renewable technologies could provide an economic boost and introduce wider environmental benefits. While she might have been critical of some elements of the widely suggested Green New Deal, a policy aimed at boosting the economy through investment in renewables, mass transit systems and insulation, it is consistent with her emphasis on the need to promote a range of environmental and economic gains from climate policies. The notion of a centrally developed green plan may have been seen as too much of a single solution panacea for her, perhaps giving rise to unintended and damaging social and ecological consequences. She was keen to imagine a society that was less consumerist and wasteful and respected future generations as part of its ethos. Policies after all were shaped by norms and can only be effectively implemented if appropriate values are widely held within a society. Climate policy also involved maintaining the key social-ecological systems necessary to maintain carbon sinks, including forests and oceans. Clean energy was thus a part of the solution but insufficient alone.

While she was cautiously optimistic, the fact that politicians rarely understood the science of climate change and that policymakers were seldom ecologically literate was highly problematic:

> In the economic emergency we are experiencing, some people think that we cannot afford it. I think it is the other way around, if we don't act now we will run into even greater economic problems in the future. And of course we still have the bad legacy of our previous president, George W. Bush. For eight years, the White House didn't consider the issue to be important. We did not have American leaders who understood that there is a scientific foundation. Obama has a much higher chance of understanding the science. But even for him it is just damn tough.
>
> (*Spiegel* Online (16 December 2009))

She believed in lobbying politicians as they had a vital role in developing policy and noted that politicians meeting face to face at internationally gatherings could learn to trust each other better. Yet policies had to be owned by citizens and demanded local implementation, along with regional and global tiers of action rather than decrees from above.

Situating the ecological economics of Elinor Ostrom

There are a number of different ways in which economists, political scientists, sociologists and others including active citizens have tried to understand the relationship between economics and environmental problems. Environmental problems can only be resolved if they are analysed and understood first. Ostrom's approach is both unique and pluralistic. Her analysis is different from approaches such as free market environmentalism, environmental economics, ecological modernism, deep ecology, ecosocialism and various other forms of social and political ecology. However, it often has points of contact and agreement with approaches that are often at odds with each other. For example, both free market environmentalists and more left leaning political ecologists hostile to the market might cite her work and can draw support from elements within it.

Free market environmentalists argue that environmental problems can be tackled using market mechanisms, stressing the role of property rights (Anderson and Leal 2001). Their perspective can be derived from Pigou's well-known example of a factory whose chimneys generate soot. The soot falls on the washing line of a local laundry, making it dirty. If the laundry owner is allowed to sue the factory for the expense caused, the problem can be remedied. Free market environmentalists are critical of most forms of environmental regulation. They argue, in the spirit of Friedrich Hayek, that such regulation is flawed because central governments lack the knowledge necessary to implement effective policies. Local people are better informed and can make better decisions. Regulation is often counterproductive and by making industrial production more expensive can reduce competitiveness. The new institutionalist economist Ronald Coase suggested that if environmental damage is necessary to promote economic welfare, companies that pollute might pay compensation to owners of private property who are damaged by their actions (Coase 1960). Overzealous regulation, even if it can be implemented, may not take into account both the costs and benefits of environmental damage, leading to a loss of economic efficiency. Proponents argue that a free market approach based on property rights is more effective, flexible and likely to better promote economic welfare than a regulatory framework. Free market environmentalists also point out that subsidies from government to polluting industries distort markets and damage the environment.

Environmental economics shares much with free market environmentalism including a concern with property rights and a belief in a broadly market based approach (Jaeger 2005). Environmental economists conceptualise environmental problems as forms of market failure caused because market prices do not include the costs of environmental damage, meaning that they are consumed excessively. While prices reflect internal costs such as the costs of producing a manufactured good they do not include the external costs which are costs to an individual other than the producer or the consumer of the good. Thus the cost of making the cars is an internal cost to the car factory, while the cost of the soot that dirties the laundry is an external cost. It may be difficult to trace all the property owners damaged by pollution and equally difficult for those economically damaged by pollution to trace the manufacturers of this third party cost. Environmental economists use a variety of policy instruments including government regulation because they are sceptical of a fully free market environmentalism. Their main instrument is environmental taxation. The negative externalities or external costs of production – whether congestion from car use or the emission of greenhouse gases – are calculated and added as a tax or charge. London's congestion charge is an almost textbook example of environmental economists' approach. The revenue from such taxes does not need to be hypothecated. For example, used to subsidise greener alternatives of public transport such as buses or trains, merely internalising the externalities will be enough to maximise net welfare gains. While private property rights are seen as environmentally important and forms of government regulation are common, environmental taxes and other market-based instruments are advocated. The tradable quotas used to combat climate change in the various international agreements are also a product of this system.

Ecological modernisation or modernism, in turn, while usually seen as a sociological perspective is allied to environmental economics (Young 2000). It is based on the assumption that environmental sustainability is vital for promoting economic welfare and environmental policies be used to promote economic growth. It evolved in Europe in the 1980s and can be seen as the basis of the policy approach of the influential German Green Party and other European green and centre left policy makers. Technological developments such as the promotion of renewable energy and new environmentally friendly forms of industrial production are vital. Indeed by cutting energy bills and reducing waste, businesses can reduce costs and promote profit. The investment needed in the new technologies required may be too expensive to be attractive to firms in the short run so the role of government is vital. The concept of a Green New Deal can be seen as a product of this approach.

Ecological economics is distinct from environmental economics because it is based on the assumption that the economy relies on the environment. It is not enough to internalise externalities or improve regulation, more fundamental action may be necessary to protect prosperity based upon the sustainability of complex ecosystems. A clear understanding of complex ecosystems is necessary and human interactions with other species must be managed with care. Notions of complexity and resilience are of growing importance within ecological economics. Ecological economics is a diverse field with considerable overlap with environmental economics, ecosocialism and green political thought (Common and Stagl 2005).

Ecosocialists in turn believe that capitalism is ecologically unsustainable because of its need for economic growth, which promotes accelerated resource extraction, and in so doing, commodifies the environment, thus reducing diversity. Ecosocialists are often critical of the traditional left for ignoring ecological problems but note a strong concern with both environmental problems and an ecological philosophy in the works of Karl Marx and Fredrick Engels. Ecosocialists are sceptical of both ecological taxation and central planning, advocating workers planning for green production and the extension of common pool property systems. Ecosocialism is also strongly linked to indigenous perspectives on economics and society (Wall 2010).

The economics of the environment have also been understood from a Malthusian perspective. The Reverend Thomas Malthus (1766–1834), along with Adam Smith and David Ricardo was one of the founders of classical market-based economics. While he studied rent, he is best known for his pessimistic musings on population. He argued that human population growth would tend to increase faster than agricultural productivity, leading to almost inevitable disaster. While Malthus did not specifically examine environmental problems, environmental concern during the 1960s and 1970s was dominated to some extent by a neo-Malthusian discourse. The biologists Anne and Paul Ehrlich popularised such an approach in their book *The Population Bomb* (Ehrlich 1968). Malthusians argue that only tough restrictions on human consumption, together with population control, provide hope for humanity.

While Elinor Ostrom took the environmental problems very seriously, she disagreed with much of the Malthusian analysis. The 'tragedy of the commons' as described by Garrett Hardin was a Malthusian concept; humans would destroy their environment unless it was controlled by enclosure. Malthusians tend to argue for centralised control and authoritarian solutions but as we have seen, Elinor Ostrom stressed that people as a whole were as likely to come up with workable solutions to environmental problems as experts, civil servants or other agents of central government.

As noted previously, free market environmentalists might see Elinor Ostrom as one of their tribe. Indeed, many of their criticisms of regulation have been echoed by her, which is unsurprising given her acknowledgement of Hayek's appreciation of the knowledge problem. However, Elinor Ostrom did see a role for government and for regulation. While she did not see commons as a panacea, she did recognise that commons often provided a very good way of sustaining local environments. Free market environmentalists, in contrast, risk seeing private property as a panacea and are often apparently unaware of common pool property regimes. Nevertheless, Anderson and Leal's account of free market environmentalism does take into account common pool property and suggests that privatisation may not always be necessary (Anderson and Leal 2001). Their optimistic embrace of the market, together with technological advance, might be mistaken for complacency from Ostrom's perspective. In turn, while Elinor Ostrom did not reject environmental economics, she did not believe that it was enough to 'internalise externalities'; conceptualising environmental problems as forms of market failure, was likely to be inadequate.

Ecological modernism is consistent with much of Elinor Ostrom's work, stressing the possibility of prosperity via a new environmental industrialism. Yet she cannot easily be seen as a 'modernist'. While she did not seek a return to a mythical ecological past, she did see human communities throughout the past as dealing intelligently with problems. Whether in the shape of Tocqueville in the nineteenth century or via the legacy of indigenous techniques, she believed that knowledge did not have to be exclusively modern to have value. Ecological modernism also tends towards blueprint thinking and imposition from the centre, which she strongly rejected. She did not address ecosocialism but would, while no doubt rejecting its account of capitalism, have noted its strong embrace of common pool property and rejection of traditional central planning.

Elinor Ostrom's work is best placed, from an environmental perspective within ecological economics, yet it is appropriate to note that she was interested in problem-solving rather than seeking to defend, extend or critique a particular school of thought or ideology. However within her work, economic factors – whether conceptualised as a product of market forces or of state intervention – shape social-ecological systems and risk being left unanalysed. Elinor Ostrom's student Michael Cox suggested that his study of the Taos Valley *acequis*, a traditional irrigation system, could have been improved by examining such economic influences (Cox 2010: 118).

Discussing economic influences on the environment, Elinor Ostrom noted what she called roving bandits (2007). The bandits, such as large fishing fleets, move into an area and extract all the fish they can before moving on. The concept of roving bandits derived from Mancur Olson (2000) illustrates a situation close to Hardin's 'tragedy of the commons' and can be seen as an unintended consequence of globalisation (Ostrom 2007). The bandits had no interest in sustainability because they could always move on to new territories. Free movement of capital, corporations and human beings may promote an economy that relies on maximising resource extraction in a given area. Once resources are exhausted, the economic actors move on to a new frontier. Elinor Ostrom (2007: 12) noted the concern of Berkes *et al.* (Berkes *et al.* 1557) that, 'roving banditry is different from most commons dilemmas in that a dynamic has arisen in the globalized world: New markets can develop so rapidly that the speed of resource exploitation often overwhelms the ability of local institutions to respond' (Berkes *et al.* 1557).

Globalisation puts pressure on local ecosystems and may erode sustainability. It also seems to describe the process of the movement of the American frontier, with homesteaders taking territory, using it and moving on. Although globalisation may give rise to benefits such as increased social diversity and increased transmission of sustainability knowledge from one part of the world to another, it may also degrade ecological diversity.

Sustainability, as Ostrom acknowledged, involved an understanding of the effects of globalisation on local and regional social-ecological systems. This, in turn, suggests that more global forces that shape production and consumption need to be examined. However, she was aware that state action to regulate globalising forces was often inadequate for a number of reasons discussed previously. A roving bandit economy needs to be made sustainable or replaced, neither of which is an easy task. Ecological considerations demand consideration of production and consumption of scare resources. Elinor Ostrom's concern with social sharing and collaborative consumptions, as methods of consuming more carefully, will be examined more fully in Chapter 7. During recent decades, technological change made discussion of the commons more relevant and her work can be applied to the economics of cyberspace and information. The next chapter deals with her contribution to discussions of the commons knowledge economy.

6 Knowledge commons

> Ideas, images, knowledges, code, languages and even affects can be privatised and controlled as property, but it is more difficult to police ownership because they are so easily shared or reproduced. There is a constant pressure for such goods to escape the boundaries of property and become common. If you have an idea, sharing it with me does not reduce its utility to you, but usually increases it. In fact, in order to realise their maximum productivity, ideas, images and affects must be common and shared. When they are privatised their productivity reduces dramatically – and, I would add, making the common into public property, that is, subjecting it to state control or management, similarly reduces productivity.
>
> (Hardt 2010: 135–6)

It is interesting to discuss the extent to which knowledge is a commons or, as the literary theorist, Michael Hardt would put it, part of the common. In his informative and entertaining history of the libertarian movement, Brian Doherty discusses the application of property rights to knowledge. Libertarians have held varied attitudes to the notion of intellectual property rights. Ayn Rand, who with her emphasis on heroic individualism and the virtues of selfishness, might be seen as the polar opposite to Elinor Ostrom, argued that copyright should protect an author during their lifetime but felt that it was 'parasitism' to maintain copyright for decades after an author's death (Rand 1967: 131). At least one libertarian took the line that knowledge could be owned and restricted to those who paid for it rather literally, Doherty notes:

> Imagine you paid for a series of lectures on liberty. You were afraid they might be a little dull, but you found yourself electrified by an entirely new way of seeing life, of conceptualizing the human social order and how to make it work best for everyone [...]. You were excited, burning to tell your associates and friends what was so special about this particular lecturer, a man of the physical sciences like yourself, a man who really got to the core of why liberty was vital and what its diligent pursuit really implied. He was a former astrophysicist by the name of Andrew Galambos, teaching in Southern California under the rubric of the Free Enterprise Institute.

> But you couldn't. You couldn't say a word. Because if one of the very interesting new ideas that Galambos had convinced you of was true, you had to honor his 'primary property' – his ideas – to the extent that you were not free to share them with someone who hadn't paid Galambos for them. You couldn't even share why you couldn't explain it.
>
> (Doherty 2007: 323–4)

While the example of Galambos is perhaps a little unusual, consideration of knowledge introduces a number of interesting questions about ownership, property rights and sharing. These have become more important in recent decades with technological innovation. In turn, the growth of cyberspace has provided a platform for a new economic model based on mass participation that moves production beyond the confines of the market and the state. To write anything about this new knowledge economy is to risk redundancy by publication because change is accelerating. Sites such as MySpace and Facebook emerge, grow and sometimes disappear. It appears that recent decades have ushered in a period of intense technological, economic and social change. Notions of an information economy or postmodern or postfordist knowledge economy may suggest a break with traditional industrial production. The tools of mainstream economics might seem inadequate to analyse economic activity that is not purely monetary and much of the knowledge economy does not involve direct monetised exchange. Elinor Ostrom's work appears, in contrast, better suited to describing these new forms of economic activity. After all, she felt that economic activity included but extended further than money, markets and states and beyond property, which was purely private, like Galambos's ideas, or purely state owned. Yet, two sets of cautions should be noted. First, the knowledge economy is not necessarily a high tech economy or even 'new'; the production and consumption of knowledge have long been an issue for economists. Caution is also necessary because Elinor Ostrom undertook relatively little specific research into the knowledge commons. She was cautious about extending findings in one area to another, feeling that sophisticated theoretical work had to be combined with detailed empirical study, before even provisional conclusions could be inferred. The natural resource commons she studied in detail were distinct from the immaterial knowledge commons under discussion here. Therefore it is misleading to suggest that she left a body of work that solves, in an off the shelf way, the practical and theoretical issues around the new knowledge commons. Nevertheless, many of the perspectives she contributed to can help us understand the new knowledge economy.

Elinor Ostrom was a knowledge common champion. She did not believe, of course, that the private sector should be excluded from the knowledge economy; firms and private individuals contributed to research and culture via the market. Nor did she believe that libraries and universities should be taken out of the hands of government. However, she saw a powerful role for non-state non-market production of knowledge. Her practical projects in this area were perhaps as significant as her theoretical contributions. Together with Vincent and other members of her faculty, she helped create a Digital Library of the Commons, encouraging academics and non-academics to contribute research that could be accessed for free by anyone on the web (http://dlc.dlib.indiana.edu/dlc/). The Digital Library was a partial antidote to the enclosure of knowledge about the commons in expensive subscription journals and a means of creating bridges between researchers. It remains an important tool for commons research. She also helped create a free online commons journal (www.thecommonsjournal.org/) and promoted open source academic publishing.

Elinor Ostrom's principal contribution to understanding as oppose to promoting the knowledge commons was in a collection of essays co-edited with Charlotte Hess, the founder and former director of the Digital Library of the Commons, entitled *Understanding Knowledge as a Commons* (Hess and Ostrom 2011).

This chapter outlines the emergence of the new knowledge commons and examines the potential contribution of Ostrom's perspectives, developed in collaboration with Hess, to understanding its emergence in terms of motivation, property rights, regulation and creativity. The notion of commons, anti-commons and 'the common' are defined in terms and discussed in relation to knowledge. The recent history of the development of the new knowledge economy is outlined and the application of theoretical perspectives from thinkers such as Stallman, Raymond, Benkler, Shirky and Lessig is briefly presented. Charlotte Hess and Elinor Ostrom's approach to the knowledge commons is examined, before moving on to the contribution of Charles Schweik and Robert English who applied Ostrom's institutional analysis to the topic of open-source software commons (Schweik and English 2012).

Commons, anti-commons and the common

Ostrom and Hess (2011: 9) suggested that it is difficult, once discovered, to exclude people from knowledge. Recipes are an example of an 'old' form of knowledge that is difficult to enclose; cooks do not pay a fee to the inventor of apple pie or spaghetti alla puttanesca every time they prepare these iconic dishes. Copyright emerged to prevent an author's work from being stolen and used without a fee, but there are fears that legal rights over immaterial objects of knowledge and culture have grown, restricting use (Bertacchini 2012).

While Elinor Ostrom has investigated the commons, both in the form of common pool resources and common pool property, other researchers have introduced the concepts of the common and anticommons to discuss property rights to knowledge. The common refers not to one particular resource or its property system but a broad category, which can be shared widely, rather than by a particular limited community. 'The common' includes something that is often shared by all such as an alphabet, periodic table or a language, while a commons in land or sea may be restricted to a particular group of people. According to Michael Hardt, economic activity is increasingly focussed on immaterial labour, which creates 'the common', including 'ideas, information, images, knowledges, code, languages' (Hardt 2010: 135).

The law professor Michael Heller, in turn, has introduced the notion of 'tragedy of the anticommons', fearing that enclosure of a resource can lead to underuse (1997). He studied the transition from state control to the creation of a market economy when the Soviet Union collapsed. Shops tended to remain shut and unused because ownership was multiple and used to exclude access:

> [...] any use of the storefront would require the agreement of multiple parties. If the parties cannot agree, then any single party may be able to block the others from exercising their rights. The Moscow storefront thus meets my definition of anticommons property, that is a property regime in which multiple owners hold rights of exclusion in a scarce resource. The tragedy of the storefront anticommons is that the resource is wasted when multiple owners fail to agree on a use.
>
> (Heller 1997: 20)

The concept of anticommons has been applied to the patenting of pharmaceutical knowledge (Heller and Eisenberg 1998). To innovate, an inventor may need to use knowledge that has already been patented. While patents and other forms of intellectual copyright may create incentives, they can also, if too strictly used, restrict invention. If a technological device or a drug relies on many different discoveries, which are legally protected, and so cannot be copied easily, innovation is slower. While Heller does not use the term 'the common', he and Hardt share a concern that enclosure leads to a tragic restriction in production. They both argue that items can be enclosed and restricted from users, reducing productive activity. There has been concern that a range of culture and knowledge has been removed from the public domain to our collective detriment. It has been suggested, for example, that Disney has taken folklore concepts which were held in common, such as the tale of Snow White and her dwarf friends, and enclosed them (Bollier 2003: 49). This has led to damaging consequences and frankly absurd situations. For example, after a public outcry Disney withdrew a 2013 application to trademark the traditional Mexican 'Day of the Dead' (Rosman and Uribe (7 May 2013)). The legal theorist James Boyle has described these attempts to create private intellectual property rights within the public domain as the 'second great enclosure'. While the first enclosure saw the legal and physical destruction of common land historically, the second has seen a push to commodify knowledge, culture and even biological material such as DNA (Boyle 2003).

There has also been discussion of the ambient commons, where fixed geographical locations that surround us are linked to data, and might be governed communally rather than by corporate bodies (McCullough 2013). Economic activity is increasingly centred around the capture and exploitation of knowledge, a trend that has accelerated rapidly with the emergence of cyberspace. At the time of writing, sites like Google and Facebook, without selling a direct product, are becoming some of the most powerful and profitable corporations on the planet, generating revenue from advertising, fuelled by the immaterial labour of millions of individuals going online. There is anxiety that such organisations are reducing the diversity of the digital environment and gaining monopoly power to shape the production and consumption of culture (McChesney 2013).

A short history of the future

Technological determinism is to be avoided, because economic, cultural, legal and political influences are all also significant in discussing social change. Nevertheless, technological innovation has promoted the new knowledge economy. Without the Internet and the World Wide Web, new forms of collaboration would have been difficult. It is perhaps impossible to trace the origins of any technology to its root; the growth of cyberspace was only possible, for example, because of the creation of a communication system between computers. Computers, in turn, have a history and were only possible because of earlier technological innovations; from the invention of electricity to the creation of plastics. It is, however, possible to outline the development of cyberspace since the 1960s.

The Internet originated in attempts to enable communication between computers pioneered by US military researchers in the 1960s. The US military sought better communication and employed developers to promote advanced computing technology, employing, amongst others the computer scientist J.C.R. Licklider (Waldrop 2002). Licklider looked towards the creation of cyberspace, noting:

> It seems reasonable to envision, for a time 10 or 15 years hence, a 'thinking center' that will incorporate the functions of present-day libraries together with anticipated advances in information storage and retrieval and the symbiotic functions suggested earlier in this paper. The picture readily enlarges itself into a network of such centers, connected to one another by wide-band communication lines and to individual users by leased-wire services. In such a system, the speed of the computers would be balanced, and the cost of the gigantic memories and the sophisticated programs would be divided by the number of users.
>
> (Licklider (March 1960))

He seemed to have seen into the future, imaging a new world, where cooperation between humans and computers, would deliver the web and the net. The Internet is a system of delivery and as such is often confused with email – a means of delivering relatively short messages – and the World Wide Web, which in turn allows large amounts of information to be transmitted.

By the 1970s, relatively small numbers of scientists used the Internet to communicate between each other. While the technology existed at a basic level, very few institutions and individuals initially had access to it. Rapid innovation improved the speed and reliability of the Internet. In 1984 Tim Berners-Lee, a contractor at the European Organization for Nuclear Research (CERN), Switzerland, brought together the relevant tools necessary and coined the phrase World Wide Web. CERN had been keen to develop a way of allowing physicists in different countries to share their research findings so that projects could move forward faster (Gillies and Cailliau 2000). Thus the World Wide Web, which is so important in promoting a peer-to-peer approach, was designed to promote interactive production by making it easier for scientists, even if they worked in different countries, to help each other with shared projects. The combination of the Internet as a means of communication between computers with the development of specific modes of communication in the form of email and the World Wide Web set the stage for transformation. The evolution of computers –from bulky machines loved by mad scientists in science fiction films to mass-produced household goods – enabled the Internet and web to take off.

The creation of cyberspace makes it easier to share information, which has had a number of interesting consequences, including the promotion of free or open source software. Software includes the programmes that instruct computers how to perform particular functions. It can be designed and patented by private companies with users asked to pay a license for it or it can be developed by individuals employed by the state. In contrast, free or open source software (FOSS) tends to be developed collaboratively via peer-to-peer processes, adapted and used freely. While economic activity is usually conceptualised as being based on either market or state provision, and property as either private or state-owned, software like resource commons, discussed in previous chapters, often moves 'beyond the state and the market'. 'Peer-to-peer' can be defined as a cooperative form of production undertaken by informal groups of individuals, often to solve precise practical problems or even for pleasure rather than for direct personal financial gain.

A new knowledge commons is a continuation of existing and less glamorous practices. Ever since human beings or imaginative hominids made stone tools designs have been adapted to make them work more effectively. The idea of a single inventor is often a romantic and misleading notion. Numerous individuals and institutions interact, often in casual and informal, experimental ways to create something new, adapt an existing design or just to solve a problem. Richard Stallman had worked as a programmer for many years, participating with others in software design before he developed the concept of free software because of a mundane practical problem (Williams 2010). An office printer he used had jammed so Stallman, who was a skilled engineer, believed that if he could adapt the printer software, he could override the jam. This was impossible because access to the software was restricted, which made his usual tinkering close to impossible. Stallman and his peers were engineers who were used to making changes in programmes and processes so that they could improve them. Because the software code was secret, Stallman's normal approach, like that of millions of other engineers and scientists throughout human history, was frustrated. Out of this frustration, he called for a social movement advocating the right to tinker with software and pass it on. Stallman is often described as a political radical. However, his key motivation in advocating free software was prosaic; to remove the barrier standing between him and solving his laser printing problem.

During the 1960s and 1970s software was essentially 'free' but by the 1980s it had begun to be commodified and its use restricted to paying customers. Stallman created the Free Software Foundation (FSF) to promote software that could be used and adapted. This was in contrast to proprietary software, which it is illegal to change. He also developed an alternative to conventional notions of patenting and copyright in the form of copyleft, first used to licence the GNU operating system. A developer can use a copyleft license to protect their software legally. Unlike copyright, copying and adaption is generally encouraged by copyleft, however the copyleft license prevents the software from being sold commercially. Thus software is made into a form of common property but the license prevents 'enclosure' which would dissolve the commons and create a private good to be bought and sold on the market. Stallman outlined a number of benefits from such an approach:

> Complete system sources will be available to everyone. As a result, a user who needs changes in the system will always be free to make them himself (*sic*), or hire any available programmer or company to make them for him. Users will no longer be at the mercy of one programmer or company which owns the sources and is in sole position to make changes.
>
> Schools will be able to provide a much more educational environment by encouraging all students to study and improve the system code. Harvard's computer lab used to have the policy that no program could be installed on the system if its sources were not on public display, [...].
>
> Arrangements to make people pay for using a program, including licensing of copies, always incur a tremendous cost to society through the cumbersome mechanisms necessary to figure out how much (that is, which programs) a person must pay for. And only a police state can force everyone to obey them. Consider a space station where air must be manufactured at great cost: charging each breather per liter of air may be fair, but wearing the metered gas mask all day and all night is intolerable.
>
> (www.gnu.org/gnu/manifesto.html)

Such free software allows individuals to improve the original design. Instead of a software project being initiated by either a state institution such as a university research department or a market institution such as a firm, individuals can collaborate voluntarily to produce software. The Internet was the technological innovation that made such shared production possible but on its own, it was insufficient. Institutional and cultural factors were also necessary in the form of an alternative to copyright and large numbers of programmers keen to participate. Indeed the Sunderland, UK-based programmer Tony Gair told me in a personal comment:

> It is also difficult to imagine Linux being successful without Stallman and the FSF. Not just the license (which Torvalds adopted) but the difficulty to

> produce compilation tools which that organisation made available. Without this, Linux would have been dead in the water. Stallman and the FSF receive little recognition of this to this day.

Stallman advocated the term 'free' to promote the freedom to adapt software as a basic right. Famously noting that 'free meant free as freedom not free as in free beer', while software might be bought and sold, the right to change it was vital. Eric Raymond, another American software designer, challenged the term, suggesting that the phrase 'open source' would be better for promoting the growth of collaborative computing projects. He argued that 'free software' was an ideologically loaded term that could also cause confusion and prevent the mainstream acceptance of such software arguing that 'open source' was more likely to be accepted commercially (Raymond 1999: 175). Many firms now use 'open source' software and many governments including Brazil have promoted it. Raymond and Stallman's political philosophies that inform their approaches to software development clearly differ but free and open source are essentially the same thing. Free/open source can be freely adapted. Such adaption promotes, according to both Raymond and Stallman, technological development. Stallman argues that patenting software can prevent much larger projects from going ahead. Incidentally as I write, large corporations such as Apple and Samsung are locked into expensive legal battles over software programmes. Such legal battles may slow innovation, reflecting the problem of the anti-commons. Raymond argues that private companies can use open source software to cut costs. Private companies who have formerly made profit from developing, patenting and selling propriety software can also be commercially successful by turning to open source. Raymond challenged both those such as Stallman, who are suspicious of software development exclusively for profit and individuals such as Microsoft's Bill Gates, who are hostile for commercial reasons to open source. Raymond suggested that alternative business models were possible. For example, while using a recipe could be free, this did not prevent people from opening restaurants and selling food for profit. The software might be provided free of charge yet companies could still create revenue by providing technical support to operate it. Indeed, the example of Google shows that while a product such as a search engine could be supplied without charge, revenue can be generated in other ways; in their case by selling advertising.

Raymond explored the benefits of peer-to-peer production, noting that, 'given enough eyeballs, all bugs are shallow'; a principle he termed Linus's Law' after the Finnish programmer (Raymond 1999: 30). Linus Torvalds started to develop Linux, a computer operating system, in 1991. He worked with many other programmers via cyberspace to create the operating system, which was entirely free to users. With many people contributing, there was a much greater chance of spotting and correcting mistakes in a programme. A free/open source culture amongst a community of programmers, appropriate licences that allowed collaborative development and the existence of the Internet which makes it fast and easy to share information, have all contributed to this form of knowledge commons. Raymond believed that the most important aspect of Linux

> was not technical but sociological. Until the Linux development, everyone believed that any software as complex as an operating system had to be developed in a carefully coordinated way by a relatively small tightly-knit group of people [...] Linux evolved in a completely different way. From nearly the beginning, it was rather casually hacked on by huge numbers of volunteers coordinating through the Internet. Quality was maintained not by rigid standards or autocracy but by the naively simple strategy of releasing every week and getting feedback from hundreds of users within days, creating a sort of rapid Darwinian selection on the mutations introduced by developers. To the amazement of almost everyone, this worked quite well
>
> (Raymond 1999: 16)

From Wikipedia to a range of other projects, peer-to-peer production has spread through society. The existence of non-monetary and decentralised forms of production is challenging to mainstream economic theory. Categories that have been largely invisible within its body of theory have an obvious presence in reality. While both market activity and state provision cannot be ignored as influences upon the growth of such new knowledge commons, they do not fully explain it. A number of ways of understanding the new knowledge economy have evolved.

Raymond has argued that while private property is sometimes impractical, it is the norm and that human beings are motivated by rational self-interest, seeking to maximise their own personal benefit. For Raymond, while immediate financial reward did not enter into open source software production, self-interest did. He argued that designers gained status amongst their peers from their contributions and the desire to promote personal reputation as a form of status satisfaction drove unpaid software contributions. In turn, alternative revenue streams from peer-to-peer production that made it potentially profitable. Raymond was keen to promote open source to profit-orientated businesses as a way of speeding innovation, cutting costs and generating revenue. Revenue, even with a free price tag, might be made from selling associated services or advertising.

There are a number of different explanations why individuals are motivated to take part in peer-to-peer production. Much peer-to-peer activity is relatively or entirely anonymous, so status promotion may be an inadequate justification. The 'new media' theorist Clay Shirky has noted the fast growth of social media such as Facebook, Flickr, Twitter, blogs and wikis (2010). Mixing music and open loading to sites like Soundcloud or making videos to place on YouTube are common at present. New technologies that have led to the mass production of cheap video and recording equipment make them possible. For example, smartphones now enable millions of people to make and edit simple films, if they so wish, on the move. Forms of crowd sourcing, where donations are collected, can be used to fund the monetised parts of such projects where necessary. Shirky has introduced the concept of 'cognitive surplus' to explain the creation of peer-to-peer participation (2010). He argues that the introduction of television acted to absorb an individual's surplus free time that they might otherwise use more creatively. He argued that television was similar to gin during the years of the gin craze in eighteenth century England, in that it absorbed and pacified individuals. The rise of social media has led to a reduction in television watching and allowed more free time for creative pursuits. Our surplus mental energy has a creative outlet rather than being absorbed by alcohol or soap operas.

Perhaps the most sophisticated approach to new knowledge commons has come from the legal theorist Yochai Benkler (2006). He has drawn upon institutional economics to explain its growth. He notes that the technologies available have made peer-to-peer possible. He also coined the term 'commons based peer production' that he linked to notions of common pool property, drawn partly from another legal theorist Carol Rose and from Elinor Ostrom's work.

He assumes that a new form of economic activity and governance has emerged which challenges mainstream economic assumptions:

> Free software is but one salient example of a much broader phenomenon. Why can fifty thousand volunteers successfully coauthor *Wikipedia*, the most serious online alternative to the *Encyclopedia Britannica*, and then turn around and give it away for free? Why do 4.5 million volunteers contribute their leftover computer cycles to create the most powerful supercomputer on Earth, SETI@Home? Without a broadly accepted analytic model to explain these phenomena, we tend to treat them as curiosities, perhaps transient fads, possibly of significance in one market segment or another. We should try instead to see them for what they are: a new mode of production emerging in the middle of the most advanced economies in the world – those that are the most fully computer networked and for which information goods and services have come to occupy the highest-valued roles.
>
> (Benkler 2006: 6–7)

He argues that human motivation is complex and cannot be reduced to the purely rational maximising model, although he does not dismiss material incentives entirely. He notes that economists' 'basic assumption is that all human motivations can be more or less reduced to something like positive and negative utilities – things people want, and things people want to avoid', noting that these are measured in money terms within the discipline (Benkler 2006: 92). He suggests that new developments in psychology and behavioural economics can help us understand motivation in a more diverse and nuanced way, arguing that human motives are extremely diverse and can be either intrinsic or extrinsic. Intrinsic motivation occurs when we do something because it is of direct value to us. For example, we may simply enjoy listening to music or making it. Extrinsic motivation occurs because we have an incentive do something not for direct value but instead as a means to an end. For example, we might make music to make money to live or to try to impress friends or potential sexual partners. According to Benkler, peer-to-peer production can result from a variety of intrinsic motivations, such as simple enjoyment of our creativity.

Benkler has argued that a number of factors have made peer-to-peer practices possible given such diverse forms of motivation. 'Modularity' is of importance for Benkler; this means being able to break a task down into smaller parts or 'modules'. In turn, '"Granularity" refers to the size of the modules, in terms of the time and effort that an individual must invest in producing them' (2006: 100). A third factor is 'integration'. The term 'integration' refers to how easy it is for individuals to interact together. The creation of the web allows individuals to link together and interact easily. Such integration is in his view vital to the creation of a new form of economy. Thus, Benkler argues if the relevant granules are small and it is possible for potential participants to choose when, where and how to contribute to a project, the costs of doing so will be trivial, so even slight motivation will promote participation. Editing a Wikipedia entry might, for example, take less than a minute. In his view, the web has allowed the growth of peer-to-peer production projects by promoting the relevant modularity, granularity and integration:

> This allows many diversely motivated people to act for a wide range of reasons that, in combination, cohere into new useful information, knowledge, and cultural goods.
>
> Together, these three characteristics suggest that the patterns of social production of information that we are observing in the digitally networked environment are not a fad.
>
> These architectures and organizational models allow both independent creation that coexists and coheres into usable patterns, and interdependent cooperative enterprises in the form of peer-production processes.
>
> (Benkler 2006: 106)

Lawrence Lessig (1999) has also, from a legal theory perspective, contributed to this discussion of the origins and growth of the new knowledge economy, arguing that the 'code is law.' Software is designed from code and, at another level, regulation acts as 'code' enabling and restricting the creation of software, cyberspace and other forms of knowledge production. In Lessig's view, government regulation can be a threat to free production but the absence of regulation may enable powerful interests to restrict peer-to-peer production. Lessig reinforces Benkler's notion in that while peer-to-peer production is likely to grow, it works within an institutional structure. They both argue that it is impossible to avoid governance, in the form of regulation, yet governance should be democratically and transparently designed. Benkler and Lessig's work, with their awareness of institutional influences, reminds us that if we are to discuss the governance of a potential new knowledge commons, it may be useful to look at Elinor Ostrom's work as a guide. It is now possible, having briefly outlined a number of conceptions of the new knowledge economy, to turn to Elinor Ostrom's work and that of her co-worker Charlotte Hess.

Crafting the knowledge economy the Ostrom way

Hess and Ostrom noted that knowledge commons research denoted 'a new way of looking at knowledge as a shared resource' (Hess and Ostrom 2011: 3). Describing knowledge as 'all intelligible ideas, information and data in whatever form in which it is expressed or obtained', they observed that it has been studied by a variety of disciplines (Hess and Ostrom 2011: 11). The diversity of approaches has, as Ostrom also noted with regard to physical commons, made it difficult to aggregate knowledge. Hess and Ostrom took a passage from Douglas R. Hofstadter's book *Gödel, Esher, Bach* to make the point that a reductionist or discipline-specific approach is likely to be misleading.

> Two monks were arguing about a flag. One said, 'The flag is moving.' The other said, 'The wind is moving.' The sixth patriarch, Zeno, happened to be passing. He told them, 'Not the wind, not the flag, mind is moving.'
>
> (Hess and Ostrom 2011: 3)

From different perspectives, the knowledge commons will be understood in different ways. Our perception determines the perspective chosen and the danger, according to Hess and Ostrom is that we forget the intellectual apparatus we use to view a phenomenon.

Hess and Ostrom noted that new knowledge commons could be understood via two pre-existing sets of institutions. The first being the common pool property systems used to govern natural resources. The second, noted by Benkler, a tradition in the United States of shared spaces that promote free speech. Such a tradition, represented by the New England town commons, were, of course, an inspiration for Tocqueville when he wrote *Democracy in America* (Hess and Ostrom 2011: 13). They observed that before the digital era, knowledge was collected in libraries and archives, and it was only with digitalisation and the development of the World Wide Web in 1992 that the notion of a knowledge commons became widespread (Hess and Ostrom 2011: 46). The arrival of the digital new knowledge economy led to a number of consequences, including distribution through the net, improved search engines, databases, word processing and software, along with 'synchronous exchange of information' (Hess and Ostrom 2011: 47). They also acknowledge threats to the knowledge commons from restrictive forms of intellectual property such as the extension in the US of copyright to 70 years after an author's death.

There are a number of insights and conceptual developments within Elinor Ostrom's work that can help us understand the growth of the new knowledge economy based on cyberspace. Craft, coproduction, institutional property rights and her use of experimental game theory to extend understanding of human economic motivation are all relevant. She and Charlotte Hess also specifically applied an IAD framework to the knowledge commons (Hess and Ostrom 2011).

The notion of 'craft' was essential to Ostrom's work. Her approach to political economy focussed on problem-solving rather than broad ideological prescriptions. Inspired by their experience of making furniture, the Ostroms created a workshop in political economy, where notions of craft were explicit: 'Just as a workshop for woodcarvers provides a forum for apprentices to hone their skills as craftsmen (*sic*), the Workshop was designed to allow faculty members and students to collaborate in productive research efforts' (Jagger *et al.* 2009: 1).

Vincent Ostrom developed the theme of artisanship, noting that all forms of human design are artifacts constructed by artisans (V. Ostrom 1980). Elinor Ostrom's enthusiasm for Herbert Simon's book *The Sciences of the Artificial* is also relevant to understanding the creation of a knowledge commons as a craft. Simon, who as well as winning a Nobel Prize in Economic Sciences for his understanding of bounded rationality, conceptualised artificial intelligence and was fascinated by computers. He examined the science behind human crafting of artificial products from administrative systems to software. The motivation of free/open source software creation as a means of solving practical problems fits well with this conception. Despite their somewhat different assumptions, Stallman and Raymond both focussed on software design as a practical activity or craft. From software coding to the institutional design of the Internet, individuals and collectives interact to craft particular projects. An archive or a library, too, can be seen as an example of craft, requiring practical design skills. Indeed Herbert Simon remarked, everyone 'designs who devises courses of action aimed at changing existing situations into preferred ones' (Simon 1996: 111).

The notion of 'craft' can be integrated with another concept in the Ostrom tool kit, that of coproduction, which she defined as 'the process through which inputs used to produce a good or service are contributed by individuals who are not "in" the same organization' (Ostrom 1996: 1073). Coproduction describes peer-to-peer processes but predates the use of the term. She first used it to describe community involvement in policing, arguing that if instead of being passive recipients of a service or 'clients', individuals were allowed to help develop the service provided, this would bring many benefits. This echoes Stallman's encounter with the dysfunctional printer. Involving consumers in the design process of a product and allowing them to customise it if necessary will lead to the creation of better items better suited to the needs of their users.

Elinor Ostrom's work, which has looked at where cooperative behaviour is more likely, aids our understanding of peer-to-peer production in a new knowledge economy. Elinor Ostrom was interested in economic motivation. She felt that the mainstream economic assumption of self-interested human beings was relevant but that human beings had a range of other motives for action. Her extensive use of behavioural game theory, illustrated that human motivation was diverse and, of course, she agreed with Herbert Simon, that even where we were self-interested, our rationality was 'bounded' rather than perfect. Economists may be a little mystified as to why individuals might contribute to free and open source software projects without being paid, but it is easier to explain from er perspective. People may contribute to software projects because they simply enjoy doing so and a host of motives from self-esteem to practical problem-solving may be relevant. The findings of Robert Axelrod (Axelrod 1984) and the development by Ostrom and her colleagues of forms of experimental game theory show that cooperation is possible, illuminating processes of motivation relevant to production within cyberspace. If individuals cooperate and are met with cooperation by others, cooperation will grow and the prisoner's dilemma will result in mutual benefit rather than a sub-optimum Nash equilibrium (Ostrom 2005: 112). A software designer with a problem to solve can place the dilemma on the web; if they are helped they will be more likely to help others with similar problems in the future.

The concept of commons, while the distinction between common pool property systems and common pool resources is less used, has been applied to cyberspace and the knowledge economy, by a number of thinkers including Benkler. Elinor Ostrom's use of the concept of property as a bundle of rights, drawn from John R. Commons, is important in this respect. Notions of property as either simply individual or state appear too crude to conceptualise free/open source property rights. The concept of copyleft, to take one example, reflects this bundle of rights concept. Property provides a number of possible rights and even duties, instead of an exclusive right of possession associated with private property. These rights can be conceptualised as rules and incorporated within an IAD analysis of a knowledge commons. An IAD framework might be used to develop design rules for promoting a robust knowledge commons, in a similar fashion to the way it has been used to investigate 'traditional' forms of common pool property.

Indeed Ostrom and Hess applied the IAD approach to constructing a framework for analysing the knowledge commons (Ostrom and Hess 2011). They suggested that a knowledge commons, given its innate complexity, can be split into three elements made up of facilities, artifacts and ideas. Facilities include libraries and archives used to store artifacts. Facilities are also digital and online in the new knowledge economy. The physical infrastructure of digital networks includes optical fibres, routers, end use computers and similar items.

Artifacts refer to 'discreet, observable, nameable representations of ideas, such as articles, research notes, books, databases, maps, computer files, and web pages' (Ostrom and Hess 2011:47). Ideas are intangible content, which are found within artifacts that might stretch from equations to grammars and other elements that are immaterial and difficult to enclose. Ideas described were by Hardt, as elements of the 'common', although Ostrom and Hess do not use the term.

The IAD analysis includes a study of users and their interactions. Users comprise information providers, information consumers and policymakers; to some extent these groups may overlap. Ostrom and Hess noted the high level of cooperation in the global digital commons between users who have never met face to face but only online.

Property rights can be understood as rules and that the use of creative commons and similar systems means that data producers can exercise a bundle of potential rights in a flexible way. Ostrom and Hess argued that the bundle of property rights relevant to knowledge includes access, contribution, extraction, removal, management, participation and exclusion.

Traditional copyright is restrictive but creative commons licenses might allow a right to access an intellectual artefact such as a piece of music but prevent its removal by enclosure by users who seeks to capture and resell it. The concept of free software can be conceptualised as a bundle of rights or indeed a bundle of different freedoms:

> A program is free software if the program's users have the four essential freedoms:
>
> - The freedom to run the program, for any purpose (freedom 0).
> - The freedom to study how the program works, and change it so it does your computing as you wish (freedom 1). Access to the source code is a precondition for this.
> - The freedom to redistribute copies so you can help your neighbor (freedom 2).
> - The freedom to distribute copies of your modified versions to others (freedom 3). By doing this you can give the whole community a chance to benefit from your changes. Access to the source code is a precondition for this.
>
> (www.gnu.org/philosophy/free-sw.html)

Action situations within the knowledge commons framework might include a particular archive. Ostrom and Hess discussed the Digital Library of the Commons as an example. The IAD framework may also include evaluative criteria; they note that commonly used criteria include increasing scientific knowledge, sustainability and preservation, participation standards, economic efficiency, equity through fiscal equivalence and redistributional equity. Alternative forms of knowledge protection such as copyleft, might be assessed accordingly. Ostrom and Hess's work on an IAD framework for the knowledge commons was, as they acknowledged, little more than a sketch. However, the IAD approach has been used to undertake a major research project which led to the publication of a book entitled *Internet Success* (Schweik and English 2012).

An IAD guide to internet success

Charles Schweik, who studied at Bloomington with the Ostroms, together with his co-worker Robert English, has used the IAD framework to investigate the success of open source software projects (Schweik and English 2012). Their five-year study, completed in 2011 was based on quantitative analysis of three very large data sets from SourceForge, an international repository of free and open source software. Schweik and English examined a data set of over 270,000 software projects, which they complemented with a more detailed survey of 1,400 SourceForge developers. Forty hypotheses and research questions dealing with the success, failure and governance of FOSS projects were investigated. Success was 'based on the idea of successful collective action rather than producing high-quality or extremely popular software' (Schweik and English 2012: 10). Schweik and English defined FOSS project, like Benkler, as based upon 'peer-production common property' (2012: 17).

They used an IAD framework to help understand the empirical and theoretical literature dealing with new knowledge commons. They surveyed the work of Hess and Ostrom, along with many of the key theoreticians of the topic including Benkler, Lessig, Stallman and Raymond. Project attributes were divided into technological, community and institutional categories. 'Technological' referred to the type of software developed and relevant technical characteristics. 'Community' dealt with the people involved but also included financial and marketing aspects. 'Institutional', referred to the rules of governance and was aided by a detailed use of the rule analysis outlined in *Understanding Institutional Diversity* (Ostrom 2005). Both formal rules and informal social norms were included in their study. The 'action arena' dealt with whether a programmer would choose to be involved in a particular project or not.

Schweik and English reached a number of conclusions from this application of an IAD framework to the question of free software success. While any summary would be an oversimplification, it is worth briefly outlining their key five conclusions. They found that motivation for taking part in a project is increased by what can be described as the theory of compound incentives. The idea of rational economic man or woman is, as one would expect, too simplistic. Reflecting Elinor Ostrom's experimental work and a large body of literature in behavioural economics, motivation was more complex than assumed by traditional economics. Surveying the diversity of motives, James Boyle asks:

> Are the motivations those of the gift economy? Is this actually a form of potlatch, in which one gains prestige by the extravagance of the resources one 'wastes?' Is open-source an implicit résumé builder that pays off in other ways? Is it driven by the species-being, the innate human love of creation that continually drives us to create new things even when *homo economicus* would be at home in bed, mumbling about public goods problems?
>
> [...] One person works for love of the species, another in the hope of a better job, a third for the joy of solving puzzles, and so on. Each person has his own reserve price, the point at which he says, 'Now I will turn off *Survivor* and go and create something.' But on a global network, there are a *lot* of people, and with numbers that big and information overhead that small, even relatively hard projects will attract motivated and skilled people whose particular reserve price has been crossed [...]. Under these conditions, this curious mix of Kropotkin and Adam Smith, Richard Dawkins and Richard Stallman, we *will* get distributed production without having to rely on the proprietary/exclusion model.
>
> (Boyle 2003: 45–6)

The need to solve practical problems was, of course, common but most likely to promote participation when it was combined with other motives; however, no specific individual motivation appeared to be linked with success or failure. The more motivations an individual had including financial gain, the more likely they were to contribute to a project and the more likely it was to succeed (Schweik and English 2012: 306).

A second finding was that governance of software projects was usually based on social norms rather than formal rules. In many of the groups Schweik and English studied, participants denied having any agreed formal governance. However, it was felt that this was because the vast majority of projects were very small, typically based on four or five individuals. It may be that larger groups, though more rarely found, might have had more formal rules of governance.

A third conclusion concerned the benefits of larger participation. While groups were generally small, they networked with many more individuals than their core members. Mancur Olson had argued that smaller groups were more likely to succeed in creating sustained collective action. Schweik and English noted that independently of Olson, Frederick Brooks had argued that a larger number of participants slowed down software production (Brooks 1975). In contrast, Eric Raymond with reference to his Linus's law argued that successful software production was a function of larger numbers of participants, because 'given enough eyeballs, all bugs are shallow' (Raymond 1999: 30). Schweik and English concluded that larger numbers of participants tend to lead to projects that are more successful; however, the number of core participants tended to remain small. As Elinor Ostrom and other researchers found, larger numbers mean greater access to labour. Thus, for example, a larger irrigation scheme is easier to maintain because it draws upon a larger potential pool of labour than a smaller system. There is a trade-off because small numbers may make it easier to gain agreement than a project involving more people. A fourth finding was that face-to-face meetings were unnecessary for successful projects. While Skype might be used to communicate, often collaborators had worked together without any formal meeting or even a shared Skype experience. Finally, their research suggested that sites like SourceForge act as key 'power-law' hubs that allow creative matchmaking to occur, so that key individuals can cooperate, despite often living on different continents. The growth of cyberspace has accelerated the importance of an existing collaborative approach to knowledge, which as we have seen promotes a new knowledge commons.

During the twenty-first century, the immaterial knowledge commons has been joined by rapid innovation in the field of physical production. While physical items are conceptualised as private goods, developments such as social sharing, coproduction and perhaps most dramatically the introduction of three-dimensional printing, are leading to new commons. Elinor Ostrom's potential contribution to understanding this area is discussed in Chapter 7.

7 The political economy of the commons in physical goods

> The industrial revolution of the late 18th century made possible the mass production of goods, thereby creating economies of scale which changed the economy – and society – in ways that nobody could have imagined at the time. Now a new manufacturing technology has emerged which does the opposite. Three-dimensional printing makes it as cheap to create single items as it is to produce thousands and thus undermines economies of scale. It may have as profound an impact on the world as the coming of the factory did.
>
> (*The Economist* 10 February 2011)

The German social critic Walter Benjamin committed suicide in 1940 in Spain. As both a Jew and a Marxist, he knew that if he returned to France he would be killed by the Nazi death machine. He wrongly believed that his application to stay in Spain had been revoked, so in desperation he took his own life. He would have been saved if he had waited. Benjamin's death was a loss; he was an insightful, non-dogmatic and often beautiful thinker (Scholem 2012). His best known essay is entitled 'The Work of Art in the Age of Mechanical Reproduction', where he argued that the ability to copy items of art was likely to have profound effects. Art would be demystified, now that technologies were emerging that made it possible to reproduce any image. He observed:

> An analysis of art in the age of mechanical reproduction must do justice to these relationships, for they lead us to an all-important insight: for the first time in world history, mechanical reproduction emancipates the work of art from its parasitical dependence on ritual. To an ever greater degree the work of art reproduced becomes the work of art designed for reproducibility. From a photographic negative, for example, one can make any number of prints; to ask for the 'authentic' print makes no sense. But the instant the criterion of authenticity ceases to be applicable to artistic production, the total function of art is reversed. Instead of being based on ritual, it begins to be based on another practice – politics.
>
> (Benjamin 2011: 218)

It is interesting to speculate what Benjamin would have thought of a process whereby not just images but physical items could be mechanically reproduced with ease, and made common. Yet the production and consumption of physical goods is being transformed as I write; virtually every day sees advances in three-dimensional printing technology. Three-dimensional printers, also known as fabricators or 'fabbers', allow simple objects to be printed by consumers. At their most sophisticated they appear to be based on a science fiction script; indeed one correspondent wrote to *The Economist* to note:

> SIR – For the 'Star Trek' fans among us, the 3D printer is old hat. There were dozens of them on the *Enterprise*, used primarily for putting together meals, one molecule at a time. In fact, that is how Captain Picard would get his favourite drink, synthesised in an instant whenever he requested, 'Tea. Earl Grey. Hot'.
>
> Agustín Barrios Gómez
> Mexico City
>
> (*The Economist*, 24 February 2011)

Before the 1970s, personal home computers were unknown. Now, instead of computers being huge expensive industrial devices associated with space exploration, they have moved into most homes. It may not be so long before we can download not just movies and songs but physical goods, cutlery, kettles and plant pots. A knowledge economy, by providing designs that can be downloaded, may lead to the transformation of the physical production of goods.

While three-dimensional printing is not, at least as I write, a reality in most households, there are other developments that give rise to potential commons in physical goods including social sharing and collaborative consumption. Examples of collaborative consumption are described by Botsman and Rogers (2010) in their book *What's Mine is Yours*. They focus on the shared use of physical goods that are normally perceived to be privately owned by individuals, including cars, clothes and kitchen appliances. *What's Mine is Yours* references Elinor Ostrom's work as inspiring the authors' approach to collaborative consumption (Botsman and Rogers 2011: 93). It might seem inappropriate to discuss Elinor Ostrom's contribution to understanding such potential commons for physical goods. She was not a commons fundamentalist, and saw a place for both the market and the state. Physical goods are described, one would have thought, quite adequately by the term 'private'. Private goods according to economists, are rival: one person's use prevents another. Richard Stallman observed 'When I cook spaghetti, I do object if someone else eats it, because then I cannot eat it' (Stallman 2002: 46).

The idea of extending commons to physical goods might appear unnecessary. Elinor Ostrom was a cautious scholar, aware of the danger of shallow understanding leading to false or partially correct conclusions (a point well illustrated by 'the tragedy of the commons' metaphor). She did not undertake, as far as I am aware, research into forms of common ownership of physical goods.

However, there are a number of reasons for examining how her approach can be applied to physical goods, as well as environmental resources and knowledge. It is important to remember that she made a distinction between items and property rights. A common pool resource such as a lake might be managed as common pool property, private property or state property. Thus private goods might be managed as private property owned by an individual or as collective property meaning that they can be shared. A microwave is a private good but might in a government office, where it is used to warm the meals of officials, be state property. In a communally shared home, the microwave could be a form of collective property. It less likely that any spaghetti left in the microwave would be communally owned, but this is not impossible, as food can be divided and shared with friends. Elinor Ostrom also felt that common property was a regime or system; by this she meant an institutional network of different rights bundled together. While common property regimes apply most obviously to common pool resources, they can also be applied to other categories of resource.

This chapter will examine how concepts of coproduction, social sharing and collaborative consumption, along with the rise of three-dimensional printing, are leading to forms of common pool property relevant to physical items. Recent research into health and financial common pool property regimes are also discussed, with reference to Elinor Ostrom's key concepts.

Sharing and sustainability

Economic growth, if it relies on ever-increasing throughput of physical goods, leading to more energy and resource use, tends to put pressure on the environment. Elinor Ostrom investigated how we could manage environmental resources sustainably. Common pool resources can, as was discussed in Chapter 4, be managed in an environmentally sustainable manner. Common pool property regimes may be conceptualised as part of wider social-ecological systems that can also work sustainably if managed correctly. Yet global economic forces put pressure on local environments, however well managed. As economies grow, we tend to use more goods and services, which in turn is likely to increase demand for metals, minerals and energy. Such rising demand for resources puts pressure on local environments. The growth in the use of fossil fuels is driving climate change, which is likely to degrade local environments, however carefully they are otherwise managed by users. The growth in demand for metals and minerals tends to raise their price, and while this promotes more careful use and recycling, it makes extraction more profitable. This means communities have a greater incentive to allow mining, which may be environmentally damaging. Increased revenues from mining mean that governments have an increased incentive to take land from local populations for extractive purposes. Technological innovation and better management can make use more sustainable but growing demand for physical goods puts more pressure on environmental resources (Bardi 2011).

There are a number of ways of making production and consumption of goods more environmentally sustainable. Writers such as the British environmentalist Jonathan Porritt in his book *Capitalism: As if the World Matters* (Porritt 2005), and Paul Hawken and his co-authors in *Natural Capitalism* have tried to develop an environmentally sustainable approach to production and consumption (Hawken *et al.* 1999). They suggest that more energy can be produced from renewables and recycling can be promoted. Sharing of physical goods is a more fundamental way of reducing the environmental impact of consumption. If we shared more items, fewer items would need to be produced and our collective impact on the environment could be sharply reduced. This approach seems consistent with Elinor Ostrom's work, and indeed when I interviewed her shortly before her death in 2012, she agreed that sharing brought environmental benefits. Collaborative consumption is increasingly used to describe the sharing of physical goods.

The term 'collaborative consumption' was first coined, apparently, by two behavioural scientists in 1978. Marcus Felson and Joe Spaeth (1978) used it to refer to shared economic practices such as 'drinking beer with friends' or family use of the washing machine. Rachel Botsman and Roo Rogers, the authors of *What's Mine is Yours*, describe collaborative consumption as an alternative to purely private ownership, which stretches from conventional forms of hiring, via bartering, to peer-to-peer coordination of access to goods and services.

> Every day people are using Collaborative Consumption – traditional sharing, bartering, lending, trading, renting, gifting and swapping, redefined through technology and peer communities. Collaborative Consumption is enabling people to realize the enormous benefits of access to products and services over ownership.
>
> (Botsman and Rogers 2011: xv–xvi)

What's Mine is Yours promotes the notion of collaborative consumption as an environmentally sustainable alternative. It is increasingly common to find luxury items, such as designer handbags, which can be rented. While this is some way from Elinor Ostrom's frugal demand that we live with less, she would surely have approved. Car sharing is one example, with car clubs emerging so that instead of owning a car, an individual can borrow one when she or he wants. Use is increasingly more important than individual private ownership, and with it environmental impact can be reduced. Like the closely related concept of social sharing, collaborative consumption has been encouraged by the growth of cyberspace in recent decades. The World Wide Web can also promote dematerialisation; cultural goods which would have previously been physically owned are often replaced with access to a service with little or no physical impact. Thus music is accessed via the web, books can be downloaded and films can be streamed. Records, tapes and CDs are no longer necessary and are increasingly seen as last century items, which are rarely consumed. Books made out of paper are being outsold by downloaded versions. Botsman and Rogers contrast the environmental impact of borrowing VHS video tapes with that of borrowing DVDs via the post from Netflix or Lovefilm or downloading them from such sources:

> It is estimated that if Netflix members drove to and from a rental store, they would consume 800,000 gallons of petrol and release more than 2.2 million tonnes of CO_2 emissions annually. And when you consider how Netflix also spares the plastic cases used by stores like Blockbuster [...]. As Netflix wades deeper into the world of online streaming, enabling consumers to watch films instantly, the dematerialized model becomes all the more environmentally friendly.
>
> (Botsman and Rogers 2011: 103)

Businesses based on sharing, such as car rental, or media downloaders like Netflix, are growing. Goods and services are also increasingly available free of charge. These too can take a commercial form; newspapers, for example, are funded by advertising and often entirely free. Free consumption can be found within a diverse institutional ecosystem, ranging from traditional businesses that raise revenue by rental or advertising rather than selling products, to voluntary peer-to-peer institutions.

Freecycle is a global scheme for the free distribution of goods that can be given to new users instead of being thrown away. Founded in Tucson, Arizona in 2003, by 2006 it had grown to a membership of '2,792,052 people comprising 3,811 communities in 77 countries' (Nelson, Rademacher and Paek 2007: 146). It explicitly promotes environmental sustainability:

> Freecycle groups match people who have things they want to get rid of with people who can use them. Our goal is to keep usable items out of landfills. By using what we already have on this earth, we reduce consumerism, manufacture fewer goods, and lessen the impact on the earth. Another benefit of using Freecycle is that it encourages us to get rid of junk that we no longer need and promote community involvement in the process.
>
> (www.uk.freecycle.org/)

Toy libraries, which are growing in popularity in the USA, UK and Canada, are another example of collaborative consumption. Joujoutheque in Montreal, Canada is one example:

> 'There are a lot of toys, a good turnover. They're toys you would like to buy, but are too big to buy, for example, a little kitchen for kids. My daughter loves that,' said Bachand-Lavallee.
>
> 'In two weeks, kids have time to play a lot and I can see after two weeks, the interest goes down, and I bring toys back,' said member Annie Brousseau.
>
> Without the hassle or the big price tag, Joujoutheque has remained popular for 30 years. It was first designed with low-income parents in mind,

> but now, a different clientele is eye the lending library, drawn by their principles.
>
> 'This is a way to be more ecologically responsible,' said Remi Masse.
>
> (CTV News (30 December, 2009))

Libraries for books have, of course, long been a state-sponsored form of collaborative consumption. The principle of usufruct is also important here, goods can be borrowed only if they are returned in as good a state as they were found. Usufruct at the point of consumption is important in contributing to a more environmentally sustainable economy. This isn't new. Elinor Ostrom noted that, during her childhood, due to the economic depression and difficult war years her family used the Goodwill store. Goodwill was established as a form of outreach for the Methodist Church. It collected clothes and other items that had been discarded by the well off and recruited impoverished citizens to repair them and make them ready for resale. In a sense, Goodwill was the eBay of Elinor Ostrom's childhood. She also noted that Vincent's mother took part in what might today be described as peer-to-peer production, or to use Elinor's own term, coproduction:

> 'My husband's mother was in a homemakers club that was started by an extension group in Washington State', recounts Ostrom. 'They met once a week for 40 years and they made quilts. Some of the quilts were put aside for community emergencies, because they were using wood stoves and house (*sic*) burned from time to time. If somebody's house burned, they had quilts made already, people would help rebuild it as a community project and they could be back into reasonable housing within a short period of time.'
>
> (Escotet Foundation (November 2010))

While sharing and coproduction have always been important for human societies but perhaps ignored by economists, Botsman and Rogers suggest that sharing has become mainstream with economic, environmental and social benefits. Drawing upon *Governing the Commons* and a number of other sources, the authors of *What's Mine is Yours* claim that four principles are necessary for successful collaborative consumption, (1) critical mass, (2) spare capacity, (3) belief in commons and (4) trust between strangers.

While Mancur Olson (1971) argued that small numbers made cooperation easier, Botsman and Rogers suggest that growth is necessary to create enough momentum to make cooperative projects self-sustaining. If the number of people contributing to a project is small, this will limit choice, and if choice is low, conventional alternatives will be more attractive. For example, if a toy library has a large number of members, who either donate good quality toys, or via a subscription allow more toys to be bought, the toy library will contain an array of attractive items. If the library is small, users will be discouraged from coming back, and the smallness will lead to further shrinkage. Critical mass also works to harness the principle of social proof. According to Botsman and Rogers, Robert Cialdini, a psychology and marketing professor, discovered that if a large enough group of participants endorsed a product or form of behaviour, other individuals would be much more willing to do so as well. They suggest that critical mass is necessary to provide evidence that a practice is safe and attractive. Small may be easier to manage, and small may enable trust, but low participation tends to lead to lower participation. The astonishing growth of the social media site Facebook seems to provide evidence of this principle.

Spare capacity refers to Benkler's notion that goods which provide excess capability beyond that needed by users have the potential to be shared with others (Benkler 2004). Often we own bicycles but only use them at weekends, or sets of tools that are taken out once or twice a year, meaning that sharing them would require little sacrifice. Private ownership is perhaps economically irrational, if a good is used only for a few minutes a year, and unlike Richard Stallman's example of spaghetti as a private good, is not diminished by direct use. Botsman and Rogers claim that 80 per cent of items owned by consumers in the UK and USA are used only once a month. Cyberspace provides a platform to make the sharing of such items far easier than was possible before its creation. The fourth principle of 'trust between strangers' draws most explicitly upon Elinor Ostrom's work, suggesting collaborative consumption works where reciprocity is promoted and free riders are discouraged (Botsman and Rogers 2011: 93). Botsman and Rogers have produced a popular rather than an academic study of social sharing, so it would be hardly fair to apply rigorous criticism to their work. It would, however, be useful if the kind of application of an IAD framework that Schweik and English (2012) used to research free/open source software was applied to collaborative consumptions, and indeed the other examples of commons for 'private' goods discussed in this chapter. Strong insights as to what makes collective action succeed in application to collaborative consumption could be developed, and assessed to generate relevant conclusions.

Coproduction of physical goods

Collaborative consumption can involve the production of goods as well as the sharing of such items. As we have seen, Elinor Ostrom coined the phrase coproduction to describe processes of providing services that involved both the consumers and producers of such services. This notion can be linked to Elinor and Vincent's advocacy of self-government. They argued that governance was a process that worked throughout society and not just at the level of a centralised state. People should, where possible, be involved in designing the rules by which they live. Consumer involvement in the production of services was beneficial. Potentially, peer-to-peer production of physical goods extends principles found in the management of common pool property, providing more democratic and collective forms of production of physical goods. Consumers can customise the goods they want, choosing their own features, rather than acting as passive recipients of mass production.

Peer-to-peer production has been extended from the production of virtual items such as operating systems (Linux) and encyclopaedias (Wikipedia) to physical goods. In a similar fashion to the concept of coproduction or peer to peer, the US futurologist Alvin Toffler coined the term 'prosumer' to describe 'those of us who create goods, services or experiences for our own use or satisfaction, rather than for sale or exchange. When, as individuals or groups, we both produce and consume our own output, we are "prosuming"' (Toffler and Toffler 2006: 163). The French green socialist André Gorz (2010) echoed this notion arguing that, with technological innovation, a host of machines could be provided to extend production to local communities:

> More than upon free time, the expansion of the sphere of autonomy depends upon a freely available supply of convivial tools that allow individuals to do or make anything whose aesthetic or use-value is enhanced by doing it oneself. Repair and do-it-yourself workshops in blocks of flats, neighbourhood centres or rural communities should enable everyone to make or invent things as they wish. Similarly, libraries, places to make music or movies, 'free' radio and television stations, open spaces for communication, circulation and exchange, and so on need to be accessible to everyone.
>
> (Gorz 1982: 87)

Gorz's vision is similar to that of earlier exponents of community or alternative technology including Karl Hess in the 1970s and Kropotkin in the nineteenth century (Hess 1979; Kropotkin 1901). Technological development may have led to the creation of new platforms that make such visions perhaps more achievable than in the 1980s, 1970s or in 1901.

It has been strongly suggested that the scope for peer-to-peer production of physical items has been accelerated by the development of three-dimensional printers (Gershenfeld 2005: 3). The printers can copy designs developed on the web using plastics or other raw materials. Also known as 'fabbers' derived from the word 'fabrication', they look likely to transform the production of physical goods. Three-dimensional printers can download designs on the web and transform them into physical items.

Fab labs have emerged in Europe and North America, where visitors can use the three-dimensional printers to make items they want. These seem similar to Gorz's conception of community workshops, containing the kind of grassroots technology advocated by Hess and other exponents of democratic production. Neil Gershenfeld, a Professor at the MIT, developed the concept of a Fab Lab, at the Center for Bits and Atoms, where a range of three-dimensional printers allow community production. He noted that mainframe computers were initially expensive and required skilled operators, limiting their market. He observed that, at first, in the same way many people laughed at predictions that personal computers would change work and leisure, they might also be sceptical of the effect of three-dimensional printers. '[As with] the earlier transition from mainframe to PCs, the capabilities of machine tools will become accessible to ordinary people in the form of personal fabricators' (Gershenfeld 2005: 3). He describes a personal fabricator as 'a machine that makes machines; it's like a printer that can print *things* rather than images' (Gershenfeld 2005: 3). They work by taking a substance and spraying it through a printhead, adding layer by layer, until the item is finished. If necessary, fusion is achieved using either a laser beam or layers of glue. A variety of substances have been used as raw materials. For example, Noy Schaal, a high school student, won first prize at her school's science fair by using a three-dimensional printer to make chocolate pieces shaped like the state of Kentucky in 2006. She assembled her own Fab home printer and customized it with a heated chocolate extruder (Lipson and Kurman 2013: 134).

Adrian Bower of the University of Bath in the UK has been developing the RepRap, a three-dimensional printer that will eventually make copies of itself. The term RepRap means 'self replicating rapid prototype' and he plans to make the software for it free online, so that it is a free/open source project which will allow users to contribute to design improvement. The RepRap machine can make a variety of simple items including children's sandals, watertight flasks, parts of a RepRap machine, fly swats, door handles, coat hooks and shot glasses. It can also now manufacture 60 per cent of its own parts. On his website Dr Bowyer shows enthusiasm for the potential of the project:

> It's potentially an extremely powerful and useful technology. Ultimately, it will give anyone the ability to make almost anything for themselves, including reproducing the machine. Will we all become *RepRappers* – jargon for people building or using RepRap machines – eventually? We are well on the way [...]. Increasingly, we are making things for ourselves that don't cost a lot of money.
>
> (www.bath.ac.uk/research/features/reprap.html)

There are now over 100 Fab Labs around the world, and they are seen as opening creative potential for all of us:

> FabLabs are neither chambers of magic nor mere accumulations of 3D printers and other fabrication devices. FabLabs are places where digital culture and material production merge and enter a new stage [...]. These machines are based on digital technologies and operated with computers. Usually, a number of 'conventional' tools, like hammers, saws, and screwdrivers, materials, like plywood, glue, and cardboard, and small electronics, like micro controllers, LEDs, and little motors, are added to the collection of machines in these workshops. In these facilities, people can create material objects that can be beautiful or practical, complex or simple, 'intelligent' or not.
>
> (Walter-Herrmann and Büching 2013: 11)

Fab Labs work on open source principles and promote shared use, but will they change the nature of production, or merely act as relatively small centres used by hobbyists? Claims that they may transform industrial manufacturing may be excessive. There are limits to fabrication, and complex items such as cars and televisions are unlikely to be produced by individual prosumers or even groups of prosumers. Indeed, while less technologically glamorous and novel, gardening and cooking can be seen as long established means of fabrication or coproduction. Many individuals leave both pursuits to others, microwave meals have swept Europe and North America, and gardening seems a lost art in some communities. Open source beer has long existed in the form of home brewing but most individuals buy mass-produced lagers and beers rather than designing their own products. Alvin and Heidi Toffler provided the example of baking a pie as a prosumer activity, and we might describe numerous activities, from DIY to cake making, as examples which are everyday and mundane (Toffler and Toffler 2006: 153). Both the benefits of economies of scale and the influence of advertising may limit the growth of prosumption. Nonetheless, peer-to-peer production of physical goods is likely to grow.

Fabbers have been developed that can copy products, disassembling the item so that they can copy the parts and assemble new or adapted copies. This has led to some concern that individuals could use fabbers to copy and make guns. It seems rather more likely that such critics are aware that manufactured items, from toasters to telephones, could be copied at home, eroding the profits of commercial companies.

Wider collective ownership of technologies that allow shared production has been seen as a source of a new or third industrial revolution. Gershenfeld has suggested:

> [...] possession of the means for industrial production has long been the dividing line between workers and owners. But if those means are easily acquired, and designs freely shared, then hardware is likely to follow the evolution of software. Like its software counterpart, open source hardware is starting with simple fabrication functions, while nipping at the heels of complacent companies that don't believe that personal fabrication 'toys' can do the work of their 'real' machines
>
> (Gershenfeld 2005: 3)

Yet such collective ownership is far from new either. For example, Robert Netting in his study of a commons system that has existed for over 1,000 years in the Alps noted that the citizens of Törbel often collectively owned large items of production equipment:

> Basic farm implements, like the various land types, were means of production that the average peasant family owned and controlled. Larger or more costly devices like the huge cheese making kettles and wine presses were owned by cooperative associations of users, or, in the case of the bread bakery, by the community as a whole.
>
> (Netting 1981:24)

This is really just an early example of Benkler's principle of social sharing, and despite technological innovation that may now make community organised production easier, sober analysis is needed to help us understand the likelihood of this occurring upon a significant scale. The researcher Peter Troxler has suggested that an IAD framework could be used to investigate the potential impact of fab labs (Troxler 2013). This might be similar to Schweik and English's study of free and open source software, briefly discussed in our previous chapter. Troxler is sceptical of the authors who have argued that 'fabbing' will extend ownership of production processes and reduce the distinction between users and makers. He argues, in contrast, that open source hardware existed historically and drove earlier industrial revolutions. Such hardware, that was initially widely copied to accelerate industrial production, was later enclosed by patents. Thus it may be that the new expansion of free and open source production, rather than diversifying and democratizing production, will also be reintegrated into conventional models of ownership. He suggests that there are number of challenges that must be overcome in order to extend peer-to-peer processes from software to hardware. Hardware, he suggests, is a much broader category than software, including, for example, ship to shore containers, circuit boards and furniture. Raw materials are also necessary, and access to them may limit the potential for 'fabbing.' It may be difficult to decompose complex processes into smaller elements that can be combined to manufacture intricate goods. Most fundamentally, an appropriate institutional understanding is necessary:

> To successfully develop the digital manufacturing ecosystem beyond a mere collection of individual tinkerers, a common understanding is needed of how such an ecosystem would function. Such a common understanding could build on a suitable theory. However, canonical knowledge in business administration, industrial engineering and organization science on 'how to run a factory' and the collective wisdom of practitioners and consultants alike will only tell us the old story of hierarchies.
>
> (Troxler 2013: 187)

Proposing an IAD approach, he suggests that fab labs, together with fabbing networks and the international community, might be seen as action situations. The criteria used in the IAD work could be used to evaluate the success of fab labs in terms of promoting control by users, the spread of knowledge and economic self-reliance for the labs. Such a study would be a very valuable extension of Elinor Ostrom's work if it were to occur.

Financial commons

Shared or open source approaches have been applied to areas beyond the traditional common pool environmental resources and the new knowledge commons. These include finance and, as will be discussed in the next section, health care.

In the wake of the financial crisis of 2008, the public's trust in banking institutions has diminished, and community forms of credit have become more attractive.

Established in the UK in 2005, ZOPA, which is derived from the term 'zone of possible agreement', is a peer-to-peer finance network (Fisher and Ury 1983: 42), through which borrowers and lenders can choose their own interest rates. A credit agency rates individuals seeking loans, and potential risk is spread across a large number of transactions. ZOPA's impact has been relatively small. By 2013 they had lent a total of £250 million, while the UK's high street banks deal in £billions. ZOPA has, however, been praised by the Bank of England Financial stability director Andrew Haldane (*Independent*, 17 December 2012).

A variety of financial experiments, based on peer-to-peer principles, is emerging. Crowd sourcing, where projects are funded by a large number of small donations, is growing. With the emergence of free cultural products, it is often difficult to fund books, films, musical performances or software. While the costs of such projects may also be reduced, in economies where access to a variety of necessities including housing, transportation, energy and food is still commodified, monetised income streams remain necessary. Alternative currencies have also been developed, one of the best known being the web-based bitcoin. Alternative forms of money and credit based on peer-to-peer principles are not new. Like the various other supposedly 'new' commons, they have been helped by the platforms provided by the development of cyberspace but are less 'new' than might be assumed. Hayek argued for the denationalisation of money, believing that privately created currencies would bring financial stability (Hayek 1976). While this is not a commons or peer-to-peer project, it reflects a desire for a more diverse financial system, similar in inspiration to the sentiments of some supporters of projects like ZOPA.

Community not for profit finance, that blurs the distinction between lenders and borrowers, also has a long history. A variety of 'utopian' financial schemes can be found throughout history, such as the *National Equitable Labour Exchange* established by the industrialist and socialist Robert Owen in 1832 (Royle 1998: 51). These were often short lived and were criticised by Hayek as inflationist (1976: 14), but some have been relatively enduring and successful. Friendly societies and credit unions emerged to help poorer individuals band together to support each other financially. In the UK, building societies emerged in a similar way to help individuals to buy homes (Leadbeater and Christie 1999). Rather than being owned by shareholders, these were mutuals which were possessed by users, including both borrowers and lenders. During the twentieth century, the number of British building societies sharply decreased and their share of the financial market declined. This was partly due to bureaucratisation, with the democratic ethos of the building societies becoming eroded and largely symbolic. The government encouraged them to demutualise and become fully fledged banks that were floated on the stock market, a process which contributed to the financial crisis of 2008 and centralization of the financial system (Klimecki and Willmott 2009).

Health commons

Health care is another area where Elinor Ostrom's work has been applied. Her colleague Michael McGinnis has discussed whether the provision of health care could be understood as a commons, and the extent to which concepts such as coproduction are relevant to improving its provision. In the USA, health care has been seen to be in crisis, with sharply rising medical bills and unequal access. Purely private provision of health care is problematic for a number of reasons. The poorest in society find it difficult to afford health care and this leads to suffering and inequality. Markets work poorly when information is unbalanced between consumers and producers, i.e information is asymmetric. Because of the problem of asymmetric information, moral hazard is a potential risk. This is often the case with health care, as doctors and other medical professionals have much better knowledge than patients, so may be tempted to exploit patients, if their salaries are linked to the number and type of procedures they undertake. Thus, over prescription is a potential problem because treatments that are unnecessary may be promoted in order to increase profits for the private health care providers (Moomaw *et al.* 2009: 172).

President Obama's attempts to improve access to health insurance for US citizens may reduce inequality of access but are unlikely to diminish moral hazard. State systems of health care, such as the National Health Service in the United Kingdom, are one alternative, though critics claim that state health care may be expensive and unresponsive to diverse local needs. In 2009 the Ostrom workshop was given a research grant to investigate health care as a commons. Elinor Ostrom noted:

> The challenge of using well our common shared resources in health and health care is of utmost importance if we are to reach the goal of a healthier population and a sustainable health system. We're thrilled at the opportunity to contribute new insights to meeting that challenge.
>
> (Hinnefeld (November 2010))

Michael McGinnis has explored how a US health care system could be viewed as a commons. He noted that, while health care has been discussed at a national level in the USA, treatment occurs locally, as patients interact with local health care workers. Outcomes are varied, with environmental, socio-economics and political governance factors all affecting the success of local health care.

He argues that health care involves shared use of a number of resources, from hospital buildings to medical equipment. A potential tragedy of the commons may occur if individuals over exploit these resources, and careful stewardship is necessary in order to overcome this. While McGinnis does not specifically note the seven-generation rule, he observes that long-term perspectives are needed to manage the health care commons. He argues that it is likely that health care which is produced more efficiently in an economic sense, where lower average costs are associated with better health, is associated with informal mechanisms of stewardship. Empirical research is being undertaken by McGinnis (2013) to determine to what extent Elinor Ostrom's eight principles of commons design can be applied to health care commons.

The notion of polycentric governance is also relevant. Diverse forms of health care provision fit with the approach of both Vincent and Elinor Ostrom, but economies of scale might be significant in reducing the costs of pharmaceuticals and high technology medical equipment. In many parts of the world, local health services are being closed to make way for hospitals based on the best technology, which are only affordable via centralization. However health care is a good example of the benefits of coproduction. If members of the community are actively involved in decisions about health care, better quality and lower cost health care provision is likely.

Ironically, from the perspective of those who believe markets always work best, given its status as one of the few remaining communist states on the planet, Cuba has been seen to provide a more cost efficient health care system than the US. According to most estimates, Cubans have the same life expectancy as US citizens 'while spending 4% per person annually of what the US does' (Fitz 2012). The Cuban system cannot be understood as a purely polycentric ecosystem of different health care institutions, but it does share other features such as decentralization and community involvement that are consistent with the Ostrom approach:

> The most revolutionary idea of the Cuban system is doctors living in the neighborhoods they serve. A doctor-nurse team are part of the community, and know their patients well because they live at (or near) the *consultorio* (doctor's office) where they work. *Consultorios* are backed up by *policlínicos* which provide services during off-hours and offer a wide variety of specialists. *Policlínicos* coordinate community health delivery and link nationally-designed health initiatives with their local implementation. Cubans call their system *medicina general integral* (MGI, comprehensive general medicine). Its programs focus on preventing people from getting diseases, and on treating them as quickly as possible.
>
> (Fitz (2012))

Thus, preventative health care has been seen as more important than investment in expensive technologies in Cuba. This is prudent, perhaps, but part of the reason that medical technologies can be expensive is because of exclusive property rights. Such high costs have helped drive, as noted previously, a centralization of health services, but the notion of health commons can also be applied to research and development of pharmaceutical drugs, which may aid necessary decentralization. Pharmaceutical companies have argued that patents are necessary for their products, as unless a new drug can be protected by a patent, companies will be reluctant to undertake new research. However the extension of patents often makes important drugs inaccessible to poorer communities, and is an important cause of rising medical bills.

While the profit motive might be thought to promote research, it can also reduce medical research progress by fragmenting knowledge. Generic drugs have emerged as a low cost alternative. In turn, the notion of a science commons has been introduced to accelerate research. Jonas Salk who discovered a polio vaccine is said to have answered, when asked if he would patent it, 'There is no patent. Could you patent the sun?' (quoted in Rowe and Barnes 2013: 65). The notion of anticommons applies to pharmaceutical research, as exclusive property rights that make sharing difficult can lead to the underutilization of new discoveries, blocking medical progress.

While this chapter has focussed on physical commons, and pharmaceutical drugs might be conceptualised as physical items, much of the debate has returned to the subject of Chapter 6, the knowledge commons. A drug contains chemicals but the essential chemicals are a product of a knowledge process. A commons in knowledge tends to produce a commons in goods, where the value of such goods is based on knowledge. While sharing has been found throughout history, the development of the web provides a platform which makes the sharing or reuse of physical goods easier. Goods are the product of design, which can be made more democratic and participatory, as theorists such as Eric von Hippel have suggested (2005). Such an approach is consistent with Elinor and Vincent Ostrom's central argument that human-created artifacts, from constitutions to chairs, are based on designs that need to be constructed, and that such construction can be made more democratic.

Common pool production and consumption

The creation of cyberspace and three-dimensional printing will have accelerating and radical economic, social, political and environmental effects, however such innovations work within a wider context. A significant contextual element is the institutional role of property rights. While we can imagine a more significant role in the future for common pool property regimes, it is also possible to argue that common pool property regimes have existed throughout history, even for the production of physical goods, and have often been reconverted into state or private ownership. In Anglo-Saxon England, commons appear to have been an important form of property ownership. With the evolution of the manorial system, local commons seem to have increasingly come under the control of private landowners. William's invasion, in 1066, introduced a feudal system; all commons were owned by an aristocratic elite, although serfs had access to them (Rodgers *et al.* 2010). In late medieval Germany, collective ownership of land and other factors of production was widespread, together with systems of collective political control (Blickle 1985). Yet many of the German commons were integrated into systems of private ownership. Common pool property regimes were close to universal amongst indigenous Americans before European colonialisation, which largely destroyed them. Netting's example of community ownership in Switzerland shows a rich institutional diversity with communal, family and individual ownership. Its production features seem as radical as the promise of three-dimensional printing (Netting 1981). What made diverse ownership including community production possible was not a technology, but democratic institutional ownership at the grassroots. Centralization, whether driven by the state or market forces, did not traditionally have much impact on the relatively remote Swiss village of Törbel that Netting studied. While institutional reductionism should be avoided as much as technological reductionism, ownership and governance are at least as significant as scientific innovation, for any potential commons of production and consumption.

While commons emerge as part of a diverse set of property rights, it seems that they are often under threat. Common pool resources often become private or state property, rather than being governed by common pool property systems. There seems to be a tendency for either the state or the market to 'crowd out' the commons. With the development of cyberspace, collaborative consumption and three-dimensional printing, a new commons-based political economy is often assumed to be the way of the future. However, common property has emerged throughout history, only to be reintegrated by the state and the market, excluding democratic self-governance. It is worth speculating as to the extent that this will happen once again and whether such reintegration matters in any fundamental sense.

Commentators on the left can point to the commodification or re-commodification of the commons; those on the right may point to the invasion of the state. Although from Rothbard on the 'right' to Marx on the left, many thinkers have shown how states and business interests often work in tandem. Certainly, at present, the emerging systems of commons can be shaped by state control or private property rights. Social media uses commons platforms but corporate forms of ownership are increasingly dominant. Twitter, Facebook and Google are currently dominant in cyberspace; all are corporate bodies based on share ownership, and seeking to make a profit. Not for profit collective institutions such as Wikipedia are thus far from universal. There is a constant battle over property rights in the form of copyright and patents to erode common pool property systems in cyberspace. Private companies often have enough money to buy out emerging commons-based alternatives, for example, peer-to-peer car sharers Zipcar were absorbed by the existing global car rental company Avis (Schwartz (January 2013)).

Regulation may also restrict commons-based alternatives, *The Economist* (9 March 2013) noted:

> In November 2012 the California Public Utilities Commission issued $20,000 fines against Lyft, SideCar and Uber for 'operating as passenger carriers without evidence of public liability and property damage insurance coverage' and 'engaging employee-drivers without evidence of workers' compensation insurance'. [...]
>
> It is not just car-sharing services that have run into legal problems. So have apartment-sharing services, which have fallen foul of zoning regulations and other rules governing temporary rentals in which the property

owner or occupier are not present. Many American cities ban rentals of less than 30 days in properties that have not been licensed and inspected.

According to Elinor Ostrom, common pool property regimes may work best, at least on a local level, if they adhere to eight broad design principles, one of which is that they are tolerated by more powerful political actors. However, this is often not the case, and even when it is, common pool property systems are shaped by external political influences. Thus commons, whether in land, seas, ideas, physical means of production or shared goods, cannot be understood without reference to politics and power. Chapter 8, entitled 'Politics without Romance' discusses Elinor Ostrom understanding of politics, power and conflict.

8 Politics without romance

> She transcended the debates found in most of the dogmatic Marxist, libertarian and heterodox economic circles by subverting the ideological divides, understanding that complex questions would require involved and complex answers, complex because the findings would have major social and economic implications:
>
> - Are individuals motivated by considerations other than crude selfishness?
> - Are individuals forever locked in a struggle against each other for power and control?
> - Can individuals overcome substantial barriers to address critical issues such as climate change?
>
> [Elinor Ostrom] explored these questions by trying to understand how the 'science and art of association' is utilized by real people situated in social dilemmas. The evidence of Ostrom's work points to yes; humankind has the capacity to develop community based solutions and act concertedly to avert disasters.
>
> (Taylor (21 June 2012))

The Whiteboys, known in Irish as *Buachaillí Bána*, so called because of the white shirts they wore, fought a small-scale war with the landlords and the authorities for several decades in eighteenth century Ireland. Brutally suppressed, this loose-knit secret society continued to reemerge between 1761 and 1786. While a number of rural abuses fuelled this peasant rebellion, the first incident was in response to an act of enclosure. T. Jackson, a historian of revolutionary Irish movements noted:

> It first appeared, near Limerick, as a reply to an attempt by the landlords to enclose stretches of waste land which had been treated as common from time immemorial. This 'waste' was indispensable to scores of peasants as grazing for their cows, sheep, goats, etc. Faced with this calamity the peasants turned out by night, threw down the walls, filled the trenches, ploughed up their meadows and restored the whole 'waste' to its original conditions. The landlords abandoned their attempts.
>
> (Jackson 1971: 103)

There was more to the conflict than enclosure. However, the Whiteboy conspiracy powerfully illustrates that common pool property rights are often associated with violent power struggles. While Elinor Ostrom engaged in careful research to challenge the notion of the 'tragedy of the commons', she can be criticised, perhaps, for failing to deal with a much greater drama. Commons have not generally been tried and proved to fail, but more often than not, they have simply been seized. Across the planet, commons owned by local communities have been stolen. Perhaps the debate between Elinor Ostrom and Garrett Hardin is a distraction. The microeconomics and politics of the institutional development of shared property appears to be of less importance than the macro picture of powerful forces taking what belongs to others. Anti-colonial, indigenous and Marxist scholars have long noted the assault on the commons (Jacobs 2006; Linebaugh 1976; Marx 1976; Shiva 1988; Thompson 1991). Corporate interests are challenging the virtual commons of the World Wide Web and land seizures continue apace in the twentieth-first century.

Elinor Ostrom was a political economist but might be criticised as being in a particular sense apolitical. It is important to discuss the extent to which her institutional analysis made reference to power, politics and social conflict. This chapter will outline the argument that the larger tragedy of the commons is one of enclosure by the rich and powerful. The underpinnings of institutional analysis and development in Vincent Ostrom's work are examined. The approach of both Vincent and Elinor can be seen as rooted in a political philosophy that promoted self-governance and was critical of attempts to centralize power. Both the Ostroms and many anti-capitalist commons scholars such as Hardt and Negri, draw upon a similar understanding of republican political thought which was transmitted via Machiavelli to the founders of the American constitution. Such republicanism and the specific political economy of the commons bring questions of methodological individuals and structural change back into the frame.

Commons, capitalism, conflict and colonialism

The environmental journalist Fred Pearce in his book *The Landgrabbers* states that millions of acres of land are being enclosed and sold to corporate investors (Pearce 2013). In Africa, much common land governed by customary rights has been re-classified by governments and sold. Ethiopia has seen huge acreage sold to corporations. Rising commodity prices have made land a valuable asset, and financial institutions, foreign governments and biofuel companies have become major buyers. Pearce concludes that:

> The world's commons are under siege. The biggest prizes for the landgrabbers are unfenced forests and pastures – and many governments are willing to sell out their inhabitants. It looks like the Earth's final round-up, the last enclosure. And with the land often comes water – a free resource being privatized. Millions of Malians suffer as their water is siphoned off for Chinese, South African and even Libyan farmers. The world's poor and

> hungry are losing their land and water in the name of development. Can this really be the way to feed the world?
>
> (Pearce 2013: 309)

The commons have been under assault for centuries. In England, between the fifteenth and nineteenth centuries, peasants found their common land enclosed and often engaged in strong resistance to get it back (Neeson 1993). Historians such as Peter Linebaugh (2008) and E.P. Thompson (1991) catalogued how commons were enclosed and how commoners fought this over many centuries. We can find episodes of resistance to enclosure, such as the Whiteboy Conspiracy discussed at the start of this chapter, in almost every European country. For example, the German peasant wars of the sixteenth century can be understood as a rebellion against enclosure (Blickle 1985). Resistance to enclosure in Britain continued into the nineteenth century. For instance, Plumstead Common in South London was preserved after boisterous protest by local women in 1870:

> 'A party of women, armed with saws and hatchets, first commenced operations by sawing down a fence enclosing a meadow adjoining the residence of Mr Hughes…' Fences belonging to William Tongue were pulled down. There was talk of pulling down Hughes' house as well. Hughes called the coppers, and some nickings followed. The next day 100s of people gathered and attacked fences put up by a Mr Jeans. When the bobbies arrived many vandals took refuge in the local pubs.
>
> (South London Radical History Group 2004)

Enclosure in Europe created 'excess' populations who, after they were deprived of land, were often resettled abroad, fuelling more enclosure in the colonies. In Ireland, prior to waves of British conquest, much land was managed as communal property. During the seventeenth century, significant numbers of English and Scottish families were 'planted' in Ireland on land taken from the local population. European colonialism in the Americas, Australia and New Zealand saw indigenous populations driven away from land, which they had governed with common pool property regimes. Property may be both freedom and theft, as the anarchist Proudhon observed, but in accounts of European colonialism, it has been entirely the latter for indigenous peoples.

In the Americas, indigenous people were, to varying degrees, removed from their customary land. In Canada and the USA, indigenous peoples were largely confined within a relatively small number of reservations. In Latin America, indigenous people were often pushed back to rainforests and other land marginal to the colonialists. Resistance was not entirely futile, for example, in what is now called Chile, the Mapuche fought the Spanish and won a peace treaty (Ray 2007). Enclosure of indigenous common property regimes continues. As I write, the Mapuche are locked into major conflict with the Chilean government. In Peru, the government of Alan Garcia attempted to lease large areas of the Amazon to gas and oil corporations, but non-violent resistance by the indigenous coalition AIDESEP defeated his plans. As many as one hundred indigenous demonstrators were killed by military police at Bagua, ironically on 5 June, 2009, World Environment Day (Wall 2010: 106). The often bloody history of enclosure, which continues today, should not be forgotten. The microanalysis of the management of the commons, while necessary, must perhaps be placed within a context of the macro analysis of global enclosure.

There is a rich literature discussing the assault on the commons. The political philosopher George Caffentzis, writing in 2004, noted that two conferences on the topic of commons were happening at the same time in Mexico. The first, held at Oaxaca under the title of 'The Commons in an Age of Global Transition: Challenges, Risks and Opportunities', was convened by the International Association for the Study of Common Property (IASCP). Elinor Ostrom was a prominent participant, and the event was supported by the Ford Foundation and the World Bank. The second, held 350 miles away in San Miguel de Allende, was entitled 'Alterglobalization', and saw social movement activists as well as academics discuss common pool property as a potential alternative to capitalism.

Caffentzis, who had studied the commons since the 1970s and published numerous articles with the autonomist Marxist collective *Midnight Notes*, delivered a paper at the second conference entitled 'A Tale of Two Conferences: Globalization, the Crisis of Neoliberalism and the Question of the Commons'. Those who attended the first conference, including Elinor Ostrom, he described as 'neo-Hardinates' who, he suggested, saw:

> [...] the problem of the commons as an issue of management requiring good institutional designs 'to help human groups avoid tragedies of the commons.' They see the property regimes regulating common-pool resources as offering different combinations of outcomes that can be measured by efficiency, sustainability and equity criteria. The solution to the problems posed by the potential for a 'tragedy of the commons' can be achieved by greater research on common-property regimes throughout the world and greater theoretical comprehension of the variables involved. It programatically rejects doctrinaire neoliberalism that assumes the superiority of private-property regimes throughout the society including the management of common-pool resources.
>
> (Caffentzis 2004)

The second approach, that of the San Miguel de Allende conference goers, according to Caffentzis, comprises social movements, indigenous and other militant advocates of social change, whom he describes as 'anti-capitalists':

> The anti-capitalist supporters of the commons see the struggle for a commons as an important part of a larger rejection of neoliberal globalizing capitalism since it is the commons in the indigenous areas, in the global sense, and in the area of collective intellectual production that is now threatened with enclosure by a capitalism bent on commodifying the planet, its

> elements, its past and future. Their key issues are how to bring together various aspects of the struggle against commodification and create 'another world' satisfying the needs of global justice.
>
> (Caffentzis 2004)

It is interesting that it is often possible to exist in one of these categories without even acknowledging the existence of the other. The 'anti-capitalist' commons scholars have often, with rare exceptions such as Caffentzis, ignored the existence of Ostrom's scholarship. Ostrom, in turn, rarely cited anti-capitalist or Marxist authors who examined the commons such as Marx himself, E.P. Thompson or Peter Linebaugh. It seems more difficult to ignore the angry elephant in the room, the large mammal trampling the commons, identified by such thinkers. The political economy of management may be obscured by the facts of enclosure and destruction of the commons. There is clearly a division in commons scholarship between the macro politics of enclosure and the micro politics of sustaining common pool property. It is important to ask why Elinor Ostrom rejected the anti-capitalist label, and the extent to which she ignored questions of power and conflict, as critics such as Caffentzis apparently imply.

Ostrom on political power

Elinor Ostrom might be criticised for failing to undertake a macro economic and macro political analysis of common pool property, yet it is wrong to dismiss her analysis as apolitical and purely managerial. She was not an anti-capitalist thinker but it is misleading to see her as acting on the side of corporate power or elites. Elinor Ostrom certainly did not advocate the removal of common pool property rights, and this is reflected in her work, but she clearly found it most useful to focus on the micro politics and economics of commons management. There are a number of reasons for this.

Elinor Ostrom has been identified as working within a tradition that follows liberal thinkers such as Adam Smith (Aligică and Boettke 2009). Her early academic work in the 1960s, 1970s and 1980s, occurred during the Cold War, when academics were often influenced by the conflict between the USA and Soviet Union. Although she drew strongly on the ideas of John R. Commons, who was a social reformer that challenged the unregulated market, she was associated with new institutionalists, who were often enthusiastic about capitalism. To explain her approach, it is worth comparing her attitudes to capitalism and social justice as broad categories with those of her colleague Amartya Sen. Both were subtle and complex thinkers who believed in the value of market mechanisms and were sceptical that governments could easily remedy market failure. Both, paradoxically or not, can be seen as critical of the extreme market-based economics of figures like Milton Friedman and other members of the Chicago school. Typically, Sen wrote a paper criticising rational choice theory entitled 'Rational Fools: A Critique of the Behavioural Foundations of Economic Theory' (1977), which Elinor encouraged her students to read. The economist

Meghnad Desai noted of Amartya Sen that he was 'peculiarly shy about talking politics publicly. It's a kind of self-denial [...]. It's also a generational thing. Good economists, when he started out, didn't get into politics. So he prefers to be subversive in a technical way' (Steele (31 March 2001)). I think this was also true of Elinor Ostrom; her work was subversive of mainstream economics in a number of ways but she avoided polemical political statements.

Both Elinor and Vincent also felt that broad categories such as 'socialism' and 'capitalism' were unhelpful. This was for at least two reasons. Firstly, language, while important, can be manipulated. 'Socialism' and 'capitalism' could be applied to very different systems of governance by self-seeking politicians. Secondly, even if applied in good faith, they tend to be too crude to represent realities on the ground. Thus Vincent Ostrom argued:

> [...] broad concepts such as 'markets' and 'states', or 'socialism' and 'capitalism', do not take us very far in thinking about patterns of order in human society. For example, when some 'market' economists speak of 'capitalism', they fail to distinguish between an open, competitive market economy and a state-dominated mercantile economy. In this, they follow Marx. He argued that 'capitalism' has a competitive dynamic that leads to market domination by a few large monopoly or monopoly-like enterprises. But what Marx called 'capitalism', Adam Smith called 'mercantilism'.
>
> (Aligică and Boettke 2009:142)

Like Adam Smith and Karl Marx, Vincent Ostrom was of course critical of concentrated market power. Elinor Ostrom was a political economist and, even at a micro level, the role of power and politics were intrinsic to her institutional analysis. The IAD approach, developed with Vincent and other colleagues, provides a way of mapping flows and structures of power. She was, of course, strongly influenced by Vincent Ostrom's approach to politics, markets and democracy. While he cannot be described as an anti-capitalist, his approach to politics and constitutions was based on a desire for radical democracy. It is essential to understand his political thinking if we are to understand Elinor Ostrom's approach to power and conflict.

The constitutional politics of Vincent Ostrom

Vincent Ostrom was hostile to forms of centralised planning aimed at improving human welfare. Like Hayek, who he often quoted, he thought that utopian revolutionary plans for society were innately oppressive. No one individual or group of individuals who created a plan for a better society were likely to get it right. Human needs were diverse and a plan from the centre, however well-intentioned, could be damaging (V. Ostrom 1997: 75). He was highly critical of Marx, Engels and Lenin (V. Ostrom 1997: 72). In 1958 he took part in 'the conference with no name' that launched public choice theory. Public choice held that economic analysis should be extended to politics, and that politicians and civil servants were often rent seeking, self-interested individuals, who were likely to exploit the public rather than to serve them. James Buchanan coined the phrase 'politics without romance' to explain his understanding that politics should not be seen as a morally pure space based on the wish to serve others (Buchanan 1984). He argued that:

> The romance is gone, perhaps never to be regained. The socialist paradise is lost. Politicians and bureaucrats are seen as ordinary persons much like the rest of us, and 'politics' is viewed as a set of arrangements, a game if you will, in which many players with quite disparate objectives interact so as to generate a set of outcomes that may not be either internally consistent or efficient by any standards.
>
> (Buchanan 1984: 20)

Public choice theorists argued that market failure could not automatically be solved by government action. Politics was part of real life, not a saintly space where the morally just tried to deal with the mess made by the rest of us.

Yet while Vincent Ostrom was not on the traditional left, a closer examination suggests that neither can he be conceptualised as a conservative figure or a free marketeer. He was, despite his rejection of Marx and Lenin, an advocate of revolutionary change where necessary. He was, unsurprisingly, a passionate supporter of the American revolution that ended British rule. However, he was also sympathetic to many anti-colonial and anti-imperialist struggles (V. Ostrom 1999). For instance, he was enthusiastic about the intellectual and practical achievements of the African revolutionary and independence leader Amilcar Cabral (V. Ostrom 1999: 182). Like Elinor Ostrom, Vincent placed ecological considerations at the centre of his analysis. Equally, while he saw value in the market, he also believed that state intervention was necessary on some occasions. Above all, like Elinor, he believed that economics extended beyond activities of exchange. He argued that political discourse had to be based on genuine choice. While agreements could be reached, it was important to respect difference. Indeed, he believed that political difference could lead to creative thinking:

> Reading a text and making one's own interpretation of the words being used is too frequently accompanied by a response of either accepting or rejecting what is being said, rather than trying sympathetically to reconstruct the formulations that the author hoped to advance.
>
> (V. Ostrom 2012: 87)

While it could be argued that, at first sight, Vincent's work centred on the US constitution was of limited application, I would argue that it is important to attempt 'to reconstruct the formulations' he hoped to advance. Without doing so it is difficult to understand fully Elinor Ostrom's political economy, and Vincent's formulations have a number of interesting implications which are worthy of consideration. Of course, we must remember that Elinor dedicated *Governing the Commons* to Vincent for 'his love and contestation' (Ostrom 1990: v). Contestation was central to their intellectual partnership. They believed in contesting or challenging each other's ideas, so while Vincent influenced Elinor's thinking she undoubtedly changed his.

While we could describe Vincent Ostrom as a liberal thinker, the description 'radical democrat' or 'republican' is perhaps closer to the heart of his political philosophy. He believed in the creation of self-governing societies and was inspired in doing so by the US constitution. He noted that '[C]onstitutions are too often viewed as abstract formulations having little or no significance for wider political activity' (V. Ostrom 2012: 85). It might be thought that constitutional documents are dry as dust and tell us little about political ideologies or political practice. Indeed, Vincent Ostrom only became enthusiastic about constitutions after he took part in the drafting of the Article on Natural Resources at the Alaska Constitutional Convention. After taking part in the process, he read *The Federalist* papers, and was particularly inspired by the opening paragraph of the first essay. Alexander Hamilton argued that the American people were embarking on a bold new experiment in democratic governance, asking whether individuals could come together to establish 'good government from reflection and choice, or whether they are forever destined to depend for their political constitutions on accident and force' (quoted by Ostrom 2012: 85).

Constitutions provide a means of creating a political framework where individuals and different groups in a society could negotiate their differences. For Vincent Ostrom, they were political documents but they could deal with ecological and economic problems. His participation in the Alaska Constitutional Convention made him aware of how important it was for contending groups to attempt to establish such frameworks. They were also experiments. Politics was about practice, not simply a set of principles outlined by scholars and implemented by politicians. The creation of the US constitution was a great experiment, and in the eyes of the thinkers that Ostrom respected most of all, like the authors of *The Federalist Papers* and Tocqueville, the first of its kind.

Vincent Ostrom believed that constitutions provided sets of rules for governance and could potentially promote human freedom. Like many other enthusiasts of the US constitution, he believed in a separation of powers. Democracy was still an innovation in the late eighteenth century, and did not extend to all groups in American society. Women, indigenous and African-Americans were excluded from participation. Yet even if a fully inclusive democracy did exist, it would have been in danger of becoming undemocratic because of the potential tyranny of the majority. The existence of a federal system that recognised the power of the American states was essential, as was a separation of power between the President, House, Congress and Supreme Court. However, Vincent Ostrom went beyond the usual mainstream enthusiasm for the US political system. He argued that politics reached beyond the state, and that governance was required at all levels of society. Human beings could potentially sit down and create systems to deal with conflicting demands from the grassroots upwards. The creation of systems of governance for commons was a good example of this thinking. Rather than being governed by a state, societies should have the maximum freedom to organise their affairs at the grassroots. Nevertheless, Vincent Ostrom argued that different levels of decision-making were necessary because not all decisions could be made at a highly localised level.

He drew strongly upon James Buchanan's constitutional ideas to understand the logical basis of such systems of governance. Ostrom found Buchanan and Tullock's *The Calculus of Consent* a useful source for understanding constitution-making at state level and throughout society. In an essay entitled 'Buchanan's Opening to Constitutional Choice', Vincent Ostrom noted four important principles. The first was methodological individualism, which meant that human beings could draw upon their individual resources to approach choices. Second, the notion of consensus, where 'participants made choices concerning, the separation of powers and a system of checks and balances were operable within the context of common knowledge and shared communities of understanding' (V. Ostrom 2012: 87). Third, Buchanan's notion of a 'cost calculus in a comparative analysis of voting rules' was instructive. Fourth, Vincent noted that such constitution-making could be 'extended to all patterns of human association and be constitutive of self-governing societies' (V. Ostrom 2012: 86).

He attempted to reconstruct the logic used by Alexander Hamilton and James Madison to create the US constitution in his book *The Political Theory of a Compound Republic* (1971). He was sharply critical of the arguments advanced by Woodrow Wilson (1856–1924) in the 1880s who suggested that a streamlined administration and a hierarchal form of political organisation were necessary. While best known as the US President who introduced progressive policies, took the USA into the First World War and advocated the creation of the League of Nations, Wilson completed his PhD on the topic of congressional government in the 1880s. Wilson admired the English parliamentary system, which concentrated power in the hands of an individual Prime Minister and felt that the US constitution was flawed because of its system of checks and balances:

> Power and strict accountability for its use are the essential constituents of good government [...]. It is, therefore, manifestly a radical defect in our federal system that it parcels out power and confuses responsibility as it does. The main purpose of the Convention of 1787 seems to have been to accomplish this grievous mistake. The 'literary theory' of checks and balances is simply a consistent account of what our Constitution makers tried to do; and those checks and balances have proved mischievous.
>
> (Wilson 1956: 187)

Vincent Ostrom challenged centralization from any quarter. Both Lenin and Wilson, in advocating a concentration of state power, stifled the opportunity for self-government, in his view. Ostrom, of course, was well aware of Marx's statement that a communist society would mean the 'withering away of the state'.

However, he noted the comments of Yugoslavian political commentator Milovan Djilas:

> Everything happened differently in the USSR and the other Communist countries from what the leaders – even such prominent ones as Lenin, Stalin, Trotsky, and Bukharin – anticipated. They expected that the state would rapidly wither away, that democracy would be strengthened. The reverse happened.
>
> (Djilas 1957: 37 quoted in V. Ostrom 1997: 6)

Wilson and many other US political thinkers were also dismissive of the political role of local government. For them, politics was about efficient management, and once elected politicians could depend upon a trustworthy bureaucracy. Local considerations were of no importance. Vincent Ostrom, in contrast, believed that all forms of administration were political and involved constitutional choice. Local democracy was vital and should be self-governing. His and Elinor Ostrom's work on local government illustrated the point that people should not be treated as passive consumers but should be co-producers of public goods such as policing. Wilson, in contrast, argued that experts at the centre should solve problems and citizens should have little or no say in governance, once they had elected politicians who would represent them.

The overlapping, messy police and local government jurisdictions, researched in particular detail by Elinor and her colleagues, provided one empirical test for this view (Ostrom *et al.* 1978). They provided a market-like alternative, because with numerous institutions, citizens might be in a position to choose the one that they most favoured. They were also decentralised, which made them more responsive to local people rather than centralised bureaucracies. Finally, messy overlap created a potential separation of powers, and a constitutional mix that made dominance by an elite more difficult.

Vincent Ostrom also argued that constitutions, at all levels of society, needed to be living things open to change. A constitution established the rules of the game, and indeed, as we have seen, can be studied using game theory. However, the good intentions of constitution writers can be perverted, and rent-seeking behaviour might be encouraged by a constitutional arrangement. Local elites could take control and political machines might squeeze out democratic input. A formal constitution may give rise to informal systems of inefficiency and tyranny. Therefore, constitutions needed to be flexible and verified by empirical evidence. Rather than accepting broad philosophical principles, Vincent Ostrom believed in logical analysis and empirical investigation. He was also inspired in this regard by the experimental approach of the American pragmatist tradition, particularly in the work of John Dewey (V. Ostrom 1997: 10). The Ostroms' student Filippo Sabetti noted:

> In the fall of 1968, I took my first graduate course with Vincent Ostrom. The course was based on readings derived largely from classical texts on

> America and the first generation of public choice scholars. It was not an easy course for me not just because that was my first introduction to readings like *The Federalist, Democracy in America, Leviathan, The Calculus of Consent* and *The Logic of Collective Action* but also because I was confronted with a novel approach to these texts. It was the approach to pursue the logic of the propositions as testable hypotheses (at least by experience, if not by rigorous field research) that set Vincent's teaching apart. No one read these books as he did.
>
> (Sabetti 2011: 74)

Buchanan's notion of 'politics without romance' runs through both Elinor and Vincent's work, but there is an important change of emphasis. Buchanan meant that we should not be idealistic about politicians, because those involved in politics were likely to be self-interested. Greed and corruption might mark a political system. Buchanan's approach suggests the need for small government, constitutional limits and a fear of political actors. While Vincent Ostrom could be said to have embraced 'politics without romance', he rejected the model of rational economic man put forward by Buchanan. As we have noted in previous chapters, the Ostroms were believers in bounded rather than perfect rationality. To the extent that humans engage in politics to maximise their personal benefit, they do so with only partial information. Some institutional economists argue that institutions are important because they make it easier to gather and transmit information. Equally, both Elinor and Vincent rejected the idea that pure self-interest was the only relevant motive for political action. States were neither servants of humanity nor cruel exploiters:

> It would be irresponsibly cynical to presume that all states are monstrous birds of prey devouring their own subjects. On the other hand, it may also be irresponsibly naive to presume that all states are benevolent creations that can always be relied upon to correct the ills of society and to get the prices right, so to speak. It is essential to address the reality that exists in human societies.
>
> (V. Ostrom 1999: 184)

For the Ostroms, politicians were no better or worse than the rest of us. Political actors who include, at best, members of entire communities, have both good and bad motives. Power issues were endemic but people were neither simply angels nor devils. Political activity could not be based on the assumption of innate cooperative qualities but a conservative belief in moral failure was also wrong, as human beings have the potential to come together for meaningful association. The Ostroms believed this might be difficult to pursue but that it was necessary to try. In their view, good political rule making provided the basis of freedom, and a libertarian or anarchist view that rejected the need for governance was just as dangerous as political centralization. Democracy was based on sets of rules that were decided by participation, different sets of rules overlapped, and democracy was a process, never a final product. The aspiration for a society without rules was seen as unrealistic and undesirable. A rigidly centralised system whether based in formal terms on liberal democracy, state socialism or any other stated ideological basis, was seen as authoritarian and something to be resisted. Vincent Ostrom went so far as to claim that any relationship between rulers and the ruled was a Faustian bargain and he rejected the very concept of sovereignty, based solely on rule by one group or individual, as an undemocratic imposition (V. Ostrom 1997: 141).

While Vincent Ostrom was not a member of the traditional left, he was also far from being a conservative. His radically democratic ideas informed Elinor's work, and her work in turn enriched his constitutional thinking. For those on the left who defend common pool property, the Ostroms' political approach is important for at least two reasons. First, it provides a warning against forms of liberation that can become stifling. Second, it makes us think about the construction of a living, radically democratic system for the governance of human society and the interaction between human society and the wider natural environment. While it might surprise both parties, there are many parallels between the Ostroms' political theories and that of Marxist defenders of the commons such as the authors Michael Hardt and Toni Negri. In fact, both Marxist and non-Marxist advocates of the commons draw upon traditions of republican political thought which demand discussion if we are to understand the political orientation of both Elinor and Vincent Ostrom.

From the republic to the commons

Republicanism has varied associations – from opposition to monarchy to the US Republican Party – but is derived from the Latin term *res publica*, referring to the public realm or more literally 'public thing'. The public realm, also often translated as 'commonwealth', can be contrasted with private property and individual interests. Vincent Ostrom believed in republican government rather than a state ruled by a monarch or an elite of any kind. He saw the efforts of the US constitution makers outlined in texts like *The Federalist Papers* as highly inspiring. US citizens constructed a constitution that they hoped would be democratic, avoid domination by a majority and guarantee human rights.

Michael Hardt and Antonio Negri, like the Ostroms, are fascinated by the commons and suspicious of centralised states and power concentrations. They are also strongly associated with Autonomist Marxism, the strain of Marxism which focusses most on the concept of the commons, or in their work 'the common', both as a resource and a property relation. Michael Hardt is a US literary theorist, while Antonio Negri is a philosopher and former political prisoner. Their wider body of intellectual work cannot be easily summarised here, drawing as it does on Marx, post-structuralist thinkers like Foucault and republican political thinkers. However it is worth discussing some shared themes from their thought and that of the Ostroms. Republican political thought can be linked to the micro politics of the management of shared things. They noted:

> The American Revolution and the 'new political science' proclaimed by the authors of the Federalist broke from the tradition of modern sovereignty, 'returning to origins' and at the same time developing new languages and new social forms that mediate between the one and the multiple.
>
> (Hardt and Negri 2000: 161)

Both Vincent Ostrom and Negri and Hardt were enthusiastic about the existence and growth of self-governed European city states in the late medieval period. Such 'free cities' emerged as partially democratic alternatives within a feudal system. An important political thinker associated with self-governing cities was, of course, the controversial Florentine author, diplomat and political philosopher Niccolò Machiavelli (1469–1527).

Machiavelli is associated most with his tract *The Prince*, which advises a ruler how to retain power (Skinner 1981). Vincent Ostrom explicitly rejected the 'moral connotations' of *The Prince* (V. Ostrom 1997: ix). The word 'Machiavellian' is a byword for political manipulation but Machiavelli also wrote extensively on republican politics. He was a passionate supporter of the independence of his home city state, Florence, which expelled the ruling Medici family in 1494 and restored self-government. He served as Secretary to the Second Chancery of the Republic of Florence but was imprisoned and tortured when the Medicis returned in 1512. Florence had a rather varied and unstable constitutional history. Originally a Roman city, it became a republic in the twelfth century. Machiavelli viewed self-rule as superior to rule by a monarch or aristocracy. The late fifteenth century saw the emergence of the Renaissance, when Greek and Roman texts were read again and learning flourished. Machiavelli wrote *Discourses on Livy* which examined the political history of the ancient Roman republic. He advocated a democratic politics, a system of checks and balances on power and other elements, which were later included in the US constitution.

Political commentators such as J.G.A. Pocock (2003) and Quentin Skinner (1998) note that Machiavelli's work inspired English revolutionaries in the seventeenth century. During the English civil war and its immediate aftermath, radicals such as those who gathered for the Putney debates proclaimed their desire for a republic. Republican ideas travelled to America where, as Negri and Hardt note, 'republican Machiavellianism that, after having inspired the protagonists of the English Revolution, was reconstructed in the Atlantic exodus among European democrats who were defeated but not vanquished' (Hardt and Negri 2000: 162).

Like Vincent Ostrom, Negri and Hardt were enthusiastic about the resulting constitution. Despite the religious references in the US constitution and *The Federalist*, this was a secular constitution that recognised no transcendent power outside of humanity but was based on the sovereignty of free individuals.

For Hardt and Negri, the numerous examples of common property systems to manage common resources, and the republican constitution of the US, were different facets of a common phenomenon: the ability of humans to come together to create systems of self-governance. They see Marx's work as based not on the drive to create a centralised state but on the demand for universal self-government. The republican demand that no individual should live at the behest of another can be linked to Marx's politics. They also note that Machiavelli held that social conflict was inevitable; different groups in society would have different demands that could not be easily reconciled. This meant that constitution making was a product of conflict. As such, politics could never be fixed but would always be in a state of flux.

Their summary of his republican views coincides strongly with the constitutional approach of Vincent Ostrom, which of course is unsurprising, given that both Machiavelli and Ostrom adhered to a republican politics of self-government:

> For Machiavelli, power is always republican; it is always the product of the life of the multitude and constitutes its fabric of expression. The free city of Renaissance humanism is the utopia that anchors this revolutionary principle. The second Machiavellian principle at work here is that the social base of this democratic sovereignty is always conflictual. Power is organized through the emergence and the interplay of counterpowers. The city is thus a constituent power that is formed through plural social conflicts articulated in continuous constitutional processes. This is how Machiavelli read the organization of republican ancient Rome, and this is how the Renaissance notion of the city served as the foundation for a realist political theory and practice: social conflict is the basis of the stability of power and the logic of the city's expansion. Machiavelli's thought inaugurated a Copernican revolution that reconfigured politics as perpetual movement. These are the primary teachings that the Atlantic doctrine of democracy derived from the republican Machiavelli.
>
> (Hardt and Negri 2000: 181–2)

According to Vincent Ostrom, political order was dependent on shared norms. Formal rules and often informal and local constitutions were vital but without shared assumptions, governance would be difficult. This touches on another of Machiavelli's principles, that civic virtue was a political necessity. While Machiavelli felt that a prince or political leader might need to take a pragmatic approach, without civic virtue a political institution was unlikely to survive. The authors of the American constitution also had such an understanding. Vincent Ostrom argued that a shared sense of cultural norms also demanded a consideration of the role of language to governance. In turn, Elinor Ostrom's work shows the importance of shared norms for maintaining commons and social-ecological systems. Institutional economists have often noted the importance of norms in maintaining economic activity.

In short, unsurprisingly perhaps, both institutionalist and anti-capitalist approaches to the commons advocate republican democracy. This does not necessarily clarify either the problem of commons management or the assault on the commons by elite groups. However the idea that either Elinor or Vincent

Ostrom's approach is somehow either apolitical or conservative can be safely rejected.

While the commons can be seen as literally *'res publica'* or public space and the radical democracy of republicanism is attractive, it is also problematic. The American constitution, as its critics noted, was the republicanism of a conquering minority (Losurdo 2011). Republicanism, paradoxically or not, has also been associated with imperialism. For example, the US state was based on an open expansionary frontier that, of course, absorbed the property of indigenous people. The federalists learnt from ancient Rome, which they saw not just as a republican but equally as an expanding imperial regime. Implicit in Machiavelli's work is patriotism for one's own republic and a demand for expansion.

Elinor and Vincent Ostrom, to their credit, have been critical of the eurocentric nature of much political discourse. The republic was too often a republic for a minority; the US constitution excluded indigenous and African-Americans. The ancient republics were male and excluded slaves and, in most cases, foreigners. Vincent Ostrom noted the importance of religious principles, such as the golden rule of treating others as you would wish to be treated yourself, derived from the Bible. However, he was at great pains to note that these principles were common to Christianity, Judaism and Islam. He noted the importance of political thought in traditional African society and from many other parts of the globe (V. Ostrom 1997). Self-government is not just for a minority.

Republics, paradoxically, given their name, have defended private property as part of a project to protect the rights of those who are citizens but have ignored alternative forms of property ownership. Instead of defending a spectrum of property rights including forms of common pool property, they have often tended to absorb and destroy commons. The founders of the US constitution borrowed the notion of a mixed constitution from the Roman author Polybius, which they saw as valuable for creating a political system that was diverse, balanced and resistant to corruption (Hardt and Negri 2000: 163). In a similar way, Vincent Ostrom can be seen as advocating a mixed constitution of property rights including state, private and communal property. Yet in the twentieth-first century land grabs continue to take communal property. The micro politics of management is vital to maintain commons, and as we have seen, is based on a demand for radical democracy, yet there is also a macro politics that needs to be conceptualised if commons are to survive.

The politics of the commons

Elinor Ostrom's work is highly political in one sense but can be seen as lacking political understanding when viewed from other angles. For Elinor Ostrom, the management of common pool resources involves negotiation between individuals. Conflict is built into the operation of the commons, because if one person gains more from a resource another may receive less. Such a zero gain assumption fits with Buchanan and Tullock's description of political constitution making. Politics is about resources, and constitutions are arrangements that acknowledge this fact. Rather than waving away such potential conflict and assuming automatic consensus, commoners need to find ways of dealing with self-interest, which if left unchecked has the potential to destroy the commons. Paradoxically, the pursuit of individual self-interest, as in the standard Nash equilibrium assumed in game theory, leads to a reduction in individual gains. *Governing the Commons* was the title of Elinor Ostrom's best-known book and looks at the governance of such resources. Governance describes the pursuit of politics.

Elinor Ostrom's work is, perhaps, innately political. She was both a political economist and an institutional economist. While her academic career might have been very different if she had been allowed to complete a PhD in economics, her work assumes that economics cannot be separated from institutions which govern our actions. The institutional analysis and development framework she developed with Vincent Ostrom and other colleagues maps power. Her wider normative concern with radical democracy grew from Vincent's analysis of constitution making. While he recognised that governance occurred throughout society and not just at a state level, Elinor developed this understanding through empirical case studies and experimental work. Both moved far beyond the starting point of the US constitution. Their micro politics mirrors that of Foucault (1980) where he indicated that power was constitutive and found everywhere.

Yet she seemed silent when it came to a macro politics of class conflict and corporate power that destroys the commons. Physical commons covering land and seas have been enclosed by force on many occasions. For example, indigenous peoples across the planet saw their communal property seized by colonialists. The seizure of commons continues in the twenty-first century, along with increasing commodification, to the extent that private property rights cover genetic material, so that it can be bought and sold (Bollier 2003). While the Ostroms saw value in a mixed system of property ownership combining private, state and collective forms of property, common pool property seems under threat of extinction. Such battles extend to the knowledge commons. The World Wide Web was established as a commons, we don't pay for each click, but large corporate bodies seek to commodify knowledge and culture, to put it behind walls, so that it can be bought and sold.

Above all, commodification is leading to the erosion of social-ecological systems. Elinor Ostrom was clearly concerned with promoting environmental sustainability, yet while communities and states might have difficulties in balancing conservation and production, a major threat is commerce. Oil and gas companies have the funds to influence the policymaking agenda, and serious action on climate change is limited because of their lobbying (Hoggan 2009). Powerful economic lobbies can shape what is possible. The Institutional Analysis and Development framework does not always seem to scale up to take into account such pressures. This is perhaps because the term capitalism, and the notion that there are wider structural forces shaping society, are absent from Elinor Ostrom's analysis.

Elinor Ostrom was clearly critical of socialism if it was top-down and statist. The Hayek caution that a plan from the centre cannot address local realities is worth taking seriously. Statism is far from being the fundamental issue. The Ostroms, after all, accepted a role for the state, and socialist politics can come in libertarian forms. Methodological individualism versus structuralism cuts to a perhaps more fundamental debate. Sex, race, gender and class influence society beyond the decision-making of individuals. Individuals act within a particular context and may be constrained in the choices that they make. The line of argument that takes us from Machiavelli's discussion of civic virtues, to Vincent Ostrom's emphasis on shared cultural meaning, to Elinor Ostrom's discussion of norms, seems to invite a macro approach. William Cronon's study of New England provides an implicit critique of Elinor Ostrom's assumptions. Cronon, in his pioneering environmental history book *Changes in the Land*, contrasted the social and ecological realities of the indigenous and the colonialists (Cronon 1983).

The indigenous and the colonialists can be internally subdivided; neither group is a uniform block. A minority of colonialists were, for example, sympathetic to the indigenous. Both groups have agency, individuals in both diverse communities made decisions and sought to shape their own futures. However, the analysis of Elinor Ostrom would seem limited in explaining how they behave, if it focussed purely on incentives, resources and payoffs. The two communities lived in different ways, had different economic systems, their attitudes to their environment were different and their effects on ecosystems were radically distinct. Cronon does not romanticise the indigenous, they did not live in a pristine wilderness but changed their environments radically, for example, through burning vegetation.

Neither group were able to sit down and negotiate a compromise or think about the most effective way of sustaining the environment. Their behaviour could not be explained, alone, by a form of game theory or rational model. While they were not prisoners of deterministic social forces, an analysis that focusses on individual interactions seems inadequate to capture how they functioned. They were part of societies that structured their reality, therefore pre-existing assumptions shaped what was possible. This was perhaps most obvious in terms of property rights; indigenous attitudes to land were alien to the colonialists. Likewise, colonial attitudes to land and the non-human environment were mysterious to the indigenous.

Individuals live in societies in which norms derived from the actions of previous individuals accumulate. Such norms interact with environmental and economic factors and shape the decisions that can be made. Given European assumptions about property, progress and 'nature', it was almost impossible for the colonialists to recognize the worth of indigenous approaches. One cannot simply switch off assumptions that are derived from the wider society in which we live. The indigenous felt that it was absurd to own land but recognised usufruct rights. Notions of property ownership on the part of Europeans were based around John Locke's principle that those who worked land could become its owners. Locke's assumptions were based on much wider and deeper traditions. Norms can be conceptualised along with rules as elements of institutions but institutions may have such weight as to shape individual action to a larger extent than is assumed by Ostrom and other institutionalist researchers.

Elinor Ostrom's approach to governance is attractive and useful. Attractive, because it respects our ability, as individuals to make decisions, to overcome conflict and to deepen democratic control. It is useful because it helps practically to overcome difficult governance dilemmas. However, its basis in methodological individualism is also flawed. Wider power structures and social forces always shape what is possible in a given social situation. It is clear that she was aware of this potential weakness and noted on several occasions the need for different levels of analysis. Social-ecological systems were tiered and needed to be investigated on different levels. Elinor, of course, moved from the micro to the macro, rather than the other way around. Macro sociological work is problematic because it obscures local variation. It is also inadequate because it suggests that human beings have little or no agency. Methodological individualism suggests that people ultimately have complete freedom.

The balance between the two approaches is a problem for all researchers investigating human society; it is not unique to Elinor Ostrom. Economists in general have made naive assumptions about human reality by failing to see changing but influential social structures. Structuralist and positivist forms of Marxism have substituted history for individual action and, at their worst, reduced human beings to puppets, mere bearers of social and economic positions. Institutional economists, in their enormous diversity from Veblen to Commons and Buchanan, have seen institutions of various forms as influential. Thus, even such a strongly market-based institutionalist as James Buchanan was perhaps more sophisticated and open to the issue of agency versus structure than 'mainstream' economists. To what extent do institutions become structures that mould human behaviour, and to what extent are we free as individuals to remake our institutions?

Elinor Ostrom made this point clear in her discussion of Ernst Mayr's title *The Growth of Biological Thought* (Mayr 1982). She noted how challenging Mayr's description of 'emergence' was to her own theoretical work. In the field of biology, explanation is inadequate if it works purely from the assumption that basic individual units can be studied. Cells cannot be explained purely by examining molecules; animals cannot be understood by solely examining cells; and ecosystems cannot be understood only by studying individual species, let alone their molecules. 'Emergence' refers to the fact that qualitatively different levels grow from previous levels. In other words, microanalysis is no substitute for macroanalysis. Elinor Ostrom was fascinated by biology and saw the biological as one, non-deterministic but shaping influence on human action. She noted that social science must also deal with this problem of 'emergence':

> I was raised on methodological individualism and the mantra 'the individual is *the* basic unit of analysis' was solidly pounded into my head. Therefore, coming from that scholarly tradition, reading Mayr's discussion was a major shock. Mayr was of course reacting to the presumption made by physical

> scientists that could reduce all biology to chemistry and physics since underlying any living system were chemical and physical elements. [...] By stressing that phenomena did not simply add up from the basic units to a system level, he was careful not to reject the importance of examining lower levels as well as higher levels of analysis.
>
> (Ostrom 2004: 44)

She noted that Douglas Hofstadter (1979) in *Gödel, Escher, Bach* discussed this issue of moving from the micro to the macro by posing the question of whether a detailed investigation of the neuronal structure of a brain could be used to predict poetry. She wrote of this:

> Reading the two books side by side made me rethink the problem of emergence in the social realm. If it took seven to ten layers to go all the way from neurons within the brain to creative structures within the mind, how many layers would it take to go all the way from an individual to a large scale society?
>
> (Ostrom 2004: 44)

Emergence is, perhaps, a potentially misleading term with which to discuss human social action. The British institutional economist Geoffrey Hodgson (2000) argues that institutions do not only emerge from the social action of human individuals, but also affect those human actions. Macro structures, whether theorised as institutions, social classes or other collective aspects of human existence, shape the 'lower levels'. Further complexity arises because different tiers of social existence interact dynamically in different ways. The notion that structures are constitutive and shape individuals, rather than emerging from preceding layers, is implicit in the work of both Elinor and Vincent. After all this is why, paradoxically, it is so important that individuals become conscious about constitution building. If institutions are conceived as sets of rules, these rules enable some forms of behaviour and constrain others. Thus they shape individuals, so individuals need to shape them. One way of viewing methodological individualism is to assume that it is a goal worthy of attainment, not a 'given'. Greater individual control is possible, but individualism may be under threat from institutions. Institutions cannot be done away with, but self-governance can be used to craft them consciously and democratically. From this perspective, the work of the Ostroms parallels some of Marx's thoughts on the relationship between structural forces and individualism. Marx largely ignored micro politics, while Elinor Ostrom never used concepts such as social class and capitalism. This, of course, causes disquiet amongst some commons activists who tend to come from the political left, and explains the divergence between Ostrom's work and Marxist-inspired discussion of property rights and common pool resources. That great Marxist scholar of the commons E.P. Thompson also worked hard to oppose structuralist interpretations of Marx's work, which he felt disposed of human action and made us prisoners of structuralism, in his polemic against the anti-humanist French philosopher Althusser (Thompson 1978).

Elinor Ostrom was aware of various forms of sociological compromise, such as Giddens' 'structuration', that combine levels of individual agency and social structure, citing his book *Central Problems in Social Theory: Action, Structure and Contradictions in Social Analysis* in *Governing the Commons* (Ostrom 1990: 253). None of these sociological compromises provide a neat and convincing answer to the issue, yet analysis that has no place for human agency seems inadequate. Human beings are capable of changing their behaviour but do so within a particular context. She believed that education was important to promote such self-governance:

> [...] the image of citizens we provide in out textbooks that presume rational citizens will be passive consumers of political life – the masses – and focus primarily on the role of politicians and officials at a national level – the elite – do not inform future citizens of a democratic polity of the actions they need to know and can undertake. While many political scientists claim to eschew teaching the normative foundations of a democratic polity, they actually introduce a norm of cynicism and distrust without providing a vision of how citizens could do anything to challenge corruption, rent seeking, or poorly designed policies.
>
> (Ostrom 1998: 3)

The politics of commons and contestation

Writing with Charlotte Hess, Elinor Ostrom noted that the history of enclosure was important to an understanding of threats to the knowledge commons. Yet while they observed that 'the narrative of enclosure is one of privatization, the haves versus the have-nots, the elite versus the masses', such statements were rare (Hess and Ostrom 2011: 12). While commons activists might criticise Elinor Ostrom for a failure to look at how issues such as class and capitalist economic structures impacted on the commons, she was well aware that macro elements were of theoretical and practical relevance. However, as a cautious scholar, she was unwilling to make judgements in areas where she had not undertaken research or read extensively. That she did not fully develop the layers of social analysis relevant to understand a society is an important silence. Just as no single scholar or group of scholars can investigate all relevant dimensions, nor can knowledge be explored effectively by just one school of thought. The 'law of the hammer' once again applies and Elinor Ostrom was open to development of her framework.

Yet in a world where powerful forces are destroying the commons and centralizing political and economic influence, Elinor Ostrom's work can seem curiously apolitical. Detailed analysis of case study situations may ignore battles at another level that threaten the commons under examination. The problem which is not easy to address is how to bring together the micro and the macro politics of the commons. Elinor Ostrom was aware of this issue. Her approach to politics was material and focussed. While informed by sophisticated social theory, she saw her academic work as practical. Political institutions were artifacts made by human action, like chairs or sausages or websites. The material had certain structural properties but could be adapted by human action. She assumed that a greater understanding of structural factors, so as to make them more visible, might lead to more effective artisanship. We know that she was keen to advance her work. If perhaps she had another 40 years, she might have integrated the microanalysis into a more developed macro approach. Indeed, the IAD framework would have allowed this integration, and is flexible enough to deal with new perspectives. It is clear that she would have valued the debate, and clearer still that she was cautious about intellectual claims that were not based on thorough empirical research combined with strong theoretical engagement. She moved some way away from assumptions of unmediated methodological individualism during her career, noting:

> Like good geographic maps, the IAD framework can be presented at scales ranging from the exceedingly fine-grained to extremely broad-grained. Human decision making is the result of many layers of internal processing [...]. Building on top of the single individual are structures composed of multiple individuals – families, firms, industries, nations, and many other units – themselves composed of many parts and, in turn, parts of still larger structures.
>
> (Ostrom 2005: 11)

While she was keen to avoid polemical statements, we must not forget she and Vincent were driven by a quest to understand how all of us, as admittedly fallible human beings, can create better systems of governance and maintain resilient, diverse social-ecological systems. Quietly spoken, she would on occasions bristle with indignation, which would fuel not anger but patient inquiry. In an interview with Margaret Levi, she noted how listening to Garrett Hardin link his 'tragedy of the commons' notion to his concern with overpopulation and the need for strong measures, revived her passion for the commons:

> I heard Garrett Hardin give a lecture, Hardin gave a speech on the IU [Indiana University, Bloomington] campus, and I went to it, [...] he really was worried about population.
>
> He indicated that every man and every woman should be sterilized after they have one child. He was very serious about it. [...] I was somewhat taken aback: 'My theory proves that we should do this,' and people said, 'Well, don't you think that that's a little severe?' 'No! That's what we should do, or we're sunk.'
>
> Well, he, in my mind, became a totalitarian. I, thus, had seen a real instance where his theory didn't work.
>
> (Ostrom in Annual Reviews Conversations 2010: 8)

In the next and final chapter I will attempt to summarize Elinor Ostrom's contribution to 'theory' that does work, examining the extent to which she promoted a sustainable economics and looking at how sympathetic critics have tried to answer some of the questions posed in this chapter.

9 A new science for a new world?

> A danger always exists that theories may proliferate to such an extent that reasoning through logical inferences is abandoned and replaced by a process of naming different theories and writing narratives about theory. The study of theory then can become little more than interesting stories about the lives, loves, and miscellaneous thoughts of political philosophers or the quaintness of different sets of ideas. We spend a great deal of time *talking about* theory and surprisingly little effort in the use of political theory. Scholars should know how to *use* theory and to do theory, not just *talk* theory.
>
> (V.Ostrom 1989: 17)

Introduction

Any interpretation of Elinor Ostrom's work is likely to be a misinterpretation. This is because she, like Vincent Ostrom, was not concerned about comparing and contrasting different schools of thought. She rejected interpretation, if interpretation meant talking about theory rather than developing and using theory. She was not interested in discussing varied discourses, instead she wanted to achieve practical results. Therefore any summary of her contribution must focus on practical consequences. In this concluding chapter, I can't wholly avoid interpretation but I am aware that a book like this tends to fall into what she would have seen as a trap. It is fascinating, of course, to relate her ideas to those of others.

Much of this book has been a narrative rather than a set of 'logical inferences', this is necessary to some extent, to make it easier to understand the kind of work that Elinor Ostrom was trying to achieve. In concluding I argue that, despite being best known for her work on common pool resources, she went beyond the commons with an emphasis on diverse forms of property and governance. In doing so she promoted a sustainable economics in the sense of an economics which is more sophisticated than the current mainstream, and an economics that deals seriously with ecological problems.

A number of commentators have looked at how her work might be developed practically in the future. Paul Dragos Aligică and Peter Boettke have argued that the Ostroms' institutional analysis is a bold challenge to prevailing social science. They suggest that the Ostroms drew upon a largely liberal tradition, from thinkers such as Adam Smith, to create a new intellectual challenge (Aligică and Boettke 2009).

The Marxist geographer David Harvey has, perhaps unsurprisingly, critiqued some of the features of the Ostroms' work that more Austrian influenced thinkers such as Aligică and Boettke (2009) value most, questioning aspects of polycentricism (Harvey 2012). Eoin Flaherty has engaged in a more detailed examination of the value of Marxist and social-ecological systems approaches to understanding the rundale, an Irish common pool property system. The difficult issues of conflict, power, structure and agency in regard to Elinor Ostroms work have been recurrent themes in this book. Arun Agrawal, a former student of the Ostroms has sought to bring Elinor Ostrom's institutional research together with other forms of political ecology, and the work of Foucault (Agrawal 2005).

These critiques and commentaries, although contradictory, would probably have been welcomed by Elinor Ostrom. Indeed she praised Aligică and Boettke's work and read drafts of Agrawal's book *Environmentality*. In particular she would have valued their practical applications to her work. Boettke and his colleagues stress the value of Elinor Ostrom's research methods particularly in the form of case studies (Boettke *et al.* 2013). Agrawal's work is both theoretically sophisticated, unusually drawing upon a French philosopher (Foucault) rather than a Scottish one (Hume or Adam Smith), but rests upon very detailed empirical work and institutional analysis. While not presented as a critique of Ostrom's work, Eoin Flaherty's examination of the Irish rundales, as social-ecological systems, is a study of common pool property regimes that utilizes both Marx and Ostrom (Flaherty 2012). While Ostrom did not engage with Marx, I am sure she would have appreciated Flaherty's empirical work, combining historical analysis and ecological resilience theory. I conclude by asking to what extent her work can provide 'a new science for a new age'.

Aligică and Boettke on challenging institutional analysis and development

Aligică and Boettke (2009) produced the first detailed study of the work of Elinor and Vincent Ostrom under the title *Challenging Institutional Analysis and Development*. They stress the challenge of the Ostroms' work to mainstream economics and its opposition to the binary state versus market division. They also stress the methodological strengths of the Ostroms' work, noting their challenge to purely mathematical analysis and their belief that language and culture are important. They conceptualise the Ostroms as working with a paradox. The Ostroms were radical in that they rejected the idea that politics is principally about government and sought to introduce new methodological approaches. Yet despite such apparent novelty, their research was rooted in the thought of political philosophers in the eighteenth century such as Hume, Adam Smith, Locke and Hobbes. These thinkers debated the problems of governance and are central to the Ostroms' work according to Aligică and Boettke. The Ostroms' relationship with public choice theory and state-sceptical approaches is outlined. In more recent work, Boettke and his colleagues have emphasised the value they see in Elinor Ostrom's use of case studies linking her perspective on the need for self-governance with her methodological approach (Boettke *et al.* 2013).

Challenging Institutional Analysis and Development is an impressive outline of the Ostroms' work with a particularly strong account of their methodological assumptions but contains a number of weaknesses. It focusses mainly on the work of Vincent Ostrom and has very little to say about the area of common pool property and common pool resources. It surprisingly makes no mention of John R. Commons' influence on the Ostroms and makes little mention of the importance of Herbert Simon to their work. The power issues around commons and the effects of enclosure are wholly ignored. The book rightly stresses the central notion of craftwork in the Ostroms' approach but tends to focus on a number of key thinkers as providing the Ostroms' tools. It is, of course, impossible to understand the Ostroms' ideas without Tocqueville and Buchanan. Nonetheless if we look at Elinor Ostrom's practice, a very wide range of influences are apparent and her work has extended into new areas such as social-ecological systems, where reliance on classical liberal theorists is insufficient. Boettke's arguments around the significance of methodological individualism and spontaneity have been challenged by Michael McGinnis from the Ostrom workshop (McGinnis 2005).

Elinor Ostrom's work was constantly evolving and while it is important to understand its origins, she was interested in practical work rather than ideological relationships. While Aligică and Boettke have produced an insightful analysis of the Ostroms' work, they seem less focussed on looking at potential weaknesses and how Elinor Ostrom's quest to understand sustainable governance could be extended. Recently, Aligică has noted:

> Yet, surprisingly often, despite Ostrom's explicit and persistent efforts to disentangle the idea of collective action from that of 'The State,' and to demonstrate that successful collective action doesn't need a Leviathan, one finds her work invoked to support state-sponsored arrangements, wrapped in vague notions of 'democracy' and 'participation,' all having nothing to do with the spirit or the letter of that work. All done, by all accounts, in good faith. The power of the 'seeing like a state' *forma mentis* among an important part of the relevant epistemic community is profound [...] the Ostroms' attempt to follow up on the public-choice revolution's insights, and to try to move studies of governance away from a state-centered view to a pluralist and polycentric one, remains a work in progress, one that sounds as radical today as it did thirty years ago.
>
> (Aligică (3 July 2013))

Critics might also suggest that while Aligică and Boettke warn against calls for paternalistic state action, falsely justified by a misreading of Elinor Ostrom's texts, they have less to say about power relations, conflict or inequality. However, there is no doubt that Aligică and Boettke appreciate the importance of Elinor Ostrom's legacy, as Aligică notes in his most recent work:

> Elinor Ostrom's work remains an enterprise of unassuming radicalism that persistently invites us to reconsider the very foundations and significance of our scientific efforts. Following the logic of institutional diversity, social heterogeneity, and value pluralism to their epistemic and normative implications, Ostrom's work both closes a cycle of research on collective action, institutions, and governance and frames the next stage or the next cycle of research.
>
> (Aligică (3 July 2013))

David Harvey's challenge to polycentricism

The geographer David Harvey comes to Elinor Ostrom's work from a Marxist perspective. Unsurprisingly, his evaluation contrasts strongly with Aligică and Boettke's. His book *Rebel Cities* (Harvey 2012) places the institution of the common or commons at the centre of his analysis of contemporary capitalism. He examines how cities can be imagined as an urban commons and praises Elinor Ostrom's work in *Governing the Commons* for challenging the 'tragedy of the commons' thesis (Harvey 2012). However her use of polycentricism at an urban level attracts his critical eye. He notes that challenging monocentricism is popular, centralised political organisations are increasingly rejected but he argues that decentralisation can lead to inequality and may be actively encouraged in neo-liberal systems because of this. Yet the target of his critique is less Ostrom and more activists on the left who reject the need for hierarchy. He argues that her work on local government rested upon the Tiebout hypothesis. In his 1956 paper the economist Charles Tiebout argued that citizens would shop for the best local government deal, moving to a new area if there were better services. One of the attractions of polycentricism is that it creates choice, encouraging local authorities to compete, like firms in a market, to provide public services. The danger of this, according to Harvey, is that richer people can move more easily and poorer areas become progressively worse off. Decentralization means that more affluent local government areas can hold on to their cash, promoting greater inequality. Richer areas of New York or London, under polycentric systems, will fail to help poorer areas, whose living standards will decline. Harvey argues, therefore, that a measure of centralisation at least in financial matters is vital but he sees much value in decentralisation, diversity and commons. His more profound argument seems to be with the autonomist Marxists, anarchists and Occupy activists:

> Decentralization and autonomy are primary vehicles for producing greater inequality through neoliberalization. Thus, in New York State, the unequal provision of public education services across jurisdictions with radically

> different financial resources has been deemed by the courts as unconstitutional, and the state is under court order to move towards greater equalization of educational provision. It has failed to do so, and now uses the fiscal emergency as a further excuse to delay action. But note well, it is the higher-order and hierarchically determined mandate of the state courts that is crucial in mandating greater equality of treatment as a constitutional right. [...]
>
> How can radical decentralization – surely a worthwhile objective – work without constituting some higher-order hierarchical authority? It is simply naïve to believe that polycentrism or any other form of decentralization can work without strong hierarchical constraints and active enforcement. Much of the radical left – particularly of an anarchist and autonomist persuasion – has no answer to this problem.
>
> (Harvey 2012: 83–4)

He also argues that central action and even enclosure of fragile environments like the Amazon might be necessary, if global ecological problems are to be solved:

> It will take a draconian act of enclosure in Amazonia, for example, to protect both biodiversity and the cultures of indigenous populations as part of our global natural and cultural commons. It will almost certainly require state authority to protect those commons against the philistine democracy of short-term moneyed interests ravaging the land with soy bean and cattle ranching.
>
> (Harvey 2012: 70)

However, Harvey does acknowledge that the both Vincent and Elinor Ostrom accepted the need for tiers of organisation to overcome potential inequality and other problems. His critique can in turn, be criticised, in that there is no necessary reason why higher level authorities will act automatically to redistribute or promote ecological sustainability. The Ostroms and their colleagues were aware that markets produced serious problems but were are also conscious that regulation was not a magic bullet. Central authorities might promote inequality and coercion and might lack the local knowledge necessary to implement effective policies, even if they were so inclined. Typically writing with Marco Janssen, Elinor Ostrom noted that rather than the state coming to the rescue of the Amazon or other threatened rainforests, as Harvey suggests, it can act to aid the roving bandits, often accepting bribes from corporation and plundering resources. She and Janssen observed, 'Many reasons can be cited for this lack of effectiveness and sustainability. One is the excessive faith in the neutrality of centralised governments' (Ostrom and Janssen 2004: 254).

Harvey notes approvingly that the green anarchist Murray Bookchin advocated a confederal system that combined the direct democracy of township meetings with delegates to regional bodies (Harvey 2012: 85). Elinor Ostrom noted that institutions at a variety of levels were necessary but was reluctant to pre-judge how these would work best. While Harvey's discussion of urban commons and critique of polycentricism can be challenged, it provides an agenda for further research. Despite the diametrically opposed ideological positions of Harvey and Aligică and Boettke, both perspectives acknowledge value in institutional diversity. For thinkers like Aligică and Boettke, the challenge is that markets can be seen evolving to homogenous corporate control, which might demand action to prevent a concentration of power. For Harvey the state might be seen as doing likewise. The Ostroms advocated both decentralised and, on occasions, more centralist governance structures. While *Governing the Commons* examined local commons, Elinor Ostrom and her associates saw local environments as nested within larger systems. Indeed the concept of social-ecological systems works on the basis that different systems interact and sustainability needs to be examined from the perspective of different tiers of analysis:

> [...] the hot debates about opposites – small-scale versus large-scale, centralised versus decentralised, top-down versus bottom-up – lead nowhere. Resilient adaptive systems need attributes of all of the above. What we do need is careful empirical research that helps us to better understand how multi-level or polycentric governance systems work, how they adapt over time, what are the major threats to their continued resilience and how we can build even better resilient, learning, complex systems in the future.
>
> (Ostrom and Janssen 2004: 255)

The problem with Harvey's critique is that the Ostroms were perhaps obsessively concerned with systems of governance rather than asserting a blanket demand to reject all hierarchy. To my mind, a more significant criticism is Elinor Ostrom's failure to analyse capitalism, explicitly, as a source of the destruction of the commons. I think it is here that Marxist thinkers like Harvey potentially are at their strongest. While it would move beyond the remit of this title to examine his work in detail, E.P.Thompson seems closest to combining a Marxist analysis of the enclosure of the commons with an Ostrom-like concern with governance. One thinker who has taken perspectives from Marx and Elinor Ostrom to study social-ecological systems is the Irish sociologist Eoin Flaherty who completed a PhD on the historical ecology of the rundales. It is to his work that I shall now briefly turn.

Eoin Flaherty on modes of production, metabolism and resilience

Eoin Flaherty has provided a sophisticated account of the Irish communal rundales, using insights from Elinor Ostrom but also introducing analysis from Marx (Flaherty 2012). Flaherty argues that macroeconomic and social influences must be examined, property systems work in a wider context and a purely ground level view is inadequate. Marx argued that property was a product of particular modes of production, noting that with the development of market-based economic systems communal property was increasingly threatened. While he acknowledged the often bloody history of direct enclosure, he also argued that markets tend to put pressure on communal systems of ownership, with commodification leading to more intensive use. Flaherty proposes that Marx's concept of modes of production can be combined with his notion of a 'metabolic rift'. Foster has argued that Marx was extensively interested in ecology and had a sophisticated understanding of the field (Foster 2000). The 'metabolic rift' creates a division between humanity and the rest of nature, resulting in severe environmental damage. Flaherty suggests that a social-ecological systems analysis is essential for understanding the degradation of the rundale system, citing Ostrom and her co-workers. In an extensive, detailed and often highly abstract discussion of environmental sociology, he argues against a dualism that separates the ecological from the social. He praises Ostrom, noting 'the seminal works of human ecologists such as Elinor Ostrom (1990), whom had advanced intriguing propositions concerning the abstract potentialities of modes of communality and customary resource governance, given their capacity for tacit augmentation' (Flaherty 2012: 508). However, he feels she and her colleagues under theorize the social. In his view, instead of labelling social groups, it is important to understand them in relational, class-based terms. Macro analysis can be abstract and misleading; to make it concrete and practical requires an interaction between sophisticated theoretical work and empirical practice. Flaherty observes that an extension of market relations placed increasing pressure upon the rundale system. Using the concept of resilience in an ecological sense, Flaherty comments that this resulted in the degradation of the rundale system in some parts of Ireland. However he notes that rundales were diverse, subject to different processes in different parts of Ireland, with some surviving into the 1950s. Flaherty's work is unique in using analytical concepts from both Marx and Ostrom to try to develop a better understanding of a system of common property. Flaherty, while developing a macro understanding, does not reduce Irish commoners to puppets of structures, but looks at how they dynamically resisted the erosion of the system. He notes that resilience ecology 'is thus concerned with the assessment of such *regime shifts*, which may be observed as systems move within particular value-ranges of identity parameters, and with *system change* or collapse as measured by loss of identity' (Flaherty 2012: 389). Many rundales were unable to cope with potato famine and resilience failed. Flaherty combines microanalysis of a communal property system, with macroanalysis of economic and social context, aided by detailed empirical work based upon historical data. He also develops a more nuanced account of the rundale as a diverse and changing system of land ownership in contrast to studies that have romanticised and homogenised it as a remnant of assumed ancient celtic peasant communism. While it is impossible to judge here the extent to which his analysis can be defended, Flaherty has provided an account that seeks to combine ground level analysis of an institution with macro considerations, using historical data to understand a social-ecological system. While he does not specifically criticise

Elinor Ostrom for failing to fully deal with problems of power, conflict and macrostructural change, he advances a framework that introduces these factors in his detailed analysis of a common pool property system.

Arun Agrawal's challenge to institutionalism

Arun Agrawal studied at the Ostrom Workshop at Indiana University and wrote a number of papers with Elinor Ostrom. As a political scientist, he argues that the institutional analysis of Elinor Ostrom is valuable for understanding environmental governance, but has a number of potential weaknesses (Agrawal 2005). He cites Jack Knight's book *Institutions and Conflict* (1992). Knight claims that institutional analysis underplays the role of politics, conflict and differential access to resources. For example, Knight noted that, under apartheid, black South Africans were systematically discriminated against and that in many societies, including ancient Rome, women had drastically deficient property rights compared to men. Mainstream economics ignores conflict and fails to see systematic inequality. Knight argued that institutions can be understood primarily as systems for distributing resources. He felt that, without structures of legal intervention to fight discrimination, gross inequality is likely to result. Knight's work is an implicit challenge to the public choice theory developed by Buchanan that is hostile to government intervention to deal with inequality. Agrawal, in turn, has argued that an institutional analysis needs to be combined with approaches from political ecology and feminism, to better deal with the problem identified by Jack Knight, that institutionalists underplay 'the importance of power' (Agrawal 2005: 99). Knight's *Institutions and Social Conflict* (1992) was read by Elinor Ostrom, and as has been discussed both in her personal experience as a woman who 'was born poor', and via her research, she acknowledged power differentials. While she was sceptical that governments would act to help those without power she affirmed the force of Knight's argument:

> Q: Libertarians have tried to co-opt your work by saying it shows the unsuitability of large scale, top-down economic arrangements.
>
> OSTROM: A question is: How do we change some of our governance arrangements so that we can have more trust? We must have a court system, and that court system needs to be reliable and trustworthy. The important thing about large-scale is the court system. For example, you would not have civil rights for people of black origin in the United States but for a federal court system and also the courage of Martin Luther King and others – people who had the courage to challenge, and a legal system where, at least in some places, the right to challenge was legitimate.
>
> We have a colleague working in Liberia. You had thugs recruiting young kids until recently. Having a legal system that does not allow thugs to capture kids, torment them, and make them use weapons is very important.
>
> (*The Progressive*, 20 June 2010)

Agrawal argues that institutionalists need to develop a more sophisticated understanding of individual subjectivity in order to deal with issues of politics, power and conflict. He suggests that institutionalism, including the work of both Jack Knight and Elinor Ostrom, fails to theorize human subjectivity. Subjectivity, he argues, is intrinsically linked both to power and ecological sustainability. Using detailed empirical work to research this area, he examined how environmental subjectivity was constructed amongst Indian forest dwellers. He embarked on a study of growing environmental consciousness on the part of villagers in Kumaon in northern India. During the 1920s the villagers lit hundreds of forest fires, which had a devastating effect, yet by the late twentieth century they had become keen conservationists. In trying to understand this shift in behaviour, he described the creation of an environmental subjectivity as 'environmentality'.

Agrawal argues that, rather than incentives being fixed or even limited by bounded rationality, changing personal identity leads to changing personal goals and action. He makes much of meeting a villager who was dismissive of conservation efforts to protect the forest but who later became an active environmentalist. Subjectivity is linked to the exercise of power, because governance can lead to changes in our self-identity, according to Agrawal. Institutions cannot be understood without understanding changes in personal subjectivity, as illustrated by villagers moving from forest burning to forest protection.

While Elinor Ostrom used experimental work to try to understand human motivation in a more subtle way than mainstream economists, Agrawal argues that the work of the French thinker Michel Foucault is useful. Foucault argued, in a way that is consistent with the Ostroms, that power is not purely negative but is universal and constitutive. Power shapes us and cannot be escaped; it is not only repressive but is also constructive. Above all, it shapes our subjectivity. Foucault further suggests that what he terms 'governmentality', can be seen as linking governance with human behaviour and institutions:

> It is changes to the practices of individual persons, with each a member of society and all of them collectively constituting the social, that are the object of regulation. Solutions to problems associated with some aspect of the social – high birth rates, low levels of industrialization, deforestation, and underdevelopment – require changes in individual behaviour. Governmental strategies achieve their effects, to the extent they do so, by becoming anchors for processes that reshape the individuals who are a part and the object of government regulation. By attending to practices, it becomes possible to see how institutions, politics and subjectivities together compromise different technologies of government.
>
> (Agrawal 2005: 219)

The suitability of Foucault's contribution to Ostrom's work can be debated. As Agrawal acknowledges, Foucault can be seen as rejecting normative concerns and, of course, he often rejected the very idea of research methodology. He went so far as to claim that his work involved the construction of 'fictions' but did note, a little obscurely, 'I do not mean to say, however, that truth is therefore absent' (Foucault 1980: 193). Foucault's contribution to research methodology is, at best, controversial.

Foucault's work does not automatically translate into a rigorous theoretical basis for understanding practical questions of governance. Equally, the precise shift from forest burning to forest conservation, identified by Agrawal, would seem to fit straightforwardly with material self-interest. Either Buchanan as a public choice theorist or Marx might have suggested that when the British colonialists excluded the Kumaon people from the forests they depended upon, they burnt those forests in revolt. While new decentralised governance of the forests may have given rise to a new environmental subjectivity, the simple notion that control over the forests would provide an incentive for self-regulation seems a more direct explanation. Yet Agrawal's claim that subjectivities demand investigation, if we are to understand governance, is difficult to challenge. Choosing how or if to use Foucault's work at all, is less important than understanding that subjectivities, institutions and governance practices interact dynamically. While the analysis of power is not absent from Elinor Ostrom's work, it demands further development. Macro structural forces interact with the micro in shaping personalities and in turn, no doubt, are shaped by them. I am sure she found her colleague Arun Agrawal's book a fascinating read.

Implicit in her work on social-ecological systems is an understanding of complex networks of causation that upset old certainties. The commons activist David Boiller notes:

> Once you venture into the world of complex adaptive systems, you enter a world where the 20th Century ontologies no longer work. The focus is more on flows rather than stocks, and on processes and relationships rather than discrete things. This shift in orientation is needed because once you acknowledge that everything is interconnected and dynamic, it no longer makes sense to view an organism in isolation. The boundaries between an organism and its ecosystem become rather indeterminate. We start to realize that everything is embedded in everything else. Biologists are discovering, for example, that we human beings are not really discrete 'individuals' so much as 'super-organisms' comprised of vast numbers of sub-organisms and -systems such as 'biomes' – vast collections of bacteria with whom we share a vital symbiotic relationship. Our very identities as a species and as individuals are not so obvious, but rather blur into the ecological context.
>
> (Bollier (12 June 2013))

Complex adaptive systems and subjectivity takes us into new and difficult areas, especially perhaps for economists, but they are, at least, implicit in the work of the Ostroms. Walking a research path between the radical indeterminacies of Foucault and dizzying allied French thinkers like Deleuze, Guttari and Lacan or the naïve certainties of mainstream economics, is extremely challenging but consistent with Elinor Ostrom's work.

Elinor Ostrom's contribution to a sustainable economics

While critics of Elinor Ostrom's work have raised a number of interesting questions, it is important to conclude by asking to what extent she has provided the basis for a new, sustainable economics. While she did not research macro-economics, her work is relevant to a more nuanced understanding of the micro foundations of a sustainable economics.

Mainstream economics has been challenged from a variety of directions, and a consensus is slowly emerging that it demands revision if it is to be fit for purpose. While such criticism is very varied, the notion of rational 'economic man or woman' looks particularly inadequate. With this foundation becoming rusty, the edifice of mainstream economics appears ever more shaky. Also, given the nature of environmental problems such as climate change, economics must help rather than hinder our efforts to promote ecological sustainability. Elinor Ostrom's work provides a good starting point for such revision.

Economics for the Ostroms was rather more complex than that of the mainstream. Switching from mainstream economics to the economic perspectives of the Ostroms is like moving from black and white television to colour, from prison food to well-prepared cuisine. The Ostroms did not view economics as purely monetary and, of course, did not believe that economics could be covered by just two types of goods and two forms of property.

Elinor Ostrom, and indeed Vincent, viewed ecological matters as fundamental to their political economy from the early days of both of their respective careers. Vincent and Elinor had observed how democratic structures had been used to manage real-life environmental problems, such as the dilemma of how to share grazing land or water basins. Yet Hardin advocated largely top-down, and potentially authoritarian, solutions to these environmental problems. Metaphors, if mobilised convincingly, can have a powerful effect. Hardin's work, based on a vivid metaphor, articulated a deep felt fear that collective action would fail and his 'tragedy of the commons' trope created much debate. Elinor Ostrom, to her credit, worked very hard to challenge it. By doing so she has helped to promote environmental sustainability and the rights of collective resource owners – from indigenous people to peasant farmers to free/open source software designers.

The reality is that there is a spectrum, or kaleidoscope, of property rights. When we move beyond the idea of the binary of state and private property, the alternative is not simply the commons. The notion of commons, both as a resource and a property right, is an advance over the binary. Commons, rather than being unowned non-property, have been identified as collectively managed resources. Yet Elinor Ostrom's work points to a conception of property beyond the commons. Items can be owned in a variety of ways and, as more sophisticated legal theorists have long understood, even privately owned items contain a bundle of rights. The insight gained from John R. Commons that property systems are diverse further opens up a new economic and legal understanding. This enhances concepts such as usufruct, the right to access a resource on the condition that it is maintained and not degraded, which are essential to creating more environmentally sustainable systems of governance. Economics can, perhaps, incorporate an understanding of usufruct rather than simple accumulation. The norms and rules of usufruct are norms and rules of sustainability. An economics of social sharing, while not investigated by the Ostroms, fits well with their research. With the social sharing of physical goods it is possible to cut the knot of the prosperity versus environment dilemma, and have access to more physical goods than we need, while reducing our use of resources. Neither usufruct nor social sharing automatically solve sustainability problems, but they are useful tools that may make them easier to face. More fundamentally, the Ostroms' concern with self-governance suggests that grassroots popular design can be promoted as a means of dealing with a range of ecological problems, including climate change.

Elinor Ostrom's approach to sustainability, therefore, cannot be reduced to a calculation of costs, or governmental regulation, or any other panacea. Social-ecological systems are complex, and purely cost considerations or centrally imposed regulatory measures are inadequate to their maintenance. The seven-generation rule is helpful in understanding her perspective. While it is unclear as to why we should consider seven generations rather than five or eight, it refers to the need to be concerned with future generations who will never meet those of us who live today. In one of her last interviews she noted that short-term profit maximisation would tend to degrade common pool resources; a longer term perspective was vital for pragmatic resource use (May and Summerfield 2012). Mainstream economics has not prioritised the welfare of future generations, and economic growth in the short term may degrade ecosystems and diminish resources, to the detriment of future generations. Elinor Ostrom's concern for environmental sustainability also distinguishes her work from most other institutional economists. However, she did not believe that a normative commitment to sustainability was sufficient, but that practical policies had to be worked out. Policies that were developed democratically were more likely to be effective, and people needed to see practical gains from such policies. Both her normative concern and her work on practical aspects of effective governance of environmental resources mean that her work advances a sustainable economics.

Her work also sustains economics in another sense. Mainstream economics is in many ways discredited and Elinor Ostrom's work contributes to a more sophisticated and realistic economics. In his last lecture before he died, Herbert Simon noted that neoclassical economics was based on a monocentric view of reality and was failing to explain economic behaviour:

> Neoclassical economics created a unified framework for 'explaining' virtually all human behaviour as produced by an Olympian process of utility maximisation that recognises no limits to the knowledge or thinking powers of the human actors. The neoclassical framework assumed a static equilibrium, and, as soon as serious attention began to be paid to dynamic phenomena and uncertainty in large, complex social systems, the structure began to deteriorate, and continues to crumble today.
>
> (Simon 2000: 750)

He further observed that while much creative work was being undertaken, detailed research on alternatives was largely absent.

> Today, economics is in an increasingly chaotic and productive state of disorganisation, searching for an alternative picture of economic mechanisms and human rationality – that is, of the genuine bounded rationality of which people are capable. There are theoretical proposals galore; what is still in short supply is detailed empirical research (of kinds that are well-known in political science) to determine how human beings actually go about solving problems and making decisions.
>
> (Simon 2000: 750)

It is worth noting how much work Elinor Ostrom performed in undertaking such empirical research. She used experiments, game theory, agent- based models and other techniques to investigate human social behaviour. Incorporating Simon's concept of 'bounded rationality', her research showed the weakness of notions of utility maximising economic agents as a universal explanatory model. Of course, her work in this area was as a network scholar rather than an individual. Most of her practical work was as part of a team, and the teams in which she was involved contributed to the wider, fast advancing fields of behavioural and neuro-economics.

The sociologist John Elster noted:

> [...] neoclassical economics will be dethroned if and when satisficing theory and psychology join forces to produce a simple and robust explanation of aspiration levels, or sociological theory comes up with a simple and robust theory of the relation between social norms and instrumental rationality. Until this happens, the continued dominance of neoclassical theory is ensured by the fact that one can't beat something with nothing.
>
> (Elster 1986: 26–7)

So to what extent did Elinor Ostrom come up with 'something?' Although she was trying to help to understand dilemmas of collective action in the context of tricky social and often ecological problems, her work focussed on precisely the point made by Elster. However she was critical of the idea that one model linking 'social norms and instrumental rationality' was sufficient. She argued that mainstream economic assumptions applied well to competitive situations for private goods in market economies, but she objected to these assumptions being extended to human behaviour in general. Focussing on common pool resource dilemmas and other problems of collective choice, she researched the link 'between social norms and instrumental rationality' that Jon Elster sees as so important. She produced a useful summary of her conclusions in 1997, in a speech she delivered as President of the American Political Science Association, which was published a year later (1998). While work on these alternatives to universal rational humanity continued up until her death, her speech provides an important overview of how she approached this area of thought.

She agreed that a broadly rational model of human behaviour was consistent with experimental and other forms of evidence. She linked this to her desire to promote a Tocqueville-inspired quest to promote human association and governance, observing:

> Consistent with all models of rational choice is a general theory of human behavior that views all humans as complex, fallible learners who seek to do as well as they can given the constraints that they face and who are able to learn heuristics, norms, rules and how to craft rules to improve achieved outcomes.
>
> (Ostrom 1998: 9)

However, as has been noted, while such broad rationality was common, the precise model of rational economic humanity, was strictly applicable only in limited circumstances. In reality our behaviour is influenced by a range of motives, and rationality is bounded because of imperfect information. She argued that, in the context of social dilemmas, 'a behavioral theory of boundedly rational and moral behavior' was more applicable (Ostrom 1998: 2). With future research, she saw the possibility of developing a more intellectually sustainable model of human behaviour. However she was sceptical that one model would suffice. The title of her speech is a reference to an earlier paper by Herbert Simon. However, whereas he talked of 'A Behavioral Model of Rational Choice' (Simon 1955) she put forward a more modest title. 'A Behavioral Approach to the Rational Choice Theory of Collective Action' was specific to collective action, rather than all human behaviour, and was an approach to a problem rather than an attempt to put forward one single superior 'model' (Ostrom 1998).

She was able, however, to draw some conclusions. First, human behaviour, at least in regard to collective action/social dilemmas, was affected by a range of factors. Her research, and that of many other experimenters in fields ranging from psychology to economics suggested that group size, group heterogeneity, dependence on benefits received, discount rates, monitoring techniques, nesting of organizational levels and the information available to participants, all influenced how the game was played. The institutional 'scaffolding' was also important. For example, competitive markets, by removing some players from the game as a result of competitive pressure, unsurprisingly promoted competitive behaviour. Other institutional forms would act to encourage other forms of behaviour. She argued that the 'thin' model of economic rationality put forward by the original game theorists and mainstream economists would apply to all human situations if such situations were governed by institutions like competitive markets. It was clear to her that this was not the case. Although advanced cautiously, this conclusion is a major challenge to mainstream economics that views all our economic behaviour as self-interestedly competitive. It also brings us back to the interesting questions about power, subjectivity and institutions that have been traced through this book.

Ostrom also noted that research had shown that while human beings, at least in the context of collective action problems, were more cooperative than economists and early game theorists had assumed, such cooperation was not sufficient to automatically solve problems such as common resource sustainability. She also observed that work by evolutionary biologists, game theorists such as Robert Axelrod, and others has suggested that human beings could develop the 'use of heuristics and norms of behavior, such as reciprocity', which were helpful in solving such collective action problems (Ostrom 1998: 3). This work also challenged the notion of universal self-interest and notions of innate behaviour.

Ostrom argued that such findings were a start towards developing a more sophisticated account of human behaviour and motivation, but would give rise to different models rather than a single universal story. However even her tentative summary, while aimed at a discussion of collective action rather than 'economics', moves us towards a more sustainable economic account of our behaviour.

She made a number of additional critical points. She was dismissive of accounts that were stuck in arguments over structure versus agency, stressing that structures were influential on our behaviour but that we could potentially change such structures. She also noted that 'if political scientists do not have an empirically grounded theory of collective action, then we are hand-waving at our central questions, I am afraid that we do a lot of hand waving' (Ostrom 1998: 1). This is a good reminder that while it is possible to strongly criticise mainstream economics, alternatives demand research and not just polemical demands for a better way. She also noted that to the extent that human beings could cooperate, this was not entirely good news, observing that, 'reciprocity norms can have a dark side' (Ostrom 1998: 17). Strong cooperation in communities could be accompanied by a 'matrix of hostile relationships with outsiders', that she feared might 'escalate into feuds, raids, and overt warfare', along with racism and other forms of discrimination. She also noted that one form of cooperation that was damaging was the creation of price fixing cartels, and stated that 'favors for favors can also be the foundation for corruption' (Ostrom 1998: 17–18).

Che Guevara talked of the new human who would be cooperative. Elinor Ostrom might have stated that humans were more cooperative than most economists believed but research and institutional design were needed to help us cooperate more. Social engineering was inappropriate, but we can redesign, democratically, what we do, and that this is necessary because we face difficult governance problems and social-ecological challenges. Elinor Ostrom suggests that politics and economics need not develop 'models' for all circumstances, because human beings are complex, but can help us to design better ways of sustaining our material welfare. This insight alone shows, I would argue, that using careful research and without claiming to put forward a fully theorised new economics, she, along with Vincent, their colleagues and an extended network of scholars, achieved something remarkable. Her challenge to economics and political science can be summarised in her own words:

> What the research on social dilemmas demonstrates is a world of possibility rather than of necessity. We are neither trapped in inexorable tragedies nor free of moral responsibility for creating and sustaining incentives that facilitate our own achievement of mutually productive outcomes.
>
> (Ostrom 1998: 16)

A new science for a new world?

Research can give rise to revolutions. The philosopher of social science Thomas Kuhn referred to these as 'paradigm shifts'. New evidence accumulates that does not fit with the prevailing assumptions; it is ignored or explained away with increasingly elaborate justifications, but eventually the evidence is so overwhelming that this leads to a shift in the framework of understanding. It might be argued that Elinor Ostrom has achieved such a paradigm shift in economics. From contributing to new understanding of the micro foundations of economics, including theorising new forms of property rights and using game theory to explore human cooperation, she challenged a number of economic fundamentals. Economists have stressed the pursuit of efficiency, a science of achieving the highest output with the lowest input. Ostrom has noted the importance of alternative goals, noting that environmental sustainability and self-governance are also essential. Economics cannot be separated from politics because economics is shaped by institutions and institutions are the subject of political science. Her emphasis on the need to maintain dialogue between social and natural science also contributes to the revolutionary implications of her work. Above all, she has advanced and transformed practical research methods in economics.

A revolution in paradigm could be linked to dramatic changes in social reality. It is easy to make a case that we are in a new world. The twenty-first century has seen the rise of cyberspace; this shapes virtually all areas of human existence. It has made it much easier to create collective systems of governance and production. Virtual platforms allow global communication. Above all, peer-to-peer forms of production have become possible. In the 1930s, Walter Benjamin noted that art could be mechanically reproduced, as photography and photocopying changed the production of aesthetic objects. The World Wide Web has allowed accelerated reproduction of information, and information conceived as codes is constitutive of everything from software to potential political constitutions. The rise and rise of three-dimensional printing could have a radical effect on economics and society.

Another novel feature of our age is the globalisation of environmental problems. While since the days of Palaeolithic over-hunting and soil erosion, as described by Plato, environmental problems have always perhaps been with us; they have been internationalised by recent changes in human society. From nuclear radiation spread by atomic tests in the upper atmosphere in the 1950s to the consequences of climate change, global environmental problems are apparent.

Attempts within mainstream economics, and even heterodox alternatives, to understand these developments can appear clumsy. Basic assumptions of plural property rights, and a practical emphasis on sustainability and shared consumption/production within Elinor Ostrom's thought makes her work essential in dealing with ecological dilemmas. What is often awkward and marginal in mainstream economics, and indeed political science, is obvious and introductory within Elinor Ostrom's science, and the wider network of scholars with whom she worked, including Vincent Ostrom. To take a typical example, while economists agonise and use convoluted explanations, she saw no mystery in production which is not for immediate individual gain. Rather than measuring environmental costs in monetary form, her work recognised the importance of understanding complex, resilient and often counterintuitive ecologies. She was not an environmentalist but an ecologist, aware of recent developments in the science that meant that assumptions had to be revised and the possibility of unintended consequences from policies acknowledged.

Thus, we live in a new world, and the new scientific contribution made by Elinor Ostrom is a starting point for understanding much of this apparent novelty. The phrase 'a new science for a new world' is derived from Tocqueville. Vincent Ostrom interpreted this in a number of linked senses. The USA was literally a new world, because colonialists had travelled to a new area of the world and made themselves independent from the British state. With reference to Kuhn's paradigm shift, Ostrom saw the construction of the US constitution as a new moment. Individuals had come together to build a new constitution; an event which, in itself, was revolutionary (V. Ostrom 1997).

So has Elinor Ostrom created a new political or economic science? Has she engineered a paradigm shift? Perhaps this is too big a claim to make. Elinor Ostrom built from within existing bodies of theoretical practice rather than rejecting them. She asked big, difficult, deep questions but used careful research to help advance some cautious answers. She designed new ways of using existing theoretical and practical tools to present alternatives.

Her overriding concern, though, was that her research was used practically. All my encounters with her work have convinced me that she would have had no interest in creating an ideological legacy. She would have wished to be remembered not in words but in practice. The construction of a tool kit which could be used to help craft human institutions that worked better was her inspiration. Her goal was not to act as an architect but to help others to self-build with more confidence.

Appendix

Institutional analysis and development: micro

August 22, 2011
POLS Y673 Fall 2011
Class #5807

Institutional analysis and development: micro

Elinor Ostrom
Tuesdays: 3:30–5:30 p.m.
Workshop in Political Theory and Policy Analysis
513 North Park Avenue
IUB
SYLLABUS

Preface

The central questions underlying this course are:

How can *fallible* human beings achieve and sustain self-governing ways of life and self-governing entities as well as sustaining ecological systems at multiple scales?

When we state that institutions facilitate or discourage effective problem-solving and innovations, what do we mean by institutions and what other factors affect these processes?

How do we develop better frameworks and theories to understand behavior that has structure and outcomes at multiple scales (e.g. household use of electricity affecting household budget and health as well as community infrastructure and investments and regional, national, and global structures and outcomes)?

How can institutional analysis be applied to the analysis of diverse policy areas including urban public goods, water and forestry resources, and healthcare?

To address these questions, we will have to learn a variety of tools to understand how fallible individuals behave within institutions as well as how they can influence the rules that structure their lives. This is a particularly challenging question in an era when global concerns have moved onto the political agenda of most international, national, and even local governing bodies without recognising the importance of the local for the global. Instead of studying how individuals craft institutions, many scholars are focusing on how to understand national and global phenomena. It is also an era of substantial political uncertainty as well as violence, terrorism, and disruption. Many of the problems we are witnessing today are due to a lack of understanding of the micro and meso levels that are essential aspects of global processes.

In our effort to understand self-governance, we will be studying the four 'I's': individuals, incentives, institutions, and inquiry.

To understand processes at any level of organization, one needs to understand the *individuals* who are participants and the incentives they face. When we talk about 'THE' government doing X or Y, there are individuals who hold positions in a variety of situations within 'THE' government. We had better understand how individuals approach making decisions in a variety of situations given the incentives they face. Those *incentives* come from a variety of sources, but a major source, particularly in the public sector, are the rules of the game they are playing. *Institutions* include the rules that specify what may, must or must not be done in situations that are linked together to make up a polity, a society, an economy, and their inter-linkages. To understand this process, we must be engaged in an *inquiry* that will never end.

The settings we study are complex, diverse, multi-scaled, and dynamic. Thus, we need to develop frameworks that provide a general language for studying these complex, multi-scaled systems. And, we can learn a variety of theories (and models of those theories) that help us understand particular settings. We cannot develop a universal theory of actions and outcomes in all settings for all time. Thus, our task of inquiry is a lifelong task. And, the task of citizens and their officials is also unending. No system of governance can survive for long without commonly understood rules and rule enforcement. Rule enforcement relies on varying degrees of force and potential use of violence. Consequently, we face a Faustian bargain in designing any system of governance.

A self-governing entity is one whose members (or their representatives) participate in the establishment, reform, and continued legitimacy of the constitutional and collective choice rules-in-use. All self-organised entities (whether in the private or public spheres) are to some extent self-governing. In modern societies, however, it is rare to find any entity whose members (or their representatives) have fashioned *all* of the constitutional and collective-choice rules that they use. Some rules are likely to have come from external sources. Many rules will have come from earlier times and are not discussed extensively among those using the rules today.

On the other hand, even in a totalitarian polity, it is difficult for central authorities to prevent all individuals from finding ways of self-organizing and creating rules of their own. Some of these may even be contrary to the formal laws of the totalitarian regime. Given that most modern societies have many different entities, let me rephrase the first question on page 1: How can fallible individuals achieve and sustain large numbers of small, medium, and large-scale self-governing entities in the private and public spheres?

We cannot thoroughly understand all of the diverse processes of self-governance in any semester-long or year-long course of study. How humans can govern themselves is a question that has puzzled and perplexed the greatest thinkers of the last several millennia. Many have answered that self-governance is impossible. In this view, the best that human beings can do is live in a political system that is imposed on them and that creates a predictable order within which individuals may be able to achieve a high level of physical and economic well-being without much autonomy. In this view, the rules that structure the opportunities and constraints facing individuals come from outside from what is frequently referred to as 'the state.'

For other thinkers, rules are best viewed as spontaneously emerging from patterns of interactions among individuals. In this view, trying to design any type of institution, whether to be imposed on individuals or self-determined, is close to impossible or potentially disastrous in its consequences. Human fallibility is too great to foretell many of the consequences that are likely to follow. Efforts to design self-governing systems, rather than making adaptive changes within what has been passed along from past generations, involves human beings in tasks that are beyond their knowledge and skills.

The thesis that we advance in this seminar is that individuals, who seriously engage one another in efforts to build mutually productive social relationships – and to understand why these are important – are capable of devising ingenious ways of relating constructively with one another. The impossible task, however, is to design *entire* social systems 'from scratch' at one point in time that avoid the fate of being monumental disasters. Individuals who are willing to explore possibilities, consider new options as entrepreneurs, and to use reason as well as trial and error experimentation, can evolve and design rules, routines, and ways of life that are likely to build up to self-governing entities with a higher chance of adapting and surviving over time than top-down designs. It takes time, however, to learn from errors, to try and find the source of the error, and to improve one part of the system without generating adverse consequences elsewhere.

Successful groups of individuals may exist in simple or complex nested systems ranging from very small to very large. The problem is that in a complexly interrelated world, one needs effective organization at all levels ranging from the smallest work team all the way to international organizations. If the size of the group that is governing and reaping benefits is too small, negative externalities are likely to occur. Further, even in small face-to-face groups, some individuals may use any of a wide array of asymmetries to take advantage of others. Individuals, who are organised in many small groups nested in larger structures – a polycentric system – may find ways of exiting from some settings and joining others. Or, they may seek remedies from overlapping groups that may reduce the asymmetries within the smaller unit. If the size of the group that is governing and reaping benefits is too large, on the other hand, essential information is lost, and further, the situation may again be one of exploitation.

Scale and complex nesting are only part of the problem. Another part has to do with how individuals view their basic relationships with one another. Many individuals learn to be relatively truthful, considerate of others, trustworthy, and willing to work hard. Others are opportunistic. Some approach governance as involving basic problem-solving skills. Some approach governance as a problem of gaining dominance over others. The opportunities for dominance always exist in any system of rule-ordering, where some individuals are delegated responsibilities for devising and monitoring conformance to rules and sanctioning rule breakers. Those who devise self-governing entities that work well only when everyone is a 'saint' find themselves invaded by 'sinners' who take advantage of the situation and may cause what had initially worked successfully to come unglued and fail.

Thus, the initial answer to the first question on page 1 is: Self-governance is possible in a setting, if…

> most individuals share a common, broad understanding of the biophysical, cultural, and political worlds they face; of the importance of trying to follow general principles of trust, reciprocity, and fairness; and of the need to use artisanship to craft their own rules;
> most individuals have significant experience in small to medium-sized settings, where they learn the skills of living with others, being responsible, gaining trust, being entrepreneurial, and holding others responsible for their actions;
> considerable autonomy exists for constituting and reconstituting relationships with one another that vary from very small to very large units (some of which will be highly specialised while others may be general purpose organizations);
> individuals learn to analyse the incentives that they face in particular situations (given the type of physical and cultural setting in which they find themselves) and to try to adjust positive and negative incentives so that those individuals who are most likely to be opportunistic are deterred or sanctioned.

The above is posed as a 'possibility', not a determinate outcome. In other words, we view self-governing entities as fragile social artifacts that individuals may be able to constitute and reconstitute over time. A variety of disturbances are likely to occur over time. A key question is to what kind of disturbances is a self-organised governance system robust? We can make scientific statements about the kinds of results that are likely if individuals share particular kinds of common understandings, are responsible, have autonomy, possess analytical tools, and consciously pass both moral and analytical knowledge from one generation to the next. These are strong conditions!

With this view, small self-governing entities may exist as an enclave in the midst of highly authoritarian regimes. This may not be a stable solution, but self-governance may provide opportunities to develop productive arrangements for those who establish trust and reciprocity backed by their own willingness to monitor and enforce interpersonal commitments. If the macro structure is not hostile or even supports and encourages self-organization, what can be accomplished by smaller private and public enclaves can be very substantial. This is initially a bottom-up view of self-governance. Productive small-scale self-organization, however, is difficult to sustain over time in a larger political system that tries to impose uniform rules, operates through patron-client networks or uses terror to sustain authoritarian rule. Having vigorous local and regional governments and many types of voluntary associations is part of the answer but not sufficient in and of itself.

Simply having national elections, choosing leaders, and asking them to pass good legislation is hardly sufficient, however, to sustain a self-governing society over the long run. Electing officials to national office and providing them with 'common budgetary pools' of substantial size to spend 'in the public interest' creates substantial temptations to engage in rent-seeking behavior and distributive politics.

The central problem is how to embed elected officials in a set of institutions that generates information about their actions, holds them accountable, allows for rapid response in times of threat, and encourages innovation and problem solving. Solving such problems involves the design of a delicately balanced system. It requires decisions from sophisticated participants who understand the theory involved in constituting and reconstituting such systems and share a moral commitment to the maintenance of a democratic social order.

Now, what is the role of the institutional analyst in all of this? Well, for one, it is essential for those who devote their lives to studying the emergence, adaptation, design, and effects of institutional arrangements to understand a very wide array of diverse rules that exist in an equally diverse set of physical and cultural milieus. To understand how various rules may be used as part of a self-governing society, one has to examine how diverse rules affect the capacities of individuals to achieve mutually productive outcomes over time or the dominance of some participants over others.

Eventually, one has to examine constellations of embedded institutional arrangements rather than isolated situations. And, one has to examine the short-run and long-run effects of many different types of rules on human actions and outcomes. Further, one has to acquire considerable humility regarding exactly how precise predictions can be made about the effects of different rules on incentives, behavior, and outcomes achieved. Design of successful institutions may indeed be feasible. Designed institutions, which tend to generate substantial information rapidly and accurately and allow for the change of rules over time in light of performance, are more likely to be successful than those resulting from 'grand designs' for societies as a whole.

To be an institutional analyst, one needs to learn to use the best available theoretical and data collection tools, while at the same time trying to develop even better theories and conducting further empirical studies that contribute to our theoretical understanding of self-governing systems. All tools have capabilities and limits. The task of the skilled artisan – whether an institutional theorist or a cabinetmaker – is to learn the capabilities and limits of relevant tools and how best to use a combination of tools to address the wide diversity of puzzles that one comes across in a lifetime of work.

Relevant tools are plentiful in the sense that we do have an extensive body of political, social, and economic theory that focuses on the impact of diverse rules on the incentives, behavior, and likely outcomes within different settings. These tools are limited, however, in that many of the most rigorous theories make questionable assumptions about both the individual and about the settings within which individuals find themselves. This can be problematic for explaining behavior in many settings. These explicit and often implicit assumptions may mask some of the deeper problems of sustaining democratic systems over time. Many of the difficult problems that human beings face in trying to develop and sustain democratic organizations are assumed away when one starts with assumptions that individuals have complete and perfect information and can make error-free calculations about expected consequences for themselves and no one else in complex, uncertain worlds

Further, when assumptions are made that the structure of the situations facing individuals are fixed and cannot be changed by those in the situation, little effort is devoted to addressing how individuals affect their own situations. Yet, these same assumptions (full information and fixed structures) are useful when the analyst wants to examine the expected short-term outcomes of an institutional and physical setting, where the options available to individuals are narrowly constrained and where individuals have many opportunities to learn about the costs and benefits of pursuing diverse options. Learning which assumptions, theories, and models to use to analyze diverse institutional arrangements combined with diverse settings is an important aspect of the training of institutional analysts.

During this seminar, we will use a variety of theoretical tools. These will help us to understand the Institutional Analysis and Development (IAD) framework that we have been developing over many years at the Workshop as well as the more recent Program for Institutional Analysis of Social-Ecological Systems (PIASES) framework. The skilled institutional analyst uses a framework to identify the types of questions and variables to be included in any particular analysis. The artisan then selects what is perceived to be the most appropriate theory available given the particular questions to be addressed, the type of empirical evidence that is available or is to be obtained, and the purpose of the analysis. For any one theory, there are multiple models of that theory that can be used to analyze a focused set of questions. Choosing the most appropriate model (whether this is a mathematical model, a simulation, a process model or the design for an experiment) also depends on the particular puzzle that an analyst wants to examine.

Further, there are multiple tools that are used in the conduct of research ranging from individual case studies, meta-analyses, large-N studies, laboratory and field experiments, GIS and remote sensing, agent based models, and others. Institutional analysts respect all of these methods when used to understand human behavior in diverse settings. No scholar can use all of these methods well nor are they all appropriate for the study of all institutional settings, but it is important to learn more about diverse tools and their strengths and weaknesses for examining diverse research questions.

(The remainder of the syllabus including the reading lists and seminar details, can be read at www.indiana.edu/~workshop/courses/Y673/y673_fall_2011_syllabus.pdf).

Bibliography

Agrawal, A. (2005) *Environmentality: Technologies of Government and the Making of Subjects*, Durham, N.C.: Duke University Press.

Aligică, P.D. (2013) *Elinor Ostrom: The Legacy and the Challenge*, Online. Available at: http://themonkeycage.org/2013/07/03/elinor-ostrom-the-legacy-and-the-challenge/ (accessed 11 July 2013).

—— (2014) *Institutional Diversity and Political Economy: The Ostroms and Beyond*, Oxford: Oxford University Press.

Aligică, P.D. and Boettke, P. (2009) *Challenging Institutional Analysis and Development*, London: Routledge.

Allen, B. and Ostrom, V. (2011) *The Quest to Understand Human Affairs*, Lanham, MD: Rowman and Littlefield Publishers.

Amadae, S.M. (2003) *Rationalizing Capitalist Democracy: The Cold War Origins of Rational Choice Liberalism*, Chicago, IL: University Of Chicago Press.

Amster, R. (2009) *Why Ostrom's Nobel is even more shocking than Obama's*, Huffington Post. Online. Available at: www.huffingtonpost.com/randall-amster/why-ostroms-nobel-is-even_b_320172.html (accessed 28 June 2012).

Anderies, J.M. and Janssen, M.A. (2012) 'Elinor Ostrom (1933–2012): Pioneer in the Interdisciplinary Science of Coupled Social-Ecological Systems', *PLoS Biol* 10 (10).

Anderson, L. and Leal, D. (2001*) Free Market Environmentalism*, New York: Palgrave.

Annual Reviews Conversations (2010) *An Interview with Elinor Ostrom*, Online. Available at: www.annualreviews.org/userimages/ContentEditor/1326999553977/ElinorOstromTranscript.pdf (accessed 30 May 2013).

Arrow, K. (1994) 'Methodological Individualism and Social Knowledge', *American Economic Review*, 84 (2): 1–9.

Ashby, W.R. (1960) *Design for a Brain; the Origin of Adaptive Behaviour*, New York: Wiley.

Axelrod, R. (1984) *The Evolution of Cooperation*, New York: Basic Books.

Bardi, U. (2011) *The Limits to Growth Revisited*, Berlin: Springer.

Benjamin, W. (2011) *Illuminations*, New York: Random House.

Benkler, Y. (2004) '"Sharing Nicely": On shareable goods and the emergence of sharing as a modality of economic production', *The Yale Law Journal*, 114: 273–358.

—— (2006) *The Wealth of Networks*, New Haven, CT: Yale University Press.

Berkes, F., Hughes, T., Steneck, R., Wilson, J., Bellwood, D., Crona, B., Folke, C., Gunderson, L., Leslie, H., Norberg, J., Nyström, M., Olsson, P., Österblom, H., Scheffer, M. and Worm, B (2006) 'Globalization, Roving Bandits, and Marine Resources', *Science*, 311: 1557–8.

Bertacchini, E. (2012) *Cultural Commons: A New Perspective on the Production and Evolution of Cultures*, Cheltenham, UK: Edward Elgar.

Bhaskar, R. (1989) *Reclaiming Reality*, London: Verso.

Blickle, P. (1985) *From the Communal Reformation to the Revolution of the Common Man*, Köln: Brill.

Boettke, P. (2009) *Boettke on Elinor Ostrom, Vincent Ostrom, and the Bloomington School*, Indianapolis, Indiana: Library of Economics and Liberty. Online. Available at: www.econtalk.org/archives/2009/11/boettke_on_elin.html (accessed 28 June 2012).

Boettke, P., Lemke, J. and Palagashvili, L. (2013) 'Riding in Cars with Boys: Elinor Ostrom's Adventures with the Police' GMU Working Paper in Economics No. 13–01.

Bollier, D. (2003) *Silent Theft: The Private Plunder of Our Common Wealth*, London: Routledge.

—— (12 June, 2013) *Applying Ostrom's Guidelines to the Design of Software Platforms*, Online. Available at: http://bollier.org/blog/applying-ostroms-guidelines-design-software-platforms (accessed 11 July 2013).

Bollier, D. and Helfrich, S. (eds) (2012) *The Wealth of the Commons*, Amherst, MA: Levellers Press.

Bookchin, M. (1986) *Radicalizing Democracy: A Timely Interview with Murray Bookchin* Conducted by the Editors of Kick It Over Magazine, Toronto, Ontario: Northern Lights Press.

Botsman, R. and Rogers, R. (2010) *What's Mine Is Yours: The Rise of Collaborative Consumption*, London: HarperCollins.

Boyle, J. (1996) *Shamans, Software, and Spleens: Law and the Construction of the Information Society*, Cambridge, MA: Harvard University Press.

—— (2003) 'The Second Enclosure Movement and the Construction of the Public Domain', *Law and Contemporary Problems*, 66 (1–2): 33–74.

Brittan, S. (1996) *Capitalism With a Human Face*, Cambridge, MA: Harvard University Press.

Brooks, F. (1975) *The Mythical Man-Month: Essays on Software Engineering*, Reading, MA: Addison-Wesley.

Buchanan, J. (1965) 'An Economic Theory of Clubs', *Economica* 32 (1): 1–14.

—— (1986) *Liberty, Market and State*, Brighton: Wheatsheaf.

—— (2007) *Economics from the Outside*, College Station, TX: Texas A&M University Press.

—— (1984) 'Politics Without Romance: A Sketch of Positive Public Choice Theory and Its Normative Implications' In Buchanan, J. and Tollison, R. (1984) *The Theory of Public Choice: II*, Ann Arbor, MI: University of Michigan Press.

Buchanan, J. and Tullock, G. (1965) *The Calculus of Consent*, Ann Arbor, MI: University of Michigan Press.

Caffentzis, G. (2004) A Tale of Two Conferences: Globalization, the Crisis of Neoliberalism and Question of the Commons A Talk Prepared for the Alter-Globalization Conference August 9, 2004 San Miguel de Allende, Mexico. Unpublished.

Callahan, G. (2010) *Methodological Individualism Reconsidered*, ThinkMarkets. Online. Available at: www. thinkmarkets.wordpress.com/2010/03/14/methodological-individualism-reconsidered.html (accessed 28 June 2012).

Callinicos, A. (2011) *The Revolutionary Ideas of Karl Marx*, London: Bookmarks.

Camerer, C. (2003) *Behavioral Game Theory: Experiments in Strategic Interaction*, Princeton, NJ: Princeton University Press.

Carlsson, L. and Berkes, F. (2005) 'Co-management: concepts and methodological implications', *Journal of Environmental Management*, 75: 65–76.
Chomsky, N. ([1957] 2002) *Syntactic Structures*, Berlin: Walter de Gruyter.
Clements, F. (1916) *Plant Succession: An Analysis of the Development of Vegetation*, Washington, DC: Carnegie Institution of Washington.
Coase, R.H. (1960) 'The Problem of Social Cost', *Journal of Law and Economics*, 3: 1–44.
Cole, D. (2013) 'The Varieties of Comparative Institutional Analysis', *Wisconsin Law Review*, no. 2: 383–409.
Common, M. and Stagl, S. (2005) *Ecological Economics: An Introduction*, New York: Cambridge University Press.
Commons, J.R. (1893) *The Distribution of Wealth*, New York: Macmillan.
—— (1968) *The Legal Foundations of Capitalism*, Madison: University of Wisconsin Press.
Cox, M. (2010) 'Exploring the dynamics of social-ecological systems: the case of the Taos Valley Acequias', unpublished thesis, Indiana University, Bloomington, Indiana, USA.
Cox, M., Arnold, G. and Villamayor Tomás, S. (2010) 'A Review of Design Principles for Community-based Natural Resource Management', *Ecology and Society*, 15 (4): 38, Online. Available at: www.ecologyandsociety.org/vol. 15/iss4/art38/ (accessed 11 July 2013).
Crawford, S. and Ostrom. E. (2005) 'A Grammar of Institutions', in Ostrom, E. *Understanding Institutional Diversity*, Princeton, NJ: Princeton University Press.
Cronon, W. (1983) *Changes in the Land: Indians, Colonists, and the Ecology of New England*, New York: Hill and Wang.
CTV News (30 December, 2009) *Toy library saves cash, environment*, Online. Available at: http://montreal.ctvnews.ca/toy-library-saves-cash-environment-1.469298 (accessed 11 July 2013).
Dale, G. (2010) *Karl Polanyi: the limits of the market*, Cambridge: Polity Press.
Dales, J.H. (1968) *Pollution Property and Prices: An Essay in Policy-Making and Economics*, Toronto, Ontario: University of Toronto Press.
Demsetz, H. (1967) 'Toward a Theory of Property Rights', *The American Economic Review*, 57 (2): 347–59.
Dietz, T., Ostrom, E. and Stern, P. (2003) 'The Struggle to Govern the Commons, *Science* 302 (5652): 1907–12.
Digital Library of the Commons (2009) Research on the Commons, Common-Pool Resources, and Common Property. Online. Available at: http://dlc.dlib.indiana.edu/dlc/contentguidelines/ (accessed 11 July 2013).
Djilas, M. (1957) *The New Class: An Analysis of the Communist System*, New York: Frederick A. Praeger.
Doherty, B. (2007) *Radicals for Capitalism: A Freewheeling History of the Modern American Libertarian Movement*, New York: Public Affairs.
Ecological Society of America (2013) Elinor Ostrom 1933–2012. *Bulletin of the Ecological Society of America*, 94: 17–19.
Economist, The (20 March 2009) *Herbert Simon*, Available at: www.economist.com/node/13350892 (accessed 11 July 2013).
—— (10 February 2011) *Print me a Stradivarius*, Available at: www.economist.com/node/18114327 (accessed 11 July 2013).
—— (24 February 2011) *Letters*, Available at: www.economist.com/node/18227161 (accessed 11 July 2013).

—— (9 March 2013) *The rise of the sharing economy*, Available at: www.economist.com/news/leaders/21573104-internet-everything-hire-rise-sharing-economy.html (accessed 11 July 2013).

Ehrlich, P. and Ehrlich, A. (1968) *The Population Bomb*, New York: Ballantine Books.

Elster, J. (ed.) (1986) Rational Choice, Oxford: Blackwell.

—— (2009) *Alexis De Tocqueville. The First Social Scientist*, Cambridge: Cambridge University Press.

Engels, F. (1972) *The Origin of the Family, Private Property and the State*, New York Pathfinder.

Epstein, J. (2006) *Alexis De Tocqueville: Democracy's Guide*, New York: HarperCollins.

Escotet Foundation (November 2010) *Interview with Nobel Laureate Elinor Ostrom*, CTV. Online. Available at: http://escotet.org/2010/11/interview-with-nobel-laureate-elinor-ostrom (accessed 11 July 2013).

European Tribune (2009). *Elinor Ostrom on Equality*, European Tribune, Online. Available at: www.eurotrib.com/story/2009/10/14/20950/185 (accessed 30 July 2013).

Felson, M. and Spaeth, J. (1978) 'Community Structure and Collaborative Consumption: A Routine Activity Approach', *American Behavioral Scientist*, 21: 614–24.

Fenton, W. (1998) *The Great Law and the Longhouse: A Political History of the Iroquois Confederacy*, Norman, OK: University of Oklahoma Press.

Fine, B. (2000) 'Economics Imperialism and Intellectual Progress: The Present as History of Economic Thought?' *History of Economics Review*, 32: 10–36.

—— (2010) 'Beyond the Tragedy of the Commons: A Discussion of Governing the Commons: The Evolution of Institutions for Collective Action', *Perspectives on Politics*, 8: 583–586.

Fisher, R. and Ury, W. (1983) *Getting to Yes*, New York: Penguin Books.

Flaherty, E. (2012) 'Modes of Production, Metabolism and Resilience: Toward a Framework for the Analysis of Complex Social-Ecological Systems', unpublished thesis, National University of Ireland Maynooth.

Fitz, D. (2012) 'Why Is Cuba's Health Care System the Best Model for Poor Countries?' *Monthly Review* Online. Available at: http://mrzine.monthlyreview.org/2012/fitz071212.html (accessed 11 July 2013).

Folke, C., Pritchard, L., Berkes, F., Colding, J. and Svedin, U. (2007) 'The Problem of Fit between Ecosystems and Institutions: ten years later', *Ecology and Society*, 12 (1): 30. Online. Available at: www.ecologyandsociety.org/vol. 12/iss1/art30/ (accessed 11 July 2013).

Foster, J.B. (2000) *Marx's Ecology: Materialism and Nature*, New York: Monthly Review Press.

Foucault, M. (1980) *Power/Knowledge: Selected Interviews and Other Writings 1972–1977*, New York: Pantheon Books.

Freecycle (2011), Freecycle Online. Available at: www.uk.freecycle.org (accessed 11 July 2013.

Gadagkar, R. (2005) 'Obituary: Ernst Mayr (1904–2005)', *Journal of Genetics*, 84 (1): 87–9.

Gamble, A. (1996) *Hayek: The Iron Cage of Liberty*, Cambridge: Polity Press.

George, P. (1995) *Dr. Strangelove, or, How I Learned to Stop Worrying and Love the Bomb*, Oxford: Oxford University Press.

Gershenfeld, N. (2005) *Fab*, Cambridge, MA: Basic Books.

Gilbert, N. (2007) *Agent-Based Models. Quantitative Applications in the Social Sciences*, London: Sage.

Gillies, J., and Cailliau, R. (2000) *How the Web was Born: The Story of the World Wide Web*, Oxford: Oxford University Press.
Gleick, P. *et al.* (2010) 'Climate Change and the Integrity of Science', *Science*, 328 (5979): 689–90.
GNU Operating System (2012) *What Is Free Software?*, Free Software Foundation, Inc. Online. Available at: www.gnu.org/philosophy/free-sw.html (accessed 28 June 2012).
—— (2012) *The GNU Manifesto*, Free Software Foundation, Inc. Online. Available at: www.gnu.org/gnu/manifesto.html (accessed 11 July 2013).
Goetzman, K. (2010) *Elinor Ostrom: The Commoner*, Topeka, Kansas: Utne Reader. Online. Available at: www.utne.com/Politics/Utne-Reader-Visionaries-Elinor-Ostrom-Commons.aspx (accessed 28 June 2012).
Gordon, H.S. (1954) 'The Economic Theory of a Common Property Resource: The Fishery', *Journal of the Political Economy* 62: 124–42.
Gorz, A. (1982) *Farewell to the Working Class: an Essay on Post-Industrial Socialism*, London: Pluto Press.
—— (2010) *Ecologica*, London: Seagull Books.
Green, D. and Shapiro, I. (1994) *Pathologies of Rational Choice Theory*, New Haven, CT: Yale University Press.
Gupta, S. (2011) *'Elinor Ostrom interview'*, Mumbai: *Indian Express*. Online. Available at: www.indianexpress.com/news/what-i-object-to-is-the-presumption-that-government-officials-have-got-all-the-knowledge-and-locals-have-none/750015/0 (accessed 28 June 2012).
Hardin, G. (1968) 'The Tragedy of the Commons', *Science*, 162: 1243–8.
Hardt, M. (2010) 'The Common in Communism', in Zizek, S. and Douzinas C. (eds) *The Idea of Communism*, New York: Verso.
Hardt, M. and Negri, A. (2000) *Empire*, Cambridge, MA: Harvard University Press.
Harter, L.G. (1962) *John R. Commons: His Assault on Laissez-Faire*, Corvallis, OR: Oregon State University Press.
—— (1965) 'John R. Commons' Modern Monopoly Theory', *Land Economics*, 41 (2): 267–70.
Harvey, D. (2012) *Rebel Cities: From the Right to the City to the Urban Revolution*, London: Verso.
Hawken, P., Lovins, H. and Lovins, A. (1999) Natural Capitalism: *Creating the Next Industrial Revolution*, London: Little Brown and Company.
Hayek, F.A. (1945) 'The Use of Knowledge in Society', *American Economic Review* 35(4): 519–530.
—— (1976) *Denationalization of Money*, London: Institute of Economic Affairs.
—— (2001) *The Road to Serfdom*, London: Routledge.
—— (2012) *Law, Legislation and Liberty, Volume Two: The Mirage of Social Justice*, Chicago, IL: University of Chicago Press.
Heller, M. (1997) 'The Tragedy of the Anticommons: Property in the Transition from Marx to the Market', The William Davidson Institute Working Paper 40, Ann Arbor, MI: University of Michigan.
Heller, M. and Eisenberg, R. (1998) 'Can Patents Deter Innovation? The Anticommons in Biomedical Research' *Science*, 280 (5364): 698–701.
Heneghan, L. (2012) 'Out of Kilter: Old Ideas of Balance and Harmony Need to Be Put Aside if We are to Save a Natural World in Constant Flux', *Aeon Magazine*. com, www.aeonmagazine.com/nature-and-cosmos/liam-heneghan-balance-of-nature/ (9 October 2012).

Hess, C. (2010) 'The Calculus of Commitment: The Ostroms, The Workshop, and The Commons', *The Commons Digest*, 9: 1–5.

Hess, C. and Ostrom, E. (2001) 'Artifacts, Facilities, And Content: Information as a Common-pool Resource', Workshop in Political Theory and Policy Analysis.

—— (eds) (2011) *Understanding Knowledge as a Commons: From Theory to Practice*, Cambridge, MA: MIT Press.

Hess, K. (1979) *Community Technology*, New York: Harper and Row.

Hinnefeld, S. (2010) *Rippel Foundation awards grant to Ostrom, IU research center, to apply insights to health care*, Indiana University Home Pages. Online. Available at: http://homepages.indiana.edu/web/page/normal/16544.html (accessed 28 June 2012).

Hildyard, N., Lohmann, L., Sexton, S. and Fairlie, S. (1993) *Whose Common Future? Reclaiming the Commons*, London: Earthscan.

Hippel von, E. (2005) *Democratizing Innovation*, Cambridge, MA: MIT Press.

Hodgson, G. (2000) 'The Concept of Emergence', *Emergence*, 2 (4): 65–77.

—— (2003) 'John R. Commons and the Foundations of Institutional Economics', *Journal of Economic Issues*, 37 (3): 547–76.

—— (2006) 'What Are Institutions?', *Journal of Economic Issues*, 40 (1): 1–25.

—— (2007) 'Meanings of Methodological Individualism', *Journal of Economic Methodology* 14 (2): 211–26.

Hoggan, J. (2009) *Climate Cover-Up: The Crusade to Deny Global Warming*, Vancouver, Canada: Greystone Books.

Hofstadter, D.R. (1999) [1979] *Gödel, Escher, Bach: An Eternal Golden Braid*, New York: Basic Books.

Indiana University (2009) *Nobel laureates discuss their education and issues in science for a Swedish TV program*, Bloomington, Indiana: The Nobel Prize Chronicles. Online. Available at: www.iu.edu/~iunews/blogs/nobel/?p=90 (accessed 28 June 2012).

Independent, The (18 December 2012) *Peer-to-peer lending 'set to double' in 2013*, Online. Available at: www.independent.co.uk/hei-fi/business/peertopeer-lending-set-to-double-in-2013-8423456.html

IRIN Global (25 April 2012) *Interview with Nobel Prize Winner Elinor Ostrom on Climate Change*, Online. Available at: www.irinnews.org/report/95355/global-interview-with-nobel-prize-winner-elinor-ostrom-on-climate-change (accessed 11 July 2013).

IU Newsroom (14 December 2009) *Ostrom for forest advocates: Sounding good is not enough*, Online. Available at: http://newsinfo.iu.edu/news/page/normal/12874.html (accessed 11 July 2013).

Jackson, T.A. (1971) *Ireland Her Own*, London: Lawrence & Wishart.

Jacobs, D.T. (2006) *Unlearning the Language of Conquest*, Austin, TX: University of Texas Press.

Jacobs, J. (1961) *The Death and Life of Great American Cities*, New York: Random House.

—— (1984) *The Death and Life of Great American Cities*, Harmondsworth: Penguin.

Jaeger, W. (2005) *Environmental Economics for Tree Huggers and Other Skeptics*, Washington, DC: Island Press.

Jagger, P., Bauer, J. and Walker, J. (2009) *Artisans of Political Theory and Empirical Inquiry: Thirty-Five Years of Scholarship at the Workshop in Political Theory and Policy Analysis*, Bloomington, Indiana: Workshop in Political Theory and Policy Analysis.

Jameson, F. (1972) *The Prison-House of Language: A Critical Account of Structuralism and Russian Formalism*, Princeton, NJ: Princeton University Press.

Janssen, M.A., Anderies, J.M. and Ostrom, E. (2007) 'Robustness of Social-Ecological Systems to Spatial and Temporal Variability', *Society and Natural Resources*, 20(4), 307–322.

Johansen, B. (1982) *Forgotten Founders: Benjamin Franklin, the Iroquois, and the Rationale for the American Revolution*, Ipswich, MA: Gambit.

Johnson, R. (2010) *Elinor Ostrom*, New York: Time Online. Available at: www.time.com/time/specials/packages/article/0,28804,2111975_2111976_2111960,00.html (accessed 28 June 2012).

Kho, J. and Agsaoay-Saño, E. (2005) *Customary Water Laws & Practices in the Philippines*, www.fao.org/legal/advserv/FAOIUCNcs/Philippines.pdf.

Kliemt, H. (2011) 'Tayloring Game Theory the Ostrom Way', *The Good Society* Volume 20, 1: 37–49.

Klimecki, R. and Willmott, H. (2009) 'From Demutualisation to Meltdown: a Tale of Two Wannabe Banks', *Critical Perspectives on International Business*, 5 (1/2): 120–40.

Knight, J. (1992) *Institutions and Social Conflict*, Cambridge: Cambridge University Press.

Korten, F. (2010) *Elinor Ostrom wins Nobel for Common(s) Sense*, Bainbridge, Washington: *Yes Magazine*. Online. Available at: www.yesmagazine.org/issues/america-the-remix/elinor-ostrom-wins-nobel-for-common-s-sense (accessed 28 June 2012).

Krader, L. (1972) *The Ethnographical Notebooks of Karl Marx*, Amsterdam: Van Gorcum and co.

Kropotkin, P. (1901) *Fields, Factories and Workshops*, New York: G.P.Putnam.

Lansing, J.S. (1991) *Priests and Programmers: Technologies of Power in the Engineered Landscape of Bali*, Princeton, NJ: Princeton University Press.

Lasswell, H. and Kaplan, A. (1950) *Power and Society*, New Haven, CT: Yale University Press.

Leadbeater, C. and Christie, I. (1999) *To Our Mutual Advantage*, London: Demos.

Leonard, M. (2009) *Nobel winner Elinor Ostrom is a Gregarious Teacher who Loves to Solve Problems*, Bloomington, Indiana: Herald Times Online. Available at: http://info.law.indiana.edu/news/page/normal/12789.html (accessed 28 June 2012).

Leonard, T. (2005) 'Retrospectives: Eugenics and Economics in the Progressive Era', *Journal of Economic Perspectives*, 19 (4): 207–24.

Lessig, L. (1999) *Code and Other Laws of Cyberspace*, New York: Basic Books.

—— (2004) *Free Culture: The Nature and Future of Creativity*, New York: Penguin.

Levi, M. (1988) *Of Rules and Revenue*, Berkeley: University of California Press.

Levitt, S. (2009) *What This Year's Nobel Prize in Economics Says About the Nobel Prize in Economics*, Online. Available at: www.freakonomics.com/2009/10/12/what-this-years-nobel-prize-in-economics-says-about-the-nobel-prize-in-economics/ (accessed 28 June 2012).

Licklider, J.C. (1960) *Man-Computer Symbiosis*, IRE Transactions on Human Factors in Electronics, Online. Available at: http://groups.csail.mit.edu/medg/people/psz/Licklider.html (accessed 28 July 2013).

Linebaugh, P. (1976) 'Karl Marx, the Theft of Wood and Working Class Composition: A Contribution to the Current Debate', *Crime and Social Justice*, 6: 5–16.

—— (2008) *The Magna Carta Manifesto: Liberties and Commons for All*, Berkeley: University of California Press.

Lipson, H. and Kurman, M. (2013) *Fabricated: The New World of 3D Printing*, New York: John Wiley & Sons.

Llewellyn, K. and Adamson Hoebel, E. (1941) *The Cheyenne Way: Conflict and Case Law in Primitive Jurisprudence*, Norman: University of Oklahoma Press.

Losurdo, D. (2011) *Liberalism: a Counter-History*, London: Verso.

Loveman, B. (2008) 'From the Cheyenne Way to the Chilean Way (of Political Reconciliation and Impunity): A Retrospective on Political Architecture, Political Culture, and Institutional Design' in Sproule-Jones, M., Allen, B.and Sabetti. F. (eds) *The Struggle to Constitute and Sustain Productive Orders: Vincent Ostrom's Quest to Understand Human Affairs*, Lanham, MD: Lexington Books.

Lyotard, J.-F. (1984) *The Postmodern Condition: A Report on Knowledge*, Minneapolis, MN University of Minnesota Press.

Marx, K. (1853) 'The Duchess of Sutherland and Slavery', The People's Paper, No. 45, March 12 1853 Online. Available at: www.marxists.org/archive/marx/works/1853/03/12.htm (accessed 10 July 2013).

—— (1976) *Capital: A Critique of Political Economy, Volume 1*, Harmondsworth, Middlesex: Penguin.

May, A.M. and Summerfield, G. (2012) 'Creating a Space where Gender Matters: Elinor Ostrom (1933–2012) talks with Ann Mari May and Gale Summerfield, *Feminist Economics*, 18 (4): 25–37.

Mayr, E. (1982) *The Growth of Biological Thought: Diversity, Evolution and Inheritance*, Cambridge, MA: Belknap Press.

McAfee, R.P. (2002) *Competitive Solutions: The Strategist's Toolkit*, Princeton, NJ: Princeton University Press.

McCay, B. (2003) 'Foreword' in Dolšak, N. and Ostrom, E. (eds) *The Commons in the New Millennium: Challenges and Adaptation*, Cambridge, MA: MIT.

McChesney, R. (2013) *Digital Disconnect – How Capitalism is Turning the Internet Against Democracy*, New York: New Press.

McCloskey, D. (1998) *The Rhetoric of Economics*, Wisconsin: University of Wisconsin Press.

McCullough, M. (2013) *Ambient Commons: Attention in the Age of Embodied Information*, Boston, MA: MIT Press.

McGinnis, M. (ed.) (2000) *Polycentric Governance and Development*, Ann Arbor, MI: University of Michigan Press.

—— (2005) 'Beyond individualism and spontaneity: Comments on Peter Boettke and Christopher Coyne', *Journal of Economic Behavior & Organization*, 57: 167–72.

—— (2013) *Caring for the Health Commons: What It Is and Who's Responsible for It*, The Vincent and Elinor Ostrom Worksop in Political Theory and Policy Analysis. Online. Available at: http://php.indiana.edu/~mcginnis/chc.pdf (accessed 28 July 2013).

McGinnis, M. and Ostrom, E. (2011) 'Reflections on Vincent Ostrom, Public Administration, and Polycentricity', *Public Administration Review*, 72 (1): 15–25.

McGovern, P. and Yacobucci, P. (1999) *'Lasswellian Policy Science and the Bounding of Democracy'*, paper posted on Theory, Policy, and Society Online Available at: www.cddc.vt.edu/tps/e-print/Lasswell.PDF (accessed 28 July 2013).

McKean, M. (1986) 'Management of Traditional Common Lands (Iriaichi) in Japan.' In National Research Council, *Proceedings of the Conference on Common Property Resource Management*, Washington, DC: National Academy Press, 559.

—— (1982) 'The Japanese Experience with Scarcity: Management of Traditional Common Lands', *Environmental Review*, 6 (2): 63–91.

Mises, L. ([1949] 1966) *Human Action. A Treatise on Economics*, Chicago: Contemporary.

Moomaw, R., Olson, K., McLean, W. and Applegate, M. (2009) *Economics and Contemporary Issues*, Boston, MA: Cengage Learning.
de Moor, M., Shaw-Taylor, L. and Warde, P. (eds) (2002) *The Management of Common Land in North West Europe,* c.*1500–1850*, Turnhout: Brepols.
Morrow, C.E. and Hull, R.W. (1996) 'Donor-initiated Common Pool Resource Institutions: The Case of the Yanesha Forestry Cooperative', *World Development*, 24 (10): 1641–57.
Neeson, J. (1993) *Commoners: Common Right, Enclosure and Social Change in England, 1700–1820*, Cambridge: Cambridge University Press.
Nelson, M., Rademacher, M. and Paek, H.-J. (2007) 'Downshifting Consumer = Upshifting Citizen? An Examination of a Local Freecycle Community', *Annals of the American Academy of Political and Social Science*, 611: 141–56.
Netting, R. (1981) *Balancing on an Alp: Ecological Change and Continuity in a Swiss Mountain Community*, Cambridge: Cambridge University Press.
Nobel Prize Org. (2009a) Economic governance: the organization of cooperation Nobelprize.org. Online. Available at: www.nobelprize.org/nobel_prizes/economics/laureates/2009/press.html (accessed 28 June 2012).
—— (2009b) *Elinor Ostrom – Biographical.* Nobelprize.org. Online. Available at: www.nobelprize.org/nobel_prizes/economics/laureates/2009/ostrom.html (accessed 28 June 2012).
Simon/Nobel Prize Org. (2013a) *Herbert Simon – Biographical.* Nobelprize.org. Online. Available at: www.nobelprize.org/nobel_prizes/economic-sciences/laureates/1978/simon-bio.html (accessed 11 July 2013).
—— (2013b) *Herbert Simon – Lecture.* Nobelprize.org. Online. Available at: www.nobelprize.org/nobel_prizes/economic-sciences/laureates/1978/simon-lecture.pdf (accessed 11 July).
North, D.C. (1996) 'Epilogue: Economic Performance Through Time', in Alston, L.J., Eggertsson, T. and North, D.C. (eds) *Empirical Studies in Institutional Change*, Cambridge: Cambridge University Press.
O' Danachair, C. (1981) 'An Ri (The King): an example of traditional social organization', *Journal of the Royal Society of Antiquaries of Ireland*, 111: 14–28.
Oakerson, R. (1986) 'A Model for the Analysis of Common Property Problems', in National Research *N.R.C. Proceedings of the Conference on Common Property Resource Management.* Washington, DC: National Academy Press.
Olson, M. (1971) *The Logic of Collective Action: Public Goods and the Theory of Groups*, Cambridge, MA: Harvard University Press.
—— (2000) *Power and Prosperity*, New York: Basic Books.
Ostrom, E. (1965) 'Public Entrepreneurship: A Case Study in Ground Water Basin Management', unpublished thesis, University of California-Los Angeles.
—— (ed.) (1982) *Strategies of Political Inquiry*, Beverly Hills, California: Sage Publications.
—— (1990) *Governing the Commons: The Evolution of Institutions for Collective Action*, Cambridge: Cambridge University Press.
—— (1996) 'Crossing the Great Divide: Coproduction, Synergy and Development', *World* Development, 24 (6): 1073–87.
—— (1998) 'A Behavioral Approach to the Rational Choice Theory of Collective Action', *American Political Science Review*, 92 (1): 1–22.
—— (2000) 'Collective Action and the Evolution of Social Norms', *The Journal of Economic Perspectives*, 14 (3): 137–58.

—— (2004) 'The Ten Most Important Books', *Tidsskriftet Politik* 4, (7): 36–48.
—— (2005) *Understanding Institutional Diversity*, Princeton, NJ: Princeton University Press.
—— (2006a) 'A Frequently Overlooked Precondition of Democracy: Citizens Knowledgeable About and Engaged in Collective Action', in Brennan, G. *Preconditions of Democracy*, The Tampere Club Series, 2: 75–89. Tampere, Finland: Tampere University Press.
—— (2006b) 'Biography of Robert Axelrod', PS: *Political Science & Politics*, 40 (1): 171–4.
—— (2007) 'Sustainable Social-Ecological Systems: An Impossibility?', unpublished paper.
—— (2008) 'Crafting Rules to Sustain Resources', The American Academy of Political and Social Science, Online. Available at: www.aapss.org/news/2008/05/29/crafting-rules-to-sustain-resources (accessed 10 July 2013).
—— (2009a) 'A Polycentric Approach for Coping with Climate Change', Policy Research Working Paper No. 5095. Background paper to the 2010 World Development Report. Washington, DC: The World Bank.
—— (2009b) 'Twelve Questions for Elinor Ostrom', *GAIA – Ecological Perspectives for Science and Society*, 15 (4): 246–7.
—— (2009) *Interview*, Cambridge, MA: The Big Think. Online. Available at: http://bigthink.com/ideas/17278 (accessed 28 June 2012).
—— (2010a) 'A Long Polycentric Journey', *Annual Review of Political Science*, 13: 1–23.
—— (2010b) 'Beyond Markets and States: Polycentric Governance of Complex Economic Systems', *American Economic Review*, 100: 641–72.
—— (2011) 'Honoring James Buchanan', *Journal of Economic Behavior and Organization*, 80 (2): 370–3.
—— (2012a) 'Coevolving Relationships between Political Science and Economics', *Rationality, Markets and Morals*, 3: 51–65.
—— (2012b) *The Future of the Commons*, London, Institute of Economic Affairs.
—— (2012c) 'Green from the Grassroots', Project Syndicate.
—— (2012d) *The books that inspired Elinor Ostrom: 'Lasswell and Kaplan's Power and Society broadened my perspective on individual choice and behaviour in a way that was very instrumental'*, LSE Review of Books. Online. Available at: http://blogs.lse.ac.uk/lsereviewofbooks/2012/04/22/academic-inspiration-elinor-ostrom/ (accessed 11 July 2013).
Ostrom/Nobel.org (2009a) *Elinor Ostrom: Biography*, Available at: www.nobelprize.org/nobel_prizes/economic-sciences/laureates/2009/ostrom-bio.html (accessed 10 July 2013).
—— (2009b) *Elinor Ostrom: Lecture*, Available at: www.nobelprize.org/nobel_prizes/economics/laureates/2009/ostrom.html (accessed 10 July 2013).
Ostrom, E. and Ahn, T.K. (2003) *Foundations of Social Capital*, London: Edward Elgar.
Ostrom, E. and Basurto, X. (2011) 'Crafting Analytical Tools to Study Institutional Change', *Journal of Institutional Economics*, 7 (3): 317–43.
Ostrom, E. and Hess, C. (2011) 'A Framework for Analyzing the Knowledge Commons' in Hess, C. and Ostrom, E. (eds) (2011) *Understanding Knowledge as a Commons*, Cambridge, MA: MIT Press.
Ostrom, E. and Janssen, M. (2004) 'Multi-Level Governance and Resilience of Social-Ecological Systems', in Spoor M. (ed.) *Globalisation, Poverty and Conflict*, Alphen aan den Rijn, Netherlands Kluwer Academic.

Ostrom, E. and Nagendra, H. (2006) 'Insights on Linking Forests, Trees, and People from the Air, on the Ground, and in the Laboratory', *PNAS*, 103: 19224–31.

Ostrom, E., Gardner, R. and Walker, J. (1994) *Rules, Games, and Common-Pool Resources*, Ann Arbor, MI: University of Michigan Press.

Ostrom, E., Parks, R. and Whitaker, G. (1978) *Patterns of Metropolitan Policing*, Cambridge, MA; Ballinger.

Ostrom, V. (1950) 'Government and Water: A Study of the Influence of Water Upon Governmental Institutions and Practices in the Development of Los Angeles', unpublished thesis, University of California-Los Angeles.

—— (1971) *The Political Theory of a Compound Republic*, Lincoln, NE: University of Nebraska Press.

—— (1980) 'Artisanship and Artifact', *Public Administration Review*, 40 (4): 309–17.

—— (1989) *The Intellectual Crisis in American Public Administration*, Tuscaloosa, AL: The University of Alabama Press.

—— (1997) *The Meaning of Democracy and Vulnerability of Democracy*, Ann Arbor, MI: University of Michigan Press.

—— (1999) 'Cryptoimperialism, Predatory States, and Self-Governance', McGinnis, M.D. (ed.) *Polycentric Governance and Development: Readings from the Workshop in Political Theory and Policy Analysis*, M.D. Ann Arbor, MI: University of Michigan Press.

—— (2012) 'Buchanan's Opening to Constitutional Choice and Meta Levels of Analysis' in Allen, B. and Ostrom, V. *The Quest to Understand Human Affairs*, Lanham, MD: Rowman and Littlefield Publishers.

Pal, Amitabh (June 2010) *Elinor Ostrom Interview, The Progressive, 20 June 2010* Online. Available at: www.progressive.org/elinor_ostrom_interview.html (accessed 11 July 2013).

Pearce, F. (2013) *The Landgrabbers*, Boston, MA: Beacon Press.

Perelman, M. (1983) *Classical Political Economy, Primitive Accumulation and the Social Division of Labor*, Totowa, NJ: Rowman & Allanheld.

Perrins, C.M. (2010) 'Introduction' in Savill, P., Perrins, C.M., Kirby, K. and Fisher, N. (eds) *Wytham Woods: Oxford's Ecological Laboratory*, Oxford: Oxford University Press.

Pettit, P. (1997) *Republicanism: A Theory of Freedom and Government*, Oxford: Clarendon Press.

Pocock, J. (2003) *The Machiavellian Moment: Florentine Political Thought and the Atlantic Republican Tradition*, Princeton, NJ: Princeton University Press.

Polanyi, K. (1957) *The Great Transformation: The Political and Economic Origins of Our Time*, Boston, MA: Beacon Press.

Polanyi, M. (1951) *The Logic of Liberty*, Chicago, IL: University of Chicago Press.

—— (2009) *The Tacit Dimension*, Chicago, IL: University of Chicago Press.

Porritt, J. (2005) *Capitalism: As if the World Matters*, London: Earthscan.

Poteete, A., Janssen, M. and Ostrom, E. (2010) *Working Together: Collective Action, the Commons, and Multiple Methods in Practice*, Princeton, NJ: Princeton University Press.

Racusin, D.J. and McArleton, A. (2012) *The Natural Building Companion: A Comprehensive Guide to Integrative Design and Construction*, White River Junction, VT: Chelsea Green Publishing.

Rand, A. (1967) *Capitalism: The Unknown Ideal*, New York: Signet.

Rapalje, S. and Lawrence, R. (1888) *A Dictionary of American and English Law, Volume One*, Jersey City, NJ: Frederick C. Linn & Co.

Rapoport, A. (1997) 'Order of Play in Strategically Equivalent Games in Extensive Form', *International Journal of Game Theory*, 26: 113–36.

Ray, L. (2007) *Language of the Land: the Mapuche in Argentina and Chile*, Copenhagen, Denmark, International Work Group For Indigenous Affairs.

Raymond, E. (1999) *The Cathedral & the Bazaar: Musings on Linux and Open Source by an Accidental Revolutionary*, Cambridge, MA: O'Reilly.

RepRap Project (2011) Rep Rap. Online. Available at: www.bath.ac.uk/research/features/reprap.html (accessed 11 July 2013).

Roberts, A. (1979) *The Self-Managing Environment*, London: Alison and Busby.

Rodgers, C., Pieraccini, M., Straughton, E. and Winchester, A. (2010) *Contested Common Land: Environmental Governance Past and Present*, London: Earthscan.

Rosman, J. and Uribe, M.O. (7 May 2013) *Disney Wants To Trademark 'Dia De Los Muertos'*, Fronteras. Online. Available at: www.fronterasdesk.org/news/2013/may/07/disney-wants-trademark-dia-de-los-muertos (accessed 11 July 2013).

Rowe, J. and Barnes, P. (2013) *Our Common Wealth: The Hidden Economy That Makes Everything Else Work*, San Francisco, CA: Berrett-Koehler.

Royle, E. (1998) *Robert Owen and the Commencement of the Millennium: The Harmony Community at Queenwood Farm, Hampshire, 1839–1845*, Manchester: Manchester University Press.

Rutherford, M. (1996) *Institutions in Economics: The Old and the New Institutionalism*, Cambridge: Cambridge University Press.

Sabetti, F. (2011) 'Constitutional Artisanship and Institutional Diversity: Elinor Ostrom, Vincent Ostrom, and the Workshop', *The Good Society*, 20 (1): 73–83.

Scholem, G. (2012) *Walter Benjamin*, New York: New York Review Books.

Schwartz, A. (January 2013) *What Happens To Zipcar Now That Avis Bought It For $500 Million?*, Fastcoexist, Online. Available at: www.fastcoexist.com/1681130/what-happens-to-zipcar-now-that-avis-bought-it-for-500-million (accessed 11 July 2013).

Schwartz-Shea, P. (2010) 'Elinor Ostrom's Fieldwork Sensibility', *Perspectives on Politics*, 8 (2): 587–90.

Schweik, C. and English, R. (2012) *Internet Success: A Study of Open-Source Software Commons*, Cambridge, MA: MIT Press.

Searle, J. (1969) *Speech Acts: An Essay in the Philosophy of Language*, Cambridge: Cambridge University Press.

Selten, R. (1994) Autobiography Online. Available at: www.nobelprize.org/nobel_prizes/economics/laureates/1994/selten-autobio.html (accessed 28 June 2012).

Sen, A. (1977) 'Rational Fools: a Critique of the Behavioral Foundation of Economic Theory', *Philosophy and Public Affairs*, 6 (4): 317–44.

Shaw, W. (1984) 'Marx and Morgan', *History and Theory*, 23 (2): 215–28.

Shepsle, K. (1989) 'Studying Institutions: Some Lessons from the Rational Choice Approach', *Journal of Theoretical Politics*, 1: 131–47.

Shirky, C. (2010) *Cognitive Surplus: Creativity and Generosity in a Connected Age*, London: Penguin.

Shiva, V. (1988) *Staying Alive: Women, Ecology and Development*, London: Zed Press.

Simon, H. (1955) 'A Behavioral Model of Rational Choice', *The Quarterly Journal of Economics*, 69 (1): 99–118.

—— (1996) *The Sciences of the Artificial*, Cambridge, MA: MIT Press.

—— (1997) *Administrative Behavior: a Study of Decision-Making Processes in Administrative Organizations* (4th ed), New York: Free Press.

—— (2000) Public Administration in Today's World of Organizations and Markets, *PS: Political Science and Politics*, 33 (4): 749–56.

Skinner, Q. (1981) *Machiavelli*, Oxford: Oxford University Press.

—— (1998) *Liberty before Liberalism*, Cambridge: Cambridge University Press.

Slater, E. and Flaherty, E. (2009) The Ecological Dynamics of the Rundale Agrarian Commune (NIRSA) *Working Paper Series*. No. 51. NIRSA – National Institute for Regional and Spatial Analysis.

Smith, A. (2010) *The Theory of Moral Sentiments*, London: Penguin.

South London Radical History Group (2004) *Down with the Fences! : Battles for the Commons in South London*, London: Past Tense.

Sovacool, B. and Brown, M. (2009) 'Scaling the Policy Response to Climate Change', *Policy and Society*, 27 (4): 317–28.

Spiegel Online (2009) *Nobel Laureate Elinor Ostrom: Climate Rules Set from the Top Are Not Enough* Spiegel Online, Online. Available at: www.spiegel.de/international/world/nobel-laureate-elinor-ostrom-climate-rules-set-from-the-top-are-not-enough-a-667495.html (accessed 26 July 2013).

Stallman, R. (2002) *Free Software, Free Society: Selected Essays of Richard M. Stallman*, Boston, MA: GNU Press.

Steber, R. (2006) *Buy the Chief a Cadillac*, New York: Carroll & Graf.

Steele, J. (31 March 2001) *Food for Thought*, Guardian, Online. Available at: www.guardian.co.uk/books/2001/mar/31/society.politics (accessed 11 July 2013).

Suk-Wai, C. (2010) *Helping People to Share Fairly, Eco Walk the Talk*, Online. Available at: www.ecowalkthetalk.com/blog/2010/09/13/elinor-ostrom-helping-people-to-share-fairly/ (accessed 11 July 2013).

Sullivan, M. (2009) *Questions for UCLA's Nobel Prize-winning economist Elinor Ostrom*, UCLA Today, Online. Available at: www.today.ucla.edu/portal/ut/PRN-10-questions-for-nobel-prize-winning-200205.aspx (accessed 11 July 2013).

The Big Think (2009) *Elinor Ostrom Interview*, Cambridge, MA. Online. Available at: http://bigthink.com/ideas/17278 (accessed 28 June 2012).

The Swedish Wire. (2009) *The story of non-economist Elinor Ostrom.* Stockholm, Sweden: The Swedish Wire. Online. Available at: www.swedishwire.com/business/1985-the-story-of-non-economist-elinor-ostrom (accessed 28 June 2012).

Taylor, K. (2012) *What Elinor Ostrom Meant for All of Us*, Centre for Stateless Societies, Online. Available at: http://c4ss.org/content/10700 (accessed 13 July 2013).

Thompson, E.P. (1978) *The Poverty of Theory and Other Essays*, London: Merlin Press.

Thompson, E.P. (1991) *Customs in Common*, Harmondsworth: Penguin.

Tiebout, C. (1956) 'A Pure Theory of Local Expenditures', *Journal of Political Economy*, 64 (5): 416–24.

Tocqueville, A. (1980) *On Democracy, Revolution and Society*, Chicago, IL: University of Chicago Press.

Toffler, A. (1980) *The Third Wave*, New York: Bantam Books.

Toffler, A. and Toffler, H. (2006) *Revolutionary Wealth*, New York: Knopf.

Toonen, T. (2010) 'Resilience in Public Administration: The Ostrom from Work of Elinor and Vincent a Public Administration Perspective', *Public Administration Review*, 70 (2): 193–202.

Trawick, P.B, (2001) 'Successfully governing the commons: principles of social organization in an Andean irrigation system', *Human Ecology*, 29 (1): 1–25.

Troxler, P. (2013) 'Making the Third Industrial Revolution – The Struggle for Polycentric Structures and a New Peer-Production Commons in the Fab Lab Community', in

Walter-Herrmann, J. and Büching, C. (eds) (2013) *Fab Lab: of Machines, Makers and Inventors*, Bielefeld, Germany: Transcript.

Udehn, L. (2002) 'The Changing Face of Methodological Individualism', *Annual Review of Sociology*, 28: 479–507.

Vogel, R. (2007) *Pharmaceutical Economics and Public Policy*, London: Routledge.

Von Neumann, J. and Morgenstern, O. (1944) *Theory of Games and Economic Behavior*, Princeton, NJ: Princeton University Press.

Wade, R. (1988) *Village Republics: Economic Conditions for Collective Action in South India*, Cambridge: Cambridge University Press.

Waldrop, M.M. (2002) *The Dream Machine: J.C.R. Licklider and the Revolution That Made Computing Personal*, New York: Penguin.

Walljasper, J. (2011) *Elinor Ostrom Outlines the Best Strategies for Managing the Commons*, On the Commons, Online. Available at: http://onthecommons.org/magazine/elinor-ostrom-outlines-best-strategies-managing-commons/ (accessed 11 July 2013).

Wall, D. (2010) *The Rise of the Green Left*, London: Pluto.

Walter-Herrmann, J. and Büching, C. (eds) (2013) *Fab Lab: of Machines, Makers and Inventors*, Bielefeld, Germany: Transcript.

Wilson, W. ([1885] 1956) *Congressional Government*, New York: Meridian Books.

Williams, S. (2010) *Free as in Freedom (2.0): Richard Stallman and the Free Software Revolution*, Boston, MA: GNU Press.

Williamson, O. (1985) *The Economics Institutions of Capitalism*, New York: Free Press.

Wohlforth, C. (2010) *The Fate of Nature*, New York: St. Martin's Press.

Young, S.C. (2000) *The Emergence of Ecological Modernisation: Integrating the Environment and the Economy*, London, Routledge.

Index

Printed in the United States
by Baker & Taylor Publisher Services